HOUSING THE
FUTURE

HOUSING THE
FUTURE

ALTERNATIVE
APPROACHES FOR
TOMORROW

SERIES EDITOR
GRAHAM CAIRNS

EDITORS
GRAHAM POTTS
RACHEL ISAAC-MENARD

First published in 2015 by Green Frigate Books

Green Frigate is an imprint of Libri Publishing

Copyright © Libri Publishing Ltd.

Authors retain the rights to individual chapters.

ISBN: 978-0-9933706-0-1

A CIP catalogue record for this book is available from The British Library

Book and cover design by Carnegie Book Production
Cover image: Via Verde, Bronx NY. ©David Sundberg/Esto

Libri Publishing
Brunel House
Volunteer Way
Faringdon
Oxfordshire
SN7 7YR

Tel: +44 (0)845 873 3837

www.libripublishing.co.uk

CONTENTS

DR GRAHAM CAIRNS

INTRODUCTION

Housing The Future – Alternative Approaches for Tomorrow confronts a critical issue at a critical time. In London, a leading capital of global finance, there is a chronic shortage of affordable housing for those that service 'the service' sector. The crisis is at levels not seen since World War II. In Beijing, capital of the 21st century's political powerhouse, the displacement of long-standing communities is a daily occurrence. In Mumbai, the biggest health risk faced by the city today has been identified as overcrowded housing, while in São Paulo, football's 2014 World Cup took place against a backdrop of community unrest and the chronic living conditions of the poor. The private sector, the state and residents themselves are searching for solutions. Whether housing refugees in conflict areas, providing safe water to the households in the developing world, or ensuring key workers can live in the cities they support in the West, the question of housing is not only global, but *critical*.

Providing affordable and decent housing provision is then, one of the most vexing and challenging problems facing designers, architects, planners and policy makers today. It affects the health, wellbeing and social aspirations of millions of people globally. It has attracted the attention of politicians, community groups, artists and architects, and was at the heart of avant-garde design thinking throughout the 20th century and needs to be today. To date, no permanent solutions have been found.

The book series, *Housing the Future,* of which this volume forms the first part, brings together theoretical essays from academics, articles that document built projects by professionals, and design proposals from students and their tutors from across the world. The objectives of the series are to raise awareness of the issue of affordable housing; highlight innovative solutions to communities and professionals from multiple perspectives; encourage the next generation of designers to address housing; and to challenge preconceptions about residential architecture. In collecting the various essays and projects that these volumes present, academics from various universities have been invited to develop essays concerned with analysing issues that affect or result from questions of design and / or the documentation of built projects. They thus relate directly with the complementary design proposals that also make up this volume. The deliberate emphasis here is on practice as opposed to theory.

The projects included are all examples, whether built or proposed, that deal with the related issues of 'affordability', quality and appropriateness. These problems are not site or issue specific and, as a result, neither are the projects in these books. Consequently, no specific site is specified and no set criteria for how to address the issue were set in advance. What results is a rich and sometimes complex set of projects dealing with issues particular to several countries including the United Kingdom, Spain, Italy, Canada, Germany, the United States, Cyprus, Greece and several Latin American contexts.

The variety of places represented in the book is mirrored in the variety of issues under consideration: *planning and strategic approaches* that consider issues of legal, finance and planning issues; *urban design initiatives* that contemplate the inevitable urban implications of housing large numbers of people in specific locations; *sustainable house initiatives* that consider housing at the level of the individual building or on a social platform; *renovating for life considerations* that underline creative and practical ideas on how to re-use existing housing (or other building stock) to meet modern housing needs, and much more.

The book, and its larger series, are both in their turn part of a larger programme of events and publications on housing called 'Housing – Critical Futures'. The overall programme is led by the research group *AMPS* (Architecture, Media, Politics, Society) and its associated and academic journal *Architecture_MPS*. The aim of the programme is to engage architects, planners, developers, policy makers, artists, academics and resident bodies on the issue of housing. This diverse and often conflictive set of partners has been asked to discuss the crisis in affordable, healthy, and sustainable housing that plagues countries across the globe. They are developing and presenting their respective solutions to providing decent and affordable living conditions to people in multiple parts of the world through various formats, including conferences, theory books, journal special issues and the present book series *Housing the Future*.

This book and its diverse projects and essays then, are premised on collaborations of universities, professional bodies, community groups, artists' networks, industry professionals and – of particular interest in this case – architects and planners, regionally, nationally and locally. It takes its place alongside the related activities of the programme. Worth pointing out in this regard is that the 'Housing – Critical Futures' programme particularly recognises the role and contribution artists and media professionals have had, do have, and will continue to have, in addressing the issue of housing worldwide – one of the most high-profile UK examples of which celebrates its fiftieth anniversary in 2016.

In 1966, the film *Cathy Come Home*, directed by the world-renowned filmmaker Ken Loach, was aired on the BBC. It led to a public outcry followed by debates in Parliament that ultimately led to the introduction of laws in the UK obliging local administrations to house the homeless. One year later, inspired by the film, the homeless charity Crisis (which would become the nation's leading voice on the issue) was established. More recently the charitable architecture group *Habitat for Humanity* organised events to engage designers, artists, activists and local community residents in projects engaging in the issue of affordable housing in some of the fastest growing cities in the world. Their 'Brick-olage' Art Festival in Yunan, China for example, saw them partnering with Shanghai's major art galleries, artists and media specialists.

In 2014 Minnesota saw one of over twenty public art installations and eleven performances around the theme of 'home is...' organised by the ARTIFY project. The Minnesota events involved occupying an abandoned car dealership and converting it to 'future housing'. More recently in the city of Liverpool, the art and architecture collaborative Assemble have worked with the local community in the Granby Street area on the redevelopment of their houses. It was shortlisted for the Turner Prize – the UK's most prestigious modern art award – in 2015. As part of this art and creative media engagement with the issue of housing provision AMPS has set up a short film competition run in conjunction with international partners and has instigated art residency programmes facilitating artists to engage with communities working on their own housing redevelopment projects.

Thus, what is represented in this book should be seen as a continuation of both practical and creative endeavours to highlight and address the need to develop more innovative, and ever more needed, solutions to what in the UK has come to be defined as 'the housing crisis'. The projects and essays collected here represent on the one hand, creative and open-ended considerations of how to move forward on his issue and, on the other, very practical approaches to dealing with issues: how to design houses that are affordable in construction, allow for a lifetime of adaptation to meet the changing needs of users and thus prevent the expense and need for moving home. They are creative but very real proposals on how to renovate and update older housing stock, so as to prevent the need for new build and to hold existing communities together. They look at urban issues, ways of living, the changing needs of ageing individuals and questions of space-saving techniques at the levels of design and construction.

Although focused on 'creative solutions through building' they are not unaware of the external factors at play in the issue of affordability – land prices, 'soft' costs, planning constraints, short-term profit motive, etc. In some cases the projects and essays presented address these issues directly, in others they start from a radical baseline, suggesting ideas that can only be implemented with small – or sometime large – shifts in these underlying 'external' factors. What they all share in common is that they are inspired by the need to deal with a *critical issue at a critical time* – the provision of affordable and decent housing. They also, either explicitly or implicitly, draw on the idea of *critical regionalism*, universalised some thirty years ago through the writings of Kenneth Frampton – a reappraisal of how global forces play out regionally and how universal approaches to design can, and should, be adapted to local conditions.

Taking these perspectives of 'critical reappraisal', the need to deal with a real issue, the value of design and new thinking, and the link between the global and the regional, the essays and projects collected in this book offer various perspectives and ideas. They come from academics, professionals and the next generation of architects and designers for site-specific interventions from eight countries. From Canada, the UN Habitat Award winning architect and founder of the Affordable Homes Programme at McGill University, Avi Friedman, gives examples of his own world-celebrated projects. From the United States the book presents the award-winning social housing project from Nicholas Grimshaw architects in New York, *Via Verde*, while from Spain it collects projects from another award-winning architect, Eusebio Alonso.

These projects foreshadow essays from a series of international academics that include some of the project architects already mentioned, as well as Carlos Garcia Vazquez from La Universidad de Sevilla, Spain; Gary Sands, Wayne State University, Detroit, USA; Charlie Smith from Liverpool John Moores University, UK; Kathrin Golda-Pongratz, the Frankfurt University of Applied Sciences, Germany; and Georgios Artopoulos with Ioannis A. Pissourios from the Cyprus Institute and Neapolis University, Cyprus. Many of these academics lead the work of the students that is also included from each of these universities. They are projects that sit alongside the work of students from La Universidad de Valladolid led by Eusebio Alonso and the Politecnico di Milano, led by Guya Bertelli, Juan Carlos Dall'Asta and Federico Jappelli.

This international perspective on the role of design and planning in affordable housing cannot of course pretend to be exhaustive. It is, on the contrary, a snapshot of the innovative global work coming from the design side of the housing debate and is intended to be read as such – an indication of the variety of solutions that can be put forward in different settings by people at different stages of their own professional trajectories. From the established architects engaged we get samples of refined and thoroughly developed proposals and projects that have been built and are currently under the interrogation of use. What lessons they ultimately offer will be determined by time. From the academic circle we get a more theoretical, but still practice focused, engagement with ideas, proposals and initiatives that have been years in development and that find their way into the projects of the next generation of architects, and designers represented here. It is to these leaders of tomorrow that the challenges, failures and successes of today will fall.

It will be this generation that is forced to address the changed needs of new societies; the possibilities of new materials and building techniques; the ongoing problems of old and failed construction methods, design approaches and models. It is of course to be hoped that the focus we see on the issue of housing today will also leave this next generation with useful templates to follow and develop, successful initiatives to build upon, and farsighted theories with which to be guided as they seek to further improvements in provision and quality of housing the world over. This book is a snapshot of all that this involves.

SECTION 1:
PROFESSIONAL PROJECTS

To begin this book, we turn in the first instance to the professional projects of three architects and their respective studios operative primarily in North America and Europe. In this brief section three award-winning studios document their work. Avi Friedman is a former UN Habitat Award winner for his affordable house designs and prototypes. He also founded the affordable homes programme at McGill University, Canada. His initial intervention in this book is entitled 'Sustainable Community in Komoka, Ontario, Canada'. As the descriptive title suggests it is the brief documentation of a project he was called upon to develop for the local community of Komoka. Drawing together his experience of house design and related urban planning issues, the project he documents is typical of his integrated, and now well-documented and much celebrated, approach.

Following this, 'Via Verde and New Housing Solutions in New York City' documents the work of one of the world's leading architectural studios operative on most continents in the world, Grimshaw Architects, offer an exposition of a recent award-winning project, the Via Verde housing complex in New York. Responding to the particular features of that city, this high-rise development, represents fairly rare, but increasing, engagement with the issue of housing by this studio. Despite the fact that it is in Australia that the studio has developed most of its housing projects, the Via Verde scheme described here is an innovative attempt at dealing with housing for mid- to low-level income groups.

Ending this brief introductory section, Eusebio Alonso Architects, document several social housing projects from across Spain that show a varied attempt at dealing with the issue that places emphasis on the quality of design. Seeking to ensure 'design quality' the approach documented here does not base itself of the overarching analysis and large-scale urban design strategies evident in the work of Avi Friedman, nor does it engage in towns and cities of great density, as is the case of Grimshaw Architects. It is focused on medium- to small-scale social housing developments in relatively small cities. Setting the architects in question a very different set of constraints and issues, the projects described also operate in a culture in which living in shared buildings is the norm.

Although all from different countries, and responding to different demographic and urban contexts, each of the the projects documented here gives an indication of current practices. They all work within the strictures of contemporary society and standard economic models of funding – whether private or state funded and thus give an indication of what can, and perhaps what cannot, be achieved under these constraints. They serve as a real and 'concrete' point of departure for the more expansive and more theoretical texts that follow in Section Two.

SUSTAINABLE COMMUNITY IN KOMOKA, ONTARIO, CANADA

In one of my sixteen books on housing, *Innovative Houses: Concepts for Sustainable Living*, I describe how housing is rapidly having to adapt to the global changes of the 21st century. These include the transformation of the family and the rise of the non-traditional households, increases in construction costs, and concerns over climate change and the depletion of natural resources. Designing residential environments that address these issues is, I suggest, an urgent priority.

That book examines the latest residential design trends that have arisen in response to these challenges and is divided into four broad areas, tightly focused thematic chapters look at twenty discrete topics, such as live/work; adaptable housing; prefabrication; water efficiency; green roofs; innovative landscaping. In other works, such as *Sustainable Residential Development: Planning and Design for Green Neighborhoods*, I have highlighted related planning and demographic issues for residential and mixed-use development at larger scales. As with all my work as a practising architect, all or most of these issues, find their way into planning, design and construction proposals. The case of the Municipality of Middlesex Centre in the Province of Ontario, Canada, is no different, although the scale of the questions dealt with are those specifically relevant to a town rather than particular streets or individual buildings.

The area has witnessed growth since the 1990s. Most notable was the development of new low-density subdivisions ever closer to the city of London. As this trend is set to continue, the municipality wanted to have a neighborhood built around the new Wellness Centre in Komoka, one of its former hamlets (Figure 1). As a result I was invited to propose a plan for the land. While the specific objectives were gathered from a consultation with members of the community and council, the general mandate was for a mixed-use residential town center based on sustainable principles.

Figure 1: Images of Komoka, Ontario, Canada

Context and History

Located 14.7 miles (23.7 km) west of the City of London, Komoka has an area of 1.2 sq. miles (1.9 sq. km) and a population of 1,190. Its close proximity to London has made the place a bedroom community surrounded by a provincial park, a number of lakes and ponds, as well as agriculture land. It is also a crossing point for three national railway lines. Country Road 14 runs along the southern edge, joining it with the neighboring district of Kilworth (Figure 2). In Komoka there are two large senior residences, two schools, and a community centre. The new Wellness Centre offers an indoor gym, ice rinks, and a library.

Komoka's urban roots date back to 1798 when the first British settlers arrived and established mills that generated power using water from the Thames River. The construction of the Great Western Railway in 1857 was the main catalyst for residential

Figure 2: The project's site is located near the neighbourhoods of Komoka and Kilworth

and hotel development. Other factors adding to the area's prosperity were the many gravel deposits and the harvesting of dense forests of red and yellow pine. Komoka continues to be a railway crossing point, although it is no longer the hub it once was, and the hotels have long since gone.

As for the site, its total area is 56 acres (22.63 hectares) made up of five parcels of a fairly flat terrain. A north–south road crosses the parcels leading to the adjacent neighborhoods. The plot west of the Wellness Centre included a filled-out former gravel pit.

Setting Objectives

In setting design objectives we examined and accounted for Komoka's current and future needs as expressed during the various consultations. In addition, Leadership in Energy and Environmental Design (LEED) criteria were considered and suitable sustainable planning principles listed as shown in Figure 3. Key aspects with implication on our planning and environmental design strategies were: to reduce automobile dependency and design a walkable community by developing an extensive network of pedestrian and bike paths; consider and include the site's natural features; have medium-density, mixed-use, and diverse housing prototypes to accommodate people of all ages; offer easy connection between the dwellings, the commercial amenities, and the Wellness Centre; orient dwellings for passive solar gain and the possibility of add-on photovoltaic (PV) panels; and include trees, native plants and landscaped xeriscaping practice, as well as allow areas for community gardens and urban agriculture.

Location: 1-10 points

Compact development: 1-6 points

Reduced automobile dependency: 1-7 points

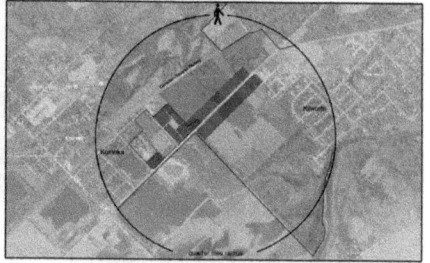

Mixed-use neighborhood: 1-4 points

Bike network and storage: 1 point

Mixed income diverse communities: 1-7 points

Walkable streets: 1-2 points

Building energy efficiency, solar orientation and
on-site renewable energy: 2-6 points

Figure 3: Some LEED criteria that guided the project's environmental performance and their ratings

Sustainable Plan

Our three key planning features were to develop a 'green' neighborhood, consider cultural, civic and recreational activities, and follow Low Impact Development (LID) principles. As for the residences, it was decided that the majority of the housing would be medium-density single and multi-family townhouses affordable for first-time buyers. Apartment buildings were located west of the Wellness Center and will provide affordable accommodations for seniors. A small percentage of the land towards north of the site was dedicated to single-family detached housing as well. The objective was to have a medium-density community of between four to nine units per acre (9.8 to 22.2 per hectare) for a diverse population (Figure 4).

To provide services to the new neighborhood and to the municipality at large, commercial amenities were located along County Road 14. It was also assumed that the location of and the accessibility to the Wellness Center would draw tourists and make them want to explore the town's other offerings. The land north of the Center had been transformed into a communal park to include a variety of outdoor recreational attractions for residents and visitors.

A covered walkway was introduced to provide access from the back of the Wellness Center to a row of shops and cafés. In the southwest corner we introduced a square,

Figure 4: Site plan

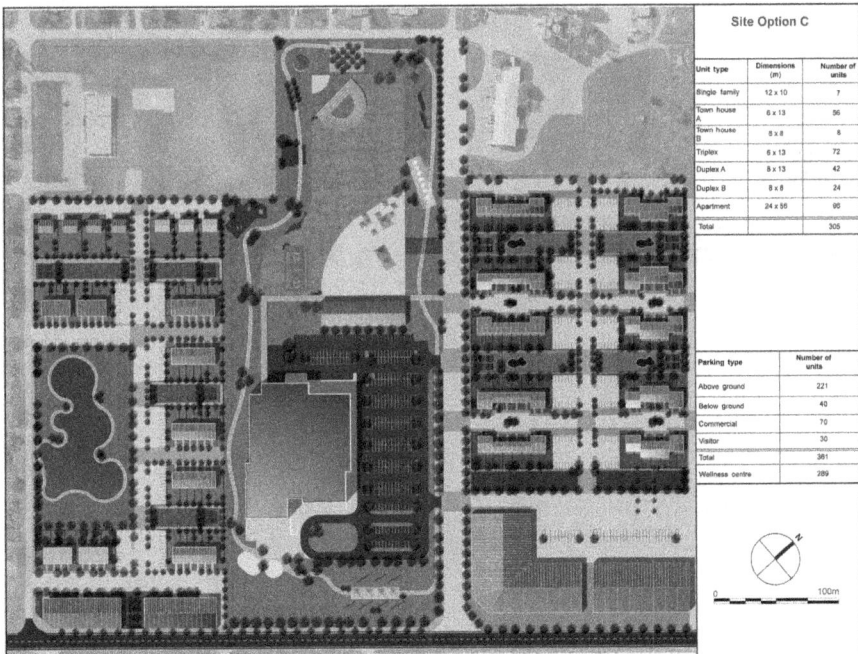

Site Option C		
Unit type	Dimensions (m)	Number of units
Single family	12 x 10	7
Town house A	6 x 13	56
Town house B	8 x 8	8
Triplex	6 x 13	72
Duplex A	8 x 13	42
Duplex B	8 x 8	24
Apartment	24 x 96	96
Total		305

Parking type	Number of units
Above ground	221
Below ground	40
Commercial	70
Visitor	30
Total	361
Wellness centre	389

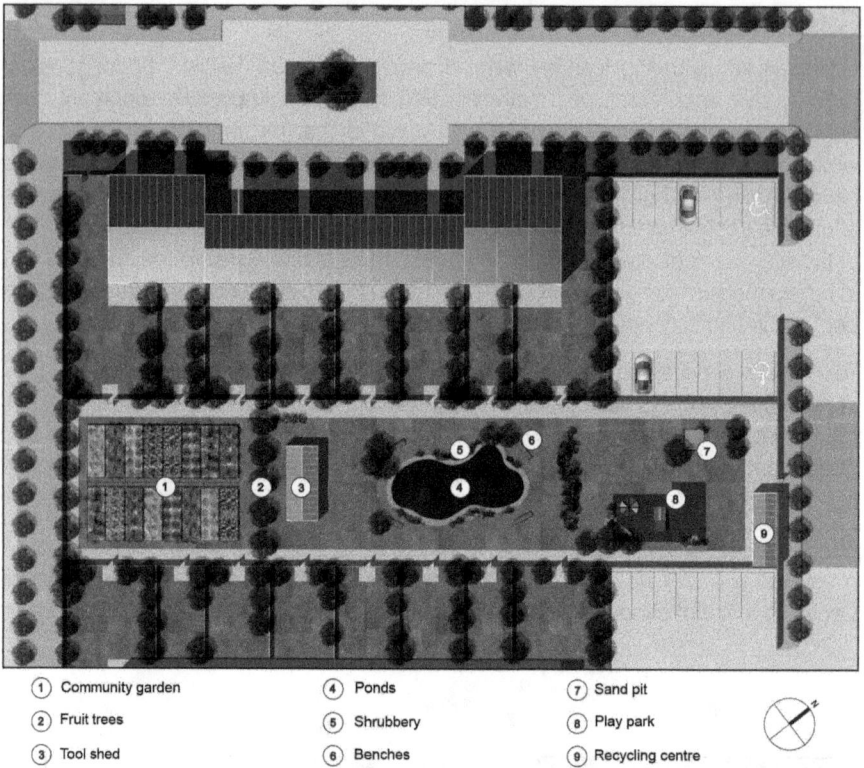

(1) Community garden	(4) Ponds	(7) Sand pit
(2) Fruit trees	(5) Shrubbery	(8) Play park
(3) Tool shed	(6) Benches	(9) Recycling centre

Figure 5: The common green area

for civic events. A path for walking, jogging, and cycling looped the park to create a link with the recreational area. Along the path, visitors would enjoy a toddlers' water spray park, local history and art display boards, sitting area in an orchard, an outdoor exercise equipment space, as well as a children's play park. In addition, an outdoor amphitheatre and a bandstand were located in the northwest.

Several pools of water from harvested sources ranging from reflection to natural ponds, will be featured in the park. Land surrounding the pools has been allotted for urban agriculture and the growing of crops (Figure 5). The water linking the pools follows a path reminiscent of the River Thames as a reminder of the town's unique sense of place.

All medium- and high-density housing has shared parking either behind or to the side of each residential block. It minimizes the amount of land dedicated to the car and improves the use and attractiveness of the street. All streets and lanes have been designed to be shared surfaces that prioritize the pedestrian and encourage cycling. In addition, a bike path runs the length of the neighborhood and connects to a bike path

Location	Guide	Illustration
Composting Centre	**Intent** To provide a cheap alternative to landfill and foster growth of more disease resistant plants that are superior in color, flavor, and reproductive capacity. **Guidelines** One composting center per 6 households, based on aeration purposes. Composting pile will be at ground level for drainage and away from uncontrollable water sources. Additional water supply will keep pile from drying out.	Bin composter Food digester
Recycling Centre	**Intent** To reduce the amount of raw material needed to make new products and as a result reduce air pollution and solid waste. **Guidelines** Recycling centres will be located in each residential block and be easily accessible to all. 1 rolling bin per 2 units will be located in each centre and a weekly collection system will be in place.	Recycling centre Composters Planting strip
Shared amenities	**Intent** To reduce energy consumption and foster neighborhood relations. The development will provide areas for shared amenities. **Guidelines** To reduce land given to parking, a common parking lot will be provided for each multi-residential unit. In addition, launderettes will be located within a close proximity of each residential unit for washing and drying clothes.	
Rain Water Collection	**Intent** To reduce effects on natural resources and reduce burdens on community water supply systems. **Guidelines** Each residential unit will be provided with a drywell to collect rainwater which will be excavated near a downspout where a barrel can also be placed. Water collected can be used for watering gardens.	

Figure 6: Guidelines for some of the project's environmental features

proposed for County Road 14 where traffic calming measures will be introduced. These measures will include a change of surface texture at the entrance to the town, planter boxes, sidewalk projections, and the inclusion of a bike lane. It was also proposed that the town considers having a 'rent-a-bike' system, which will include a station at the Wellness Center.

Architectural guidelines have been prepared to offer design principles of massing, exterior façade, windows, doors, streetscape, and parking. They were developed while considering the various housing types listed in the master plan. In addition, a separate set of environmental recommendations has been introduced to address orientation, nature, public health, urban agriculture, landscaping, and composting and recycling (Figure 6 and Figure 7).

Location	Guide	Illustration
Community Gardens	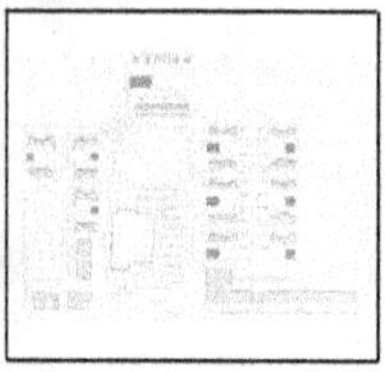 **Intent** Promote community-based agriculture, improve nutrition with fresh produce, support small farms local economy. Permanent and viable spaces for community gardens and agriculture. **Guidelines** Provide solar access, fencing, watering systems, garden bed enhancements, secure tool storage and pedestrian access. The project will ensure that these spaces are owned and managed by an entity that includes residents using the space. 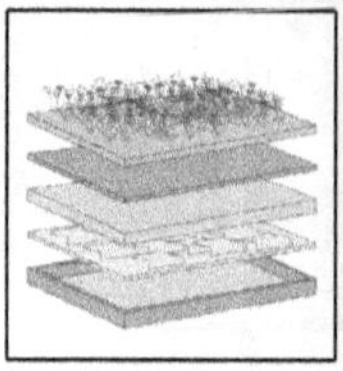 	
Private Gardens	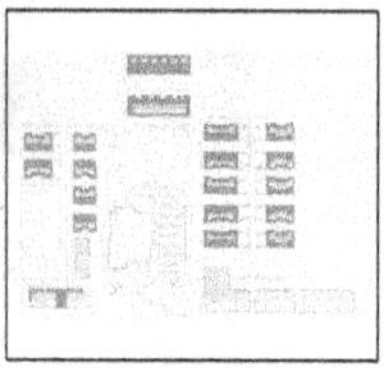 **Intent** To encourage healthy living and improve nutrition through increased access to fresh produce. **Guidelines** The projects will establish *convenants, conditions, and restrictions* (CC&R), which will state that the growing is not prohibited in the project area. This will allow use of private greenhouses and food production in front and back yards, balconies, and rooftops. 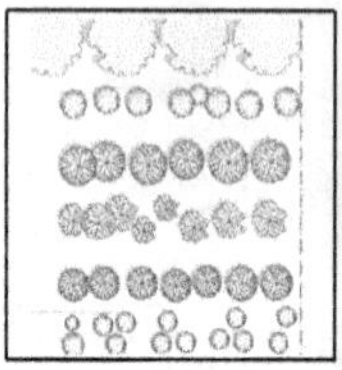 	
Green Roofs	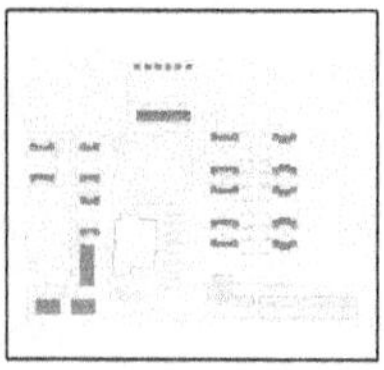 **Intent** To promote the social, economical, and environmental benefits of green roofs. **Guidelines** The project will permit rooftop gardens for growing fruit, vegetables, herbs, and flowers. 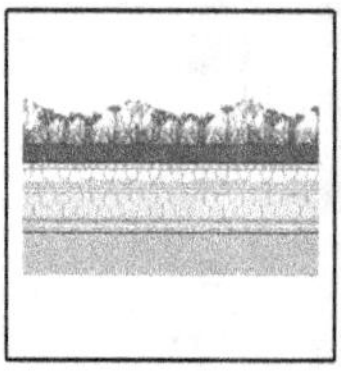 	
Farmer's Market	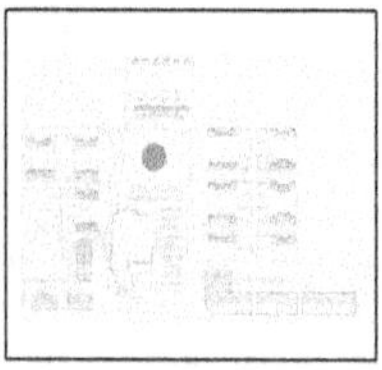 **Intent** Improve nutrition with increased access to fresh produce, support small farms and local economy. **Guidelines** The project will housea farmer's market that will operate oncea week for 5 months a year. Only items grown within 241 km of site may be sold. The market must have firm commitment from farmers and vendors to meet above requirements. 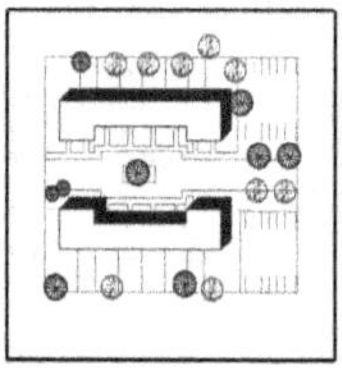 	

Figure 7: Guidelines for the project's additional environmental features

VIA VERDE AND NEW HOUSING SOLUTIONS IN NEW YORK CITY

New York City, in an effort to curb a growing housing crisis, has executed a variety of programs, competitions, and schemes in an effort to increase the number of housing units available in the city, particularly those geared towards mid and lower income residents. Grimshaw has participated in a number of these competitions and bid processes, often in concert with additional architects, developers, landscape architects, and other consultants. Over time, separate initiatives and competitions have addressed a range of design solutions tailored to specific local and demographic circumstances. What unites these developments is not only an increased commitment to design, but increasing demand and competition for the few units that are available.

In Long Island City, a formerly industrial waterfront neighborhood in Queens, the city has erected towering residential buildings, Hunter's Point South, that offer stunning views of Manhattan and easy access to public transportation. The number of applications for the 924 available units exceeded 92,700 before the lottery's closing date in December, 2014. Grimshaw's unsuccessful competition entry for the project, executed with Jonathan Rose Companies and Fetner Properties, proposed a project with 100% permanently affordable units available at a mix of income levels (Figures 1–3). Even in this seemingly best case scenario, approximately half of families in Queens earn below the minimum income threshold that imparts eligibility for subsidized units. The final project, anticipating residents in mid-2015, is anticipated to set aside 60% of units as affordable to low- and moderate-income families.

Rising on Manhattan's east side is another City-led project, AdAPT NYC, the city's first endeavor in microhousing. The building, containing 55 apartments that range from 250 to 370 square feet, is meant to accommodate New York's growing number of one- and two-person households who are willing to share some amenities, like gardens, storage space, a lounge, and a gym, with other tenants. The team behind the winning entry, to

Figure 1. Hunters Point South 2nd St: 'View of proposed Hunter point South development as approached from the Subway' (Grimshaw Architects)

Figure 2. Hunters Point South Courtyard: 'Overlooking central courtyard of proposed Hunters Point South development toward the East river and Manhattan beyond' (Grimshaw Architects)

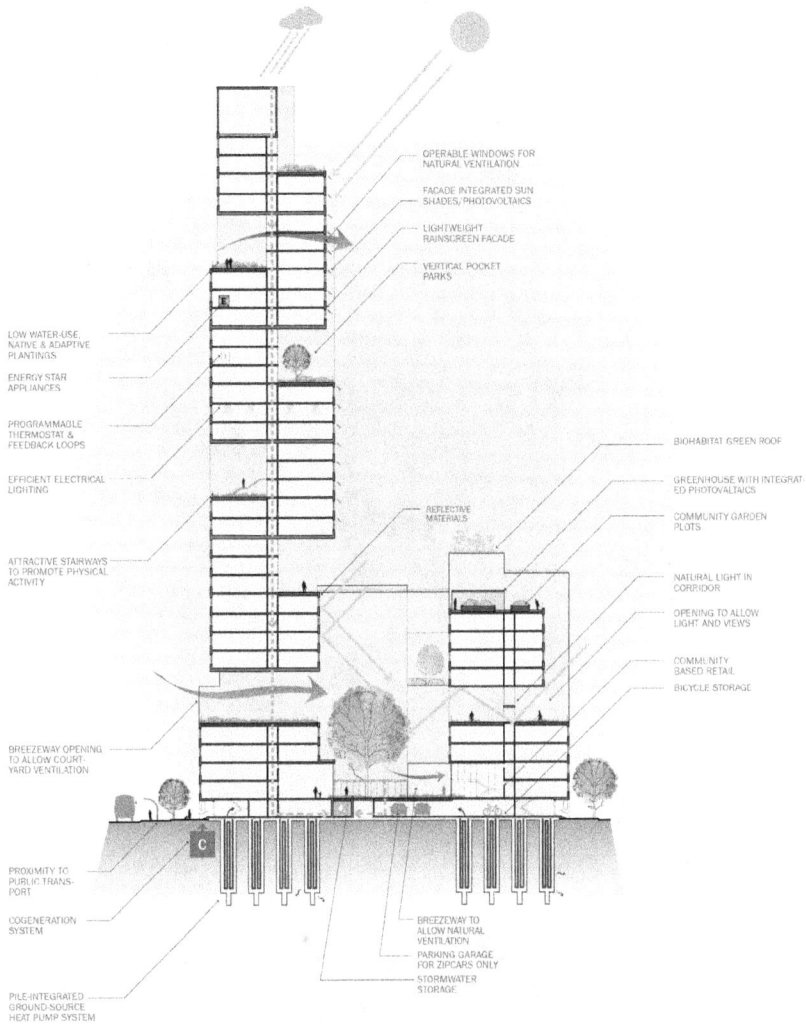

OPERABLE WINDOWS FOR
NATURAL VENTILATION

FACADE INTEGRATED SUN
SHADES/PHOTOVOLTAICS

LIGHTWEIGHT
RAINSCREEN FACADE

VERTICAL POCKET
PARKS

LOW WATER-USE,
NATIVE & ADAPTIVE
PLANTINGS

ENERGY STAR
APPLIANCES

PROGRAMMABLE
THERMOSTAT &
FEEDBACK LOOPS

EFFICIENT ELECTRICAL
LIGHTING

ATTRACTIVE STAIRWAYS
TO PROMOTE PHYSICAL
ACTIVITY

BREEZEWAY OPENING
TO ALLOW COURT-
YARD VENTILATION

PROXIMITY TO
PUBLIC TRANS-
PORT

COGENERATION
SYSTEM

PILE-INTEGRATED
GROUND-SOURCE
HEAT PUMP SYSTEM

BIOHABITAT GREEN ROOF

GREENHOUSE WITH INTEGRAT-
ED PHOTOVALTAICS

COMMUNITY GARDEN
PLOTS

NATURAL LIGHT IN
CORRIDOR

OPENING TO ALLOW
LIGHT AND VIEWS

COMMUNITY
BASED RETAIL

BICYCLE STORAGE

REFLECTIVE
MATERIALS

BREEZEWAY TO
ALLOW NATURAL
VENTILATION

PARKING GARAGE
FOR ZIPCARS ONLY

STORMWATER
STORAGE

Figure 3. Hunters Point South Section: 'Summary section of sustainability strategies for Hunters Point South' (Grimshaw Architects and Atelier Ten)

be completed by the end of 2015, includes Monadnock Development LLC, Actors Fund Housing, Corcoran Sunshine, and architects nARCHITECTS.

Prior to both Hunter's Point South and AdAPT NYC, a consortium of high-level organizations introduced the New Housing New York Ideas competition. The competition was initiated by the New York City Department of Housing Preservation and Development (HPD), New York State Energy Research and Development Authority, the American Institute of Architects New York Chapter, and Enterprise Community Partners. The brief called for affordable housing that exhibits innovative design solutions to New York City's pressing housing production problems. The proposal stressed that submitted designs address the importance of affordability, sustainability, transferability, and viability.

Figure 4. Via Verde Courtyard: 'Elevated view over courtyard looking south' (David Sundberg/Esto)

Figure 5. Via Verde Façade: 'Street view of Brook side façade looking north' (David Sundberg/Esto)

Via Verde, the winning scheme from co-developers Jonathan Rose Companies and Phipps Houses, and co-architects Dattner Architects and Grimshaw, reflects a commitment to create the next generation of social housing that addresses poverty, health, and the environment (Figures 4–6). Arranged on a long, narrow, former brownfield lot, Via Verde activates the challenging site with a development that wraps around the perimeter, creating and framing open space for the residents' use. An integrated approach enabled the project to creatively address site constraints, navigate the public approvals process, and become a beacon for this developing community.

Three building types - a 20-story tower to the north, a 6- to 13-story mid-rise duplex apartment component in the middle, and 2- to 4-story townhouses to the south – make up the complex. The 222 apartments include 71 work force housing cooperatives for residents earning 80–100% of the Area Median Income (AMI) and 151 low-income rentals for residents earning 60% or less of AMI. The project provides both affordable rental and ownership housing.

The building envelope consists of a prefabricated rain screen panel system that provides a well-insulated, 'breathing' enclosure with a contemporary aesthetic. The innovative structure came equipped with windows, sunshades, and balconies, all in one piece. Comprised of metal and cement board panels, with wood panel accents, the facades create a lively, distinct appearance. Via Verde is one of the first housing developments to use this type of panelized system at this scale. Increased quality control from the

Figure 6. Via Verde Gardening: 'Residents working in roof top community garden overlooking central courtyard' (David Sundberg/Esto)

outset allowed the construction team to install the modules at a faster-than-normal rate, enclosing the building far sooner than typical construction methodologies.

The ground floor features a private medical facility and a pharmacy alongside live-work units, creating a lively street presence. A main entry portal leads to residential lobbies and townhouse entries. Stairwells with natural lighting and colorful finishes are prominently placed at each entry point with signs encouraging residents to save electricity and get exercise by forgoing use of the elevators.

At the heart of Via Verde are a series of gardens that begin in the courtyard and then spiral up through a series of green roofs and south facing solar panels. The rooftop gardens dissipate heat and absorb rainwater runoff, using a reclamation system that recycles water for irrigation, while providing opportunities for active gardening, fruit and vegetable cultivation, relaxation, and social gathering. A landscaped courtyard, the green roofs, a fitness center, and day-lit stairs promote healthy lifestyles and provide opportunities for physical fitness.

The terraced roof gardens and various public spaces were designed, in part, in response to community feedback sessions advocating for communal activity spaces. Growing food on site also reinforces healthy living principles that are further encouraged through the availability of an attractive exercise room, and a continuous walking path amongst many of the garden terraces. These multifunctional gardens create opportunities for gardening, recreation, and social gathering, all with an increased connection to the outdoors.

The Dattner and Grimshaw team was appointed to the project in June 2007, with construction commencing in March 2010. Prior to the start of construction, the site underwent extensive remediation due to a previous gas station on the corner of the development site, which, after the station's closure, was used as an abandoned railroad yard that lay below street level. The project's structure topped out in January 2011, and the completed building was officially opened by then New York City Mayor Michael Bloomberg in June 2012.

The project continues the work of the studio which, since its establishment by Sir Nicholas Grimshaw in 1980, has strived to achieve bespoke, carefully crafted design solutions utilizing up-to-the-moment material and building capabilities across nearly all building sectors and across the globe. The Grimshaw studio is founded on analysis and exploration, rather than the imposed application of a pre-ordained stylistic architectural solution. This method allows us to explore design in a much more organic way. The studio is a place of innovation, invention, and imagination – a place where the atmosphere is more that of a laboratory or think-tank than of a typical architecture office. This group boldly engages in design from first principles, and their solutions are often unexpected, but, once understood, resonantly clear.

Our solutions evolve out of broad investigation and a thorough understanding of a project's program – the careful balancing of elements that make up architecture. The investigation continues right down to the finest detail, so that each detail element has the DNA signature of the overall concept. We believe that beauty arises through functionality, and often see our most integrated and unique architecture achieved through this pragmatic approach. The Via Verde project is just one example of this.

Via Verde Project Team:

Dattner Architects, Grimshaw Architects, Jonathan Rose Companies, Phipps Houses

Hunters Point South Proposal Team:

Grimshaw Architects, Starr Whitehouse Landscape Architects, SLCE Architects, Atelier Ten, Jonathan Rose Companies, Fetner Properties

EUSEBIO ALONSO GARCÍA ARCHITECTS

Eusebio Alonso García Architects was established over 30 years ago. It pays special attention to the issue of housing and has won several public awards. It is interested in creating contemporary and flexible domestic space and beneficial relationships between the interior and exterior in the context of public and collective housing. Among its projects are a 48-unit public housing project in Benta Berri, San Sebastian, which won First Award in a national competition in Spain and a proposal for public housing that was shortlisted for the European III Award in 1994.

Other projects include a nine-house unit in Valladolid in Delicias Street, 1993, which respected the scale and context of its popular district. The project explores the possibility of generating public space on the ground floor while linking to the dwelling units themselves, operating as a point of access as well as a social space for meeting neighbours. A later project to build 12 public housing units in Ciudad de Osma (Soria), 1998, won first prize in the competition of the Council of Castilla and León. The houses are arranged in a continuous and compact block that is articulated volumetrically to reflect the complex topography of the site. Key to the project was the reinstallation of a small square to the village which also doubles as access to the publicly funded housing units.

The concerns for the integration of daily life into the infrastructure of the housing units and the incorporation of public social space into the fabric of the housing block that characterized previous projects was also evident in 19 public houses built on the outskirts of the village of Santa Cristina de la Polvorosa (Zamora) in 1998–2001. Receiving awards from the Council of Castilla y León, the VI brick Architecture Prize, and Hispalyt, this project was designed to incorporate the three distinct courtyards accessible from each of the dwellings, thereby helping to articulate different levels of privacy and facilitate urban gardening.

In recent years, the studio has been interested in typological research, developments necessary in housing for new social contexts, and the increasing importance of

Figures 1–3. 16 Public Houses in San Adrián Las Villas in Valladolid.

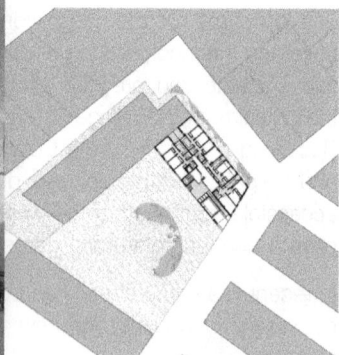

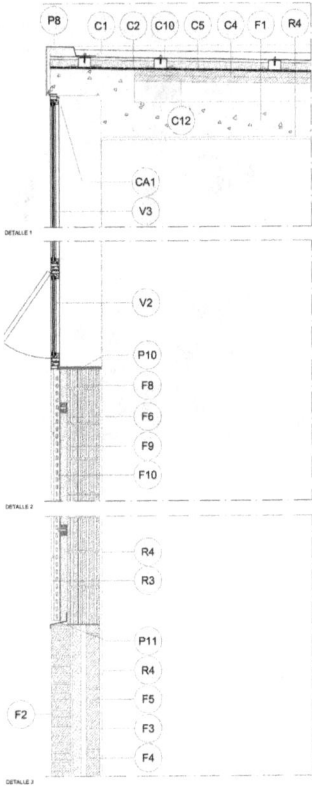

environmental issues. This is reflected in a project for 50 homes for young people in Palencia, 2007, and 16 public housing units constructed for the City Council of Valladolid, 2006 (Figures 1–3). Both these projects received multiple national awards. In the latter of these, the layout formed a square in a neighbourhood that was in the beginning stages of regeneration, the materials were seen to reflect its 'urban condition' and the plan permitted different forms and levels of accessibility by designing steps from the square and a ramp from the street, as well as a lift for people and a separate one for cars.

The Project for Valladolid adopts various strategies including attention to the structures and characteristics of the existing urban context through reducing the circulation systems of the site to a single clearly defined route; opening up views to the more traditional areas of the district; and creating new useable public space for residents. In addition, its aesthetic treatment is based on combing brick with vertically orientated windows on the north and east facades along with ecologically sound and energy efficient materials – a concern for the environment reflected in the project's incorporation of solar panel

Figures 4–6. 48 Public Houses in Santos
Pilarica in Valladolid.

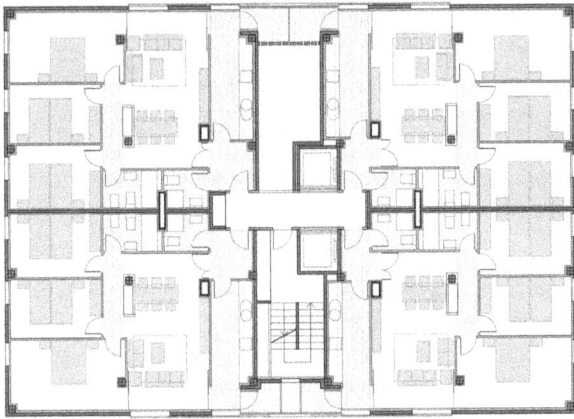

Planta Tipo.

systems as naturally as possible. In short, it is a project that on a limited design and construction budget has helped regenerate the neighbourhood; that integrates with, and improves its public spaces; and which limits running costs for low income residents by its use of energy efficient materials and systems.

Built at the same time, the Santos Pilarica project in Valladolid involved the development of two small towers containing 48 public housing units next to the ring road of Valladolid (Figures 4–6). The recipient of multiple awards, these towers form a landmark whilst also respecting the small scale of the typical housing unit. Designed to have a versatile and flexible plan, they respond to changing lifestyle preferences and create visual interest externally through the incorporation of mobile shutters on the curtain wall, enabling the formal resolution of two scales: landmark block and individual house.

The principal issue in the design of this project is the fact that it is a new community. In this context it is necessary to create an 'identity' for particular buildings but also, and more importantly, for the wider area and neighbourhood. It is an area that, as with all new urban residential projects, has a quickly growing community, often with young families whose needs change as the family grows – and ages. Consequently, the adaptability of the interiors is a primary concern. In terms of visual identity as a means of facilitating community identity, the project uses visibly recognizable perforated aluminum sheets contrasted with brick and has two towers that are immediately recognizable. In addition, these define an area of common public space between them, intended to create a sense of shared space and shared form.

More recently, the studio has engaged with designs for institutions: a Health Centre in Mombuey, 2010, and a Centre for Entrepreneurs in Torrelavega, Santander, 2013. It has also participated in international competitions, including the Gosan Public Library in Daegu, Korea, 2012 and the ZIM Residential complex in Samara, Russia, 2014. In all of these projects the studio's ethos of integrating public and private space, of allowing for changing uses and ways of living remains paramount.

When dealing with housing one is obliged to think beyond the house as a unit and consider the context in which people are housed – their neighbourhoods and urban settings. It is thus a question of operating at various scales – of creating spaces adequate for the way an individual lives, and spaces adequate for how we interact as communities at the urban scale. These are generic themes that have only been underlined in recent years in countries like Spain where the economic conditions in which housing is produced have been extremely difficult.

In these conditions, as with many other countries across Europe, this has focused attention somewhat away from new build and towards the renovation of existing housing stock which, in the context of the social housing of Spain, was largely built in the 1960s and 1970s. This raises a series of further issues that the projects described here have all engaged with in their distinct ways. This housing stock, although designed and built according to norms that are now out-of-date, do have an advantageous commonality – they are generally located near the centre of Spanish cities. This, together with the fact that are large in scale, makes the question of housing inseparable from the question of the urban.

To deal specifically with these issues in the Spanish context, it is arguable that there are three principal lines of action required. Firstly, we have to adapt the domestic spaces of these complexes so they meet the needs of today's smaller, more individual-focused and multi-cultural families that increasingly see the home as a workplace. Secondly, we have to deal with ways of improving the public spaces that were built during this period and which have to now host quite different social activities at different times of day, and involving different types of people and communities. Thirdly, it is unquestionable today that any work we do on actual houses or their urban settings, has to have an awareness of limited energy use at its core. These three strands are evident in every project outlined here and will be essential to what is likely to be the next wave of housing projects in countries like Spain – projects focused on renovation.

SECTION TWO:
THEORETICAL–PRACTICAL ESSAYS

The previous brief project descriptions offer a practice-based sense of what is possible working to the standard constraints of relatively large-scale commercially focused housing projects in developed economies. Innovation is possible, but in reality, is severely tempered by the broader economic, cultural and social contexts in the countries in question. Those contexts set the time of the style of architecture possible, the size of the projects, the money available and the models of living accommodated. Despite their attempts to push those boundaries, their commercial imperatives inevitably limit possibilities.

In part as a response to those constraints it is typical of the academic field to search for alternatives through theory, research and the analysis of approaches that could, at least conceptually, operate outside these restrictions. That said, academia is not a rarefied world in which utopias are the only models sought as alternatives to commercial imperatives. On the contrary, it is often the place where commercial and practical research takes place with a view very firmly on the real world scenarios that produce the projects just described. Free – in these cases – of the immediate time and commercial imperatives of practice, this type of research very often has immediate and practical import.

It is in the spirit of this practice-orientated research and theoretical exploration that the essays incorporated in this section of the book have been developed. Considering, in some cases, the economics and urban decline of places like Detroit, or the need to renovate the deteriorating housing stock of the recent past, or in other instances, looking at practical ways of improving design quality whilst still providing affordability, these essays are extended explorations of real issues. They cover a geographical terrain that is as broad as that of their thematic content: North America, Europe and Latin America. They are written by academics from several countries and consider issues as they relate to specific places and sites – whether they be countries or regions of countries.

As is typical of the academic essay, they are more extensive engagements in their areas of concern than the brief project outlines of Section One. They develop their arguments according to standard scholarly tropes and formats and offer the reader access to multiple additional sources of research, documentation and investigations. In some cases, they document real projects, in others they analyse data and, in some instances, they present social and critical theory. They all offer a very different perspective and approach to the issue of housing affordability, quality and supply than seen in Section One. They also offer the conceptual framework for the design proposals that follow in Section Three. They begin in the United States and end by crossing the Atlantic from Lima to Madrid.

GARY SANDS

HOPE FOR BETTER THINGS: HOUSING MARKET FAILURE IN DETROIT

Introduction

At the beginning of the 20th century, Detroit was the fastest growing major city in the United States. Rapid growth of the automobile industry helped to bring more than one million new residents to the city between 1900 and 1930. As Detroit expanded its boundaries and population, much of today's built environment and public infrastructure were created. The automobile industry also helped to create a prosperous working class, many of whom were able to own their own homes. By 1950, the majority of Detroit households (54 percent) were owner occupants; single- and two-family homes dominate Detroit's housing stock. Public (government owned) housing represented less than five percent of the total; privately owned rental housing made up the balance.

The story of the collapse of Detroit's housing market starts with the loss of employment opportunities that began half a century ago.[1] The manufacturing employment that was largely responsible for Detroit's growth in the first part of the 20th century was a major factor in the city's decline in the latter half. In 1970, there were 735,000 jobs in the city of Detroit. By 2000, there were 390,000 fewer jobs left in the city. Many jobs relocated to the suburbs, where employment increased from 1.2 million in 1970 to 2.3 million in 2000. Detroit's share of total metropolitan employment fell from 38 percent to 13 percent. In 1950, there were almost 760,000 Detroit residents with jobs, divided between the city and its suburbs. Almost 28 percent of these jobs were in the motor vehicle manufacturing industry. Fifty years later, the number of Detroiters with jobs was just 331,000, a decline of over half.

This employment collapse brought about a decline in Detroit's population and households. From a peak population of 1.85 million in 1950, the number of Detroit

---

1   Reese, L., Sands, G. and Skidmore, M. (2014) "Memo from Motown: Is Austerity Here to Stay?" *Cambridge Journal of Regions, Economy and Society* 7(1): 99-116.

residents fell to 951,000 in 2000. The number of households fell from a high of 515,000 in 1960 to an estimated 256,600 in 2013. The residential vacancy rate in Detroit was just over ten percent.

Detroit in the 21st Century

Economy and Employment

Between 2000 and 2012, the number of private sector jobs in the city declined by 30 percent, to 180,300. Job losses were particularly severe in the city's neighborhoods, where the number of jobs fell by over 74,000 (Table 1); city center employment, in contrast, declined by just five percent. Annual payroll of downtown workers actually rose by a third during this period, partially offsetting the substantial decline in annual payroll in the rest of the city. By 2013, the downtown core accounted for 49 percent of jobs and 62 percent of payrolls.

	Employees			Annual Payroll (000,000)		
	2000	2012	Change	2000	2012	Change
Core	93,168	88,055	-5.5%	$4.176	$6.257	49.8%
Balance	166,171	91,814	-44.7%	$6.566	$3.775	-42.5%
Total	259,339	179,869	-30.6%	$10.742	$10.032	-6.6%

Table 1. Employment and Income in Detroit, 2000–13
Source: County Business Patterns

Job losses outside the core were affected by the continuing decline of the manufacturing sector (Table 2). The net loss of manufacturing establishments was just over 40 percent; the number of manufacturing workers fell by more than 22,000. The 51 percent decline in manufacturing payrolls is equivalent to almost a 62 percent decline when adjusted for inflation. Other businesses, such as retail trade, personal and business services, have had similar declines. The number of Detroiters with jobs declined by more than 30 percent, while the unemployment rate doubled, from 13.8 percent to 28.5 percent.

	2002	2007	2012	Change
Establishments	647	472	382	-40.1%
Employees	38,019	22,962	17,013	-55.3%
Payroll (000,000)	$2.054	$1.486	$1.009	-50.9%

Table 2. Detroit Manufacturing Trends, 2002–12
Source: US Economic Census

Population and Housing

Current estimates put Detroit's population at 689,000. Many of these residents have limited education and skills; the proportion of Detroiters with a bachelor's degree is just 12.7 percent, less than half the national average. The proportion of Detroiters with a disability (19.5 percent) is significantly above the national average of 12.1 percent. It is not surprising that Detroit residents find it increasingly difficult to qualify for the dwindling number of jobs that are available. Median household income in Detroit declined by more than 11 percent in current dollars; the decline was 34.3 percent adjusted for inflation. Poverty rates in the city are well above both the corresponding values in 2000 and the current national averages.

	2000	2013	Change
Median Household Income	$29,626	$26,325	-$3,301
Persons in Poverty	28.1%	39.3%	+11.2 points
Children in Poverty	37.5%	53.3%	+15.8 points
College Graduates	11.0%	12.7%	+1.7 points
With a Disability	11.4%	19.5%	+8.1 points
Households with No Vehicle	21.9%	24.1%	+2.2 points

Table 3. Detroit Population Characteristics, 2000–13
Source: American Community Survey

Since the turn of the century, Detroit has issued permits for 9,500 residential units, mostly multi-family housing. During the same period, the City demolished more than 37,400 housing units, resulting in a net decline of almost 27,900 units in Detroit. Despite the reduction in the housing stock, the city's residential vacancy rate tripled, to 29.3 percent, as the number of occupied housing units fell by 80,000, a decline of more than 27 percent.

Detroit Housing Market Activity

Virtually every metropolitan area in the United States experienced a housing market collapse in 2008–09.[2] While Detroit was no exception, the causes and consequences of the housing crash are distinct. For Metropolitan areas like Phoenix or Las Vegas, the price collapse was truly the result of bursting of a speculative price bubble. In other metropolitan areas, such as Charlotte, the housing price index declined less and recovered more rapidly. Although the sharp drop in prices was painful for many households, especially those whose homes were lost to foreclosure, there has been a significant price recovery in recent years.

Nationally, average home prices recovered almost two-thirds of their post-2007 losses by 2014 (Figure 1); Charlotte's home price index, for example, had regained more than 70 percent of its losses. Detroit, on the other hand, had regained just half of its losses,

---

2   Blinder, A. (2013) *After the Music Stopped* (New York, Penguin Books).

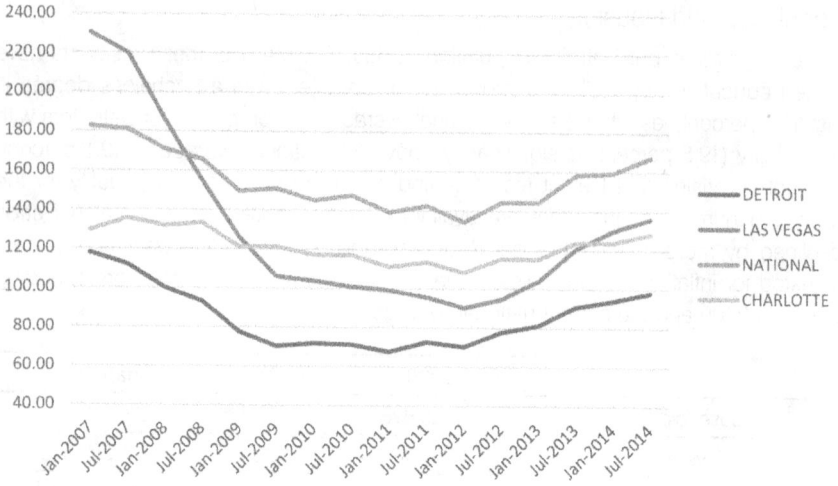

Figure 1. Metropolitan House Price Index, 2007–13
Source: S&P Case-Schiller Housing Price Index

Figure 2. City of Detroit Residential Sales Price Trends
Source: Realty Trac

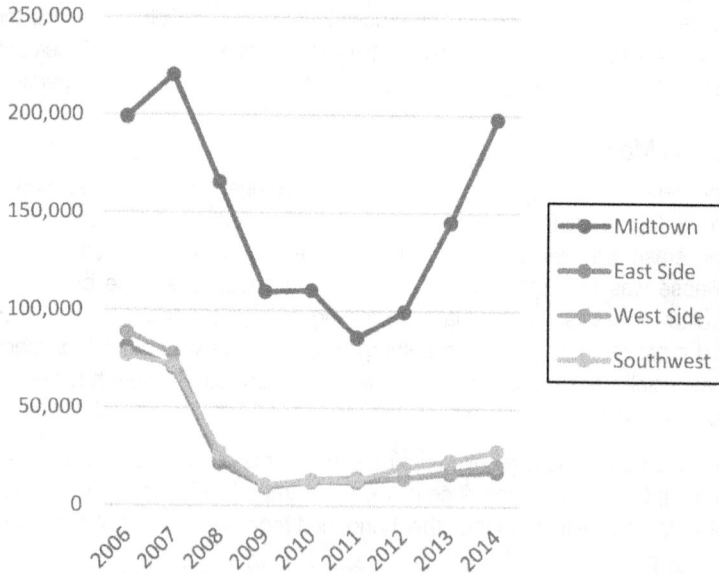

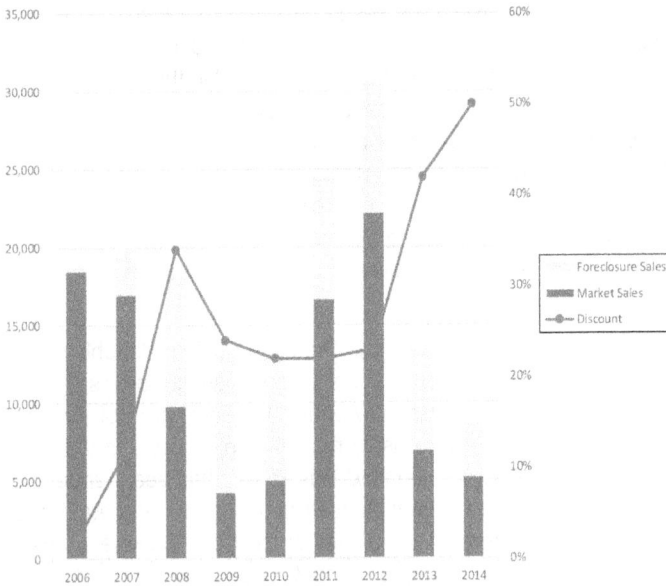

Figure 3. Detroit Market and Foreclosure Home Sales, 2006–14 Source: Realty Trac

and continues to have the lowest home price index among the 20 metropolitan areas surveyed by Case-Schiller.

Detroit's housing collapse is the result of fundamental structural weakness in the housing market. The decline in employment in Detroit led to a reduction in population and incomes that has pushed housing prices down. As a result, the recovery in Detroit home prices has proceeded more slowly than elsewhere in the metropolitan area.

Figure 2 illustrates housing price trends in Detroit's core area and in the rest of the city from 2006 – just prior to the Great Recession – to 2014. In all four parts of the city, home prices dropped sharply between 2006 and 2009. Home prices in the Midtown/Downtown core area of the city continued to decline until 2011, when a sharp recovery began. By 2014, core area home sale prices were less than one percent below the 2006 average. In Detroit's neighborhoods, average sales prices were at their low point in 2009. Since then, prices have recovered, but at a much lower rate than in Midtown/Downtown; average sales prices in 2014 were just 22 percent to 36 percent of the corresponding 2006 average.

Detroit, like other American cities, was plagued by a large number of mortgage foreclosures in this period. In 2009–10, foreclosure sales depressed prices, crowding out most market sales. Beginning in 2008, foreclosure sales prices have been at least 22 percent less than the market sales prices. Because foreclosure rates were also high in Detroit's suburbs, prices declined there as well, allowing many Detroit residents to afford a house in the suburbs.

Currently, the City of Detroit is experiencing a second wave of foreclosures, this time for unpaid property taxes. Over half of Detroit taxpayers are delinquent in their property tax payments.[3] As many as 62,000 properties could be included in this year's auction; the actual number may be considerably less because the volume exceeds the capacity to process all of the potential sales.[4] There are two important differences between the mortgage and tax foreclosures. The mortgage foreclosure process is relatively short, usually about six months; about three years are required to complete a tax foreclosure. Moreover, property tax payments continue to be made for mortgage foreclosures, while tax foreclosed properties generate no revenue until they are returned to private ownership.

The physical evidence of housing abandonment in Detroit is striking. Roughly 80,000 (23 percent) of the city's housing units, 36 percent of commercial parcels, and 22 percent of industrial properties are now vacant. About 20 square miles of the city's land area is now vacant.[5] The collapsing housing market significantly impacted City services; the litany of service reductions is lengthy.[6] Bus service has been reduced by almost 22 percent. The number of city recreation centers has been reduced from 30 to 17, and public swimming pools from 18 to 10. Half of the City's parks are closed. Water, sewage and other public infrastructure developed prior to 1950 for two million residents over 139 square miles now serves a population under 700,000 in the same space. A key challenge is how to maintain old infrastructure, much of which is now serving largely vacant areas, without the necessary tax revenues.

As property values dwindle, the City, public schools, and other government entities that rely on the property tax experience sharp reductions in their revenues, and local businesses have fewer customers. The widespread vacancies and abandonments have a perverse effect on the neighborhoods. Longtime residents see their property values decline and receive poor quality public services for their property tax dollars. They may also feel threatened by the growing number of vacant and vandalized structures in their neighborhoods. Many households who are able to maintain their property and pay their taxes choose instead to abandon it if they cannot sell it at any price.[7] This accelerates the process of neighborhood decline. Aggregate Detroit property tax revenues declined by over $143 million (58 percent). Only about 80 to 85

3   MacDonald, C. "Half of Detroit Property Owners Don't Pay Taxes." *The Detroit News*, 12 February 2013.

4   MacDonald, C. "Wayne County Overwhelmed by Foreclosures." *The Detroit News*, 21 February 2013.

5   Data Driven Detroit, "Motor City Mapping" http://datadrivendetroit.org/projects/Motor-City-Mapping/ accessed: January 9, 2015.

6   Detroit Office of the Emergency Manager. (2013). *Proposal for Creditors. Executive Summary*. Detroit MI: City of Detroit.

7   Raleigh E. and Galster, G. (2014) "Neighborhood Disinvestment, Abandonment and Crime Dynamics." *Journal of Urban Affairs* DOI: 10.1111/juaf.12102

percent of the property tax levy is actually collected in the year that it is due.[8] It is not at all surprising that the City of Detroit was declared bankrupt in 2013.[9]

Discussion

Detroit's current situation remains grim. There are, however, positive indicators that point to an improved future for Detroit and its residents:

- *Financial Stability.* The recently concluded bankruptcy hearings have left the City with a much-improved balance sheet. The approved Plan of Adjustment calls for improvements in critical public services that will enhance the quality of life for Detroiters.

- *Home Price Stability.* While Detroit's housing market continues to be severely distressed, with a significant imbalance between supply and demand, there are at least some indications of increasing stability. Despite high vacancies and limited demand, average sales prices for non-foreclosure sales have increased slightly in each of the last three years.

- *Improved Public Services.* Through a combination of privatization, new funding, and reductions in service levels, the City has already begun to experience improved public service delivery. Although substantial improvements are reported in police emergency response times, public lighting, and blight removal, there has been little change in other critical areas such as public education and transportation.

- *Strategic Vision.* For decades land use and development decisions in Detroit have been ad hoc, frequently ignoring a long-range master plan that envisioned the city's return to the prosperity of the 1950s.[10] The *Detroit Future City* report, on the other hand, recognizes that Detroit will never be able to return to its past. This report has been accepted by many as the framework for the redevelopment of the city.[11] This combination of realism and commitment has not been seen in Detroit for a very long time.

Despite these promising developments, a number of significant obstacles remain:

- *Financial.* It is not at all clear that Detroit will have access to sufficient resources to implement the necessary changes. The modest improvements in public

---

8   City of Detroit (2014) *Comprehensive Annual Financial Report 2013.*

9   Bomey N. and Gallagher, J. "How Detroit Went Broke." *Detroit Free Press.* 14 September 2013.

10   Walsh, T. "Can Duggan change history of failed master plans?" *Detroit Free Press* 28 February 2015. http://www.freep.com/story/money/business/columnists/tom-walsh/2015/02/26/can-duggan-change-history-failed-master-plans/24087915/

11   Detroit Future City, *Strategic Framework.* Detroit: Detroit Future City Implementation Office. http://detroitfuturecity.com/framework/ accessed February 20, 2014.

services that have been achieved have been funded by borrowing and extraordinary revenue (for example, foundation grants); it is not at all clear how the present efforts can be sustained in the long run. Traditional revenue sources, such as the property and income taxes, have limited potential for growth in the near term. Increasing tax rates will likely be counter-productive; increasing the tax base may not happen quickly enough.

- *Demographic*. While much has been made of recent population growth in Midtown and other select areas of Detroit,[12] the city is still experiencing a net loss of population. The 95 percent of the city that is not in the favored core area continues to be unable to attract or retain residents in recent years.

- *Employment*. Despite low labor force participation rates, Detroit has had double-digit unemployment rates for several decades. There were more than 83,000 unemployed Detroiters in 2013, according to the American Community Survey reports. If Detroit employment was average (that is, if Detroit's labor force participation and unemployment rates matched the national averages), more than 108,000 jobs would have to be added. This would be a 52 percent increase over the current total of 208,400. Job growth on this scale would be difficult to achieve in a metropolitan area that has suffered a net loss of employment since 2000.[13]

- *Education*. Public education is perhaps the most critical public service in terms of improving economic prospects. Neither the Detroit Public Schools, nor the numerous public school academies (charter schools) provide the quality of education that is required.

- *Spatial*. The City of Detroit covers almost 140 square miles. Although the aggregate population of the city would be sufficient to support amenities and private services, many neighborhoods are too thinly populated to support adequate retail and commercial services.[14] Private investment in these areas is limited; low amenity levels make them unattractive to new residents. Increasing blight and poor public and private services are contributing to the abandonment of good quality housing.

---

12   Hudson-Weber Foundation, (2013) *7.2 Square Miles. Detroit: Hudson-Weber Foundation: A Report on Greater Downtown Detroit*. Detroit: Hudson-Weber Foundation.

13   Parilla, J. et al. (2015) *Global Metro Monitor 2014: An Uncertain Recovery*. (Washington: Brookings Institute).

14   Urban N. and Sands, G. (2014) *City of Change*. Data Driven Detroit blog post. http://blog.datadrivendetroit.org/2014/11/

Conclusions

Detroit's current housing market crisis has been developing over the past 60 years; the problems will not be quickly or easily resolved. The city housing market continues to be dysfunctional, with excess supply and insufficient demand. Even though housing prices appear to have 'bottomed out' in some neighborhoods, the fundamental problems have not been addressed, let alone resolved. The complex causes of this housing market collapse will require systemic, multifaceted changes. Improving housing affordability is an essential first step. But housing is unaffordable to many Detroiters, not because of high prices, but because of their low incomes. Addressing this income deficit will require not only the creation of tens of thousands of new jobs, but also significant improvements in the education and skill levels of Detroiters. Access to mortgage funding must also be improved. Many Detroiters have poor credit ratings and low property valuations limit the amount of mortgage funding that is available. Renovation costs often exceed the market value of residential properties. These factors contribute to the accelerated decline of many neighborhoods in Detroit.

Recovery of the Detroit housing market will require more than improvements to individual homes; neighborhood and community development improvements are also necessary. This will require a significant improvement in public services, not only public safety and education, but also public transit and health. Although there have been substantial improvements in some areas, often as a result of privatization, regionalization, and external funding, most public services are not yet at acceptable levels. To eliminate current service deficits, considerably higher levels of public spending will be required. If this can be achieved only through higher taxes, the private investment and employment growth that the city needs, as well as the additional population, is unlikely to happen. Even a strategy of shrinking the footprint of the occupied territory (as proposed by Detroit Future City) will require substantial expenditures to create and maintain the new open spaces and ecological preserves. Simply continuing to concentrate on a low-income population will do little to create a viable, self-sufficient city.

Will Detroit continue to be dragged down into the maelstrom of economic collapse? Or will the City be able to break free and return to a more stable course? Will the prevailing culture of racism/mistrust/antipathy that exists in Southeast Michigan trump the efforts to address the financial and political issues? With continued external financial support and strong leadership, a modest recovery is possible, but by no means certain. A brighter future will be possible only if the long-standing crisis of confidence in Detroit as a place to live, work, and invest can be overcome.

Bibliography

Bomey, N. and Gallagher, J. "How Detroit Went Broke." *Detroit Free Press*. 14 September 2013. http://www.freep.com/article/20130915/NEWS01/ 130801004/Detroit-Bankruptcy-history-1950-debt-pension-revenue Accessed October 1, 2013.

City of Detroit. *Comprehensive Annual Financial Report 2013*. http://www.detroitmi.gov/ Portals/0/docs/finance/CAFR/Final%202012%20Detroit%20Financial%20Statements.pdf Accessed February 20, 2015.

Detroit Future City. *Strategic Framework*. http://detroitfuturecity.com/framework/ accessed February 20, 2014.

Detroit Office of the Emergency Manager. *Proposal for Creditors. Executive Summary*. Detroit MI: City of Detroit, 2013.

Hudson Weber Foundation. *7.2 Square miles: A report on greater downtown Detroit*. Detroit MI: Hudson Weber, 2013.

MacDonald, C. "Half of Detroit Property Owners Don't Pay Taxes." *The Detroit News*, 12 February 2013, page 1A.

Macdonald, C. "Wayne County Overwhelmed by Foreclosures." *The Detroit News*, 21 February 2013, page 13A.

Parilla, J., Trujillo, J. L., Berube, A. and Ran, T. *Global Metro Monitor 2014: An Uncertain Recovery*. Washington: Brookings Institute, 2015.

Raleigh, E. and Galster, G. "Neighborhood Disinvestment, Abandonment, and Crime Dynamics." *Journal of Urban Affairs*. 2014. DOI: 10.1111/juaf.12102.

Reese, L. A., Sands, G. and Skidmore, M. "Memo from Motown: Is Austerity Here to Stay?" *Cambridge Journal of Regions, Economy and Society* 7, no. 1 (2014): 99-118.

Sands, G. and Skidmore, M. "Making Ends Meet: Options for Property Tax Reform in Detroit." *Journal of Urban Affairs*, 36, no. 4 (2014): 682-700.

Urban, N. and Sands, G. *City of Change*. Data Driven Detroit blog post, accessed October 1, 2014. http://blog.datadrivendetroit.org/2014/11/

Walsh, Tom "Can Duggan change history of failed master plans?" *Detroit Free Press*, accessed February 21, 2014. http://www.freep.com/story/money/business/columnists/ tom-walsh/2015/02/26/can-duggan-change-history-failed-master-plans/24087915/

CARLOS GARCÍA VÁZQUEZ

OBSOLESCENCE OF SPANISH POSTWAR SOCIAL HOUSING ESTATES – MISMATCHES WITH CONTEMPORARY NEEDS

Introduction

The obsolescence of the periphery is one of the latest challenges faced by contemporary public administrations across Europe which, until recently, were more concerned with the decline of historic centres. The 1973 petrol crisis brought about the appearance of a first generation of obsolete areas, the industrial periphery, and over recent years this has spread to postwar residential neighbourhoods[1]. As a result of this, governments the world over have begun to establish organizations to analyse the problem and, in this regard, the work of the Observatoire National des Zones Urbaines Sensibles (ONZUS) in France is worth noting. Also noteworthy is the Design for London planning office in the United Kingdom. These think tanks have provided the conceptual support for iconic interventions such as Park Hill in London (2011), Le Lignon in Geneva (2009), La Viste in Marseille (2014), Le Grande Parc in Bordeaux (2011), and Bois-le-Prête, Les Courtilliéres, and La Grande Borne in Paris (between 2011 and 2014).

This chapter is concerned with issues similar to those dealt with in these projects and stems from the R&D&i project 'Intervención en barriadas residenciales obsoletas: Manual de Buenas Prácticas' ('Intervention in obsolete residential neighbourhoods: Good Practice Handbook'). It was carried out in Spain by two research groups from

---

1   Probably, the most well-known case of this kind of obsolescence is the one of Pruitt-Igoe, a social housing neighbourhood built in 1955 in St. Louis, that was in a radical state of decay in 1970, and was demolished in 1972, seventeen years after being built.

the University of Seville[2] and funded by the Department of Development and Housing of the Council of Andalucía and the European Union[3].

The initial hypothesis was that the buildings in question were no longer suitable for or aligned with the requirements and expectations of contemporary society and ways of living. In order to confirm this hypothesis this chapter analyses the mismatch and seeks to identify the strengths and weaknesses of the typologies that emerged during their retrofitting process.

Contemporary Social Change and Obsolescence of Residential Polígonos

The 'physical body' of this research is the social housing built during the Franco era in Spain, specifically that constructed between 1939, when the Subsidised Housing Law was passed, and 1976, which saw the end of the last National Housing Plan of the dictatorship. It was during this period, specifically the 1950s, that the conceptual and administrative foundations of 'polígonos residenciales', an urban-architectural model widely implemented in the 1960s and 1970s, was laid[4].

Three years after the death of the dictator Francisco Franco in 1975 the establishment of a democratic constitution marked the start of a veritable sociocultural revolution. Between the late 1980s and early 1990s a change took place in Spain that was unique in Europe – the end of the dictatorship was almost immediately followed by entry into the European Union. This radical change triggered all sorts of processes: immigration, geographical mobility, the appearance of new family models, modifications of the age pyramid, fall in birth rates, etc. All this had an impact on the polígono architectural type, originally designed as working class housing for an industrial society with moral and cultural guidelines imposed by a dictatorship. Today, the profile of individuals seeking housing is completely different from that of the original residents, and as a result, it is suggested that the architectural type is a major contributing factor to the current obsolescence of polígonos.

---

2   Groups HUM-666 (*Ciudad, Arquitectura y Patrimonio Contemporáneos*) and TEP-130 (*Arquitectura, Patrimonio y Sostenibilidad: Acústica, Iluminación y Energía*).

3   In order to collaborate in this task, both research groups proposed to the Regional Government of Andalusia the elaboration of a Good Practices Handbook that would systematize criteria, assume a compromise with the social and cultural values of these neighbourhoods, and confront all the phases involved in the process of renewal: evaluation of the level of obsolescence, design, construction, management, and monitoring.

4   The publications about this topic have proliferated in the last fifteen years, fostered by an interesting revision process of the architecture built during the Franco times, as well as by the rebirth of interest in the social housing question. However, most of these publications have tackled the issue with specific approaches, focusing on concrete problems or on geographical locations. A more holistic approached is missed.

In order to put this hypothesis to the test we carried out studies that applied the residential requirements and expectations of contemporary society to the polígonos. The main precedent study used as reference in the process was *Habitar el Presente. Vivienda en España: sociedad, ciudad, tecnología y recursos* by Josep Maria Montaner and Zaida Muxí, produced for the Spanish Ministry of Housing in 2006[5]. After identifying the mismatches between the housing in the polígonos and contemporary needs, we focused on what could be called physical-spatial needs – where architectural type is a determining factor. Two of these factors, size and functionality, are quantitative, while the rest are essentially qualitative and stem from changes in culture and ways of life.

Size of housing

Three parameters come into play with regard to house size: the floor area of the residential units, the number of people living there, and the number of rooms each unit has. It should be noted that floor area was constantly reduced during the Franco era and in the first half of the 1950s. The architect and researcher Miguel Fisac even proposed residential units of 40 m² for eight people, with an average useable surface area per inhabitant of 5 m². The Social Housing Plan (1954) established a standard and was followed by many other regulations: 42 m² for a three-bedroom residential unit, that is to say, approximately 7 m² per inhabitant. Subsequently the 1961 National Housing Plan increased the surface area to 50 m², 8.3 m² per inhabitant, although it is worth noting that the 10 m² per inhabitant set as an 'existential minimum' in interwar Germany was never reached.

The second and third parameters, number of people and rooms, are connected. According to the 1958 census carried out by the National Statistics Institute, the percentage of inhabitants per residential unit was 4.51. There is no specific data on the particular case of social housing, but it is assumed that this percentage was higher – as residents were mostly married couples of child-bearing age. The four children per family average explains why most of the housing of the period had three bedrooms. This was actually stipulated by the 1954 Social Housing Plan and the 1955 National Housing Plan. The 1961 Plan gave complete priority to three-bedroom housing and referred to housing with two, four, or five bedrooms as 'exceptional' (houses with one bedroom were not mentioned at all).

According to the 2006 study by Montaner and Muxí, at present the average floor and number of inhabitants per housing unit have decreased. The biggest change noted has been the increase in single-person dwellings as more young people live alone from an earlier age, and the residential autonomy of older people has increased. There has also been a major increase in the number of childless couples with two incomes. As a result of these demographic shifts currently 20% of Spanish homes are single-person households, 25% are made up of two people, while three- and four-member families account for 21% each. From this point in the scale, the percentage numbers

5   Montaner, J. M. y Muxí, Z. (2006), *Habitar el Presente. Vivienda en España: sociedad, ciudad, tecnología y recursos*, Madrid, Ministerio de Vivienda: 20-57.

decrease drastically: 7.7% five-member homes, and only 2.5% being six-person homes. In conclusion, current demographic trends suggest the need to increase one- and two-bedroom homes.

Functionality of residential units

In terms of functionality there are two major factors that need to be considered: an over emphasis on spatial hierarchies and the mono-functionality of spaces.

The Francoist family model was very stable. Society was ruled by the precepts of 'National-Catholicism', which forbade divorce, and condemned any type of cohabitation, other than that of the traditional family. The seemingly permanent nature

Figure 1. Examples of flexibility and hybridisation of uses in contemporary housing
On the floorplan on the left (housing in Rabassa, by L. F. Herrero, M. Pérez and C. Calle) hierarchies have been eliminated: the bedrooms are similar in size and wardrobes and bathrooms open onto common areas. In the floorplan on the right (housing in Mataró, by Durán & Grau Arquitectes), there is a room designed as a possible work space kept separate from rooms for domestic use and connected to the entrance.
(Montaner, J. M. y Muxí, Z. (2006), *Habitar el Presente. Vivienda en España: sociedad, ciudad, tecnología y recursos*, Madrid, Ministerio de Vivienda).

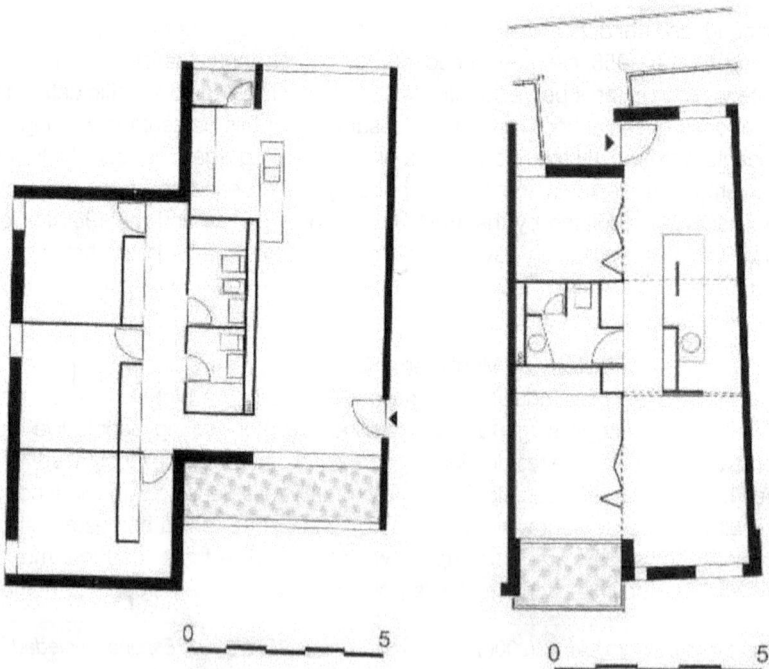

of this traditional family model was reflected in housing floorplans. Bedrooms were hierarchical: the largest one designated for the parents, and smaller ones for the children. In more expensive housing this hierarchy was further reinforced by adding built-in wardrobes or en-suite bathrooms to the master bedrooms.

As stated by Montaner and Muxí, at present the plan arrangement of these homes is often crudely modified as a result of interpersonal relationships which do not fit the 'plan'. In the light of this, it is argued that housing should adapt to this new situation and designs should be as flexible as possible. Furthermore, it is advisable that hierarchies be kept to a minimum: bedrooms should be of similar sizes; bathrooms should be shared; and built-in wardrobe spaces should open out onto communal areas.

In addition, the mono-functionality of these houses resulted from modernist architectural precepts being applied through regulations, instructions, and ordnances of the Law of Limited Income Housing in 1954. As these buildings were assumed to be exclusively for residential use, they were divided into day areas (living room and kitchen, facing west and connected to the entrance) and night areas (bedrooms and bathrooms, facing east and relegated to the most private part of the residential unit).

The growth of telecommuting and the increasing number of professionals working from home are just two of the reasons why this model is now incompatible with current living styles and arrangements. Consequently, we argue that it is necessary to allow for work spaces that can operate separately from the rest of the residential unit, to provide spaces with bathrooms and vestibules that are independent of the private rooms (Figure 1).

Changes in culture and ways of life

Residential polígonos were designed for a society of the masses: family units made up of older parents of the same nationality, race, religion, and culture; where the men worked in industry or construction, and women were housewives. Their urban image faithfully reflected this homogeneity: endless successions of functionally organised blocks, modulated in size, aesthetically standardised and sun-orientated; and residential blocks which were made up of highly standardised units varying only in surface area and number of bedrooms[6].

Various thinkers from the field of 'cultural studies' – a branch of critical thought which advocates, amongst other things, analysing the cultural production processes for the lower classes – have discussed these issues. For example, it has been argued that

6   Ignacio Paricio ('Las razones de la forma en la vivienda masiva', in *Cuadernos de Arquitectura y Urbanismo, nr. 96, 1973*) has shown the case of four polígonos in Barcelona (Can Badía, Ciutat Meridiana, La Mina and Bellvitge) with 20.000 apartments, and about 100.000 inhabitants. However, the spatial distribution and the surface of the apartments, as well as the dimension of the façade and the depth of the construction are almost the same (http://www.raco.cat/index.php/CuadernosArquitecturaUrbanismo/article/viewFile/111631/160968).

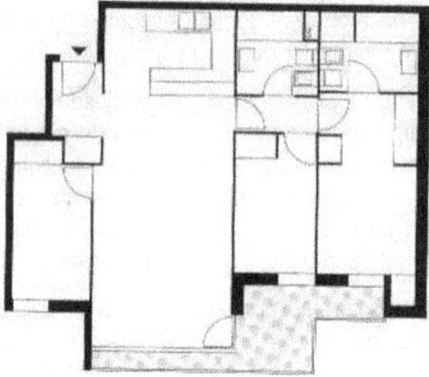

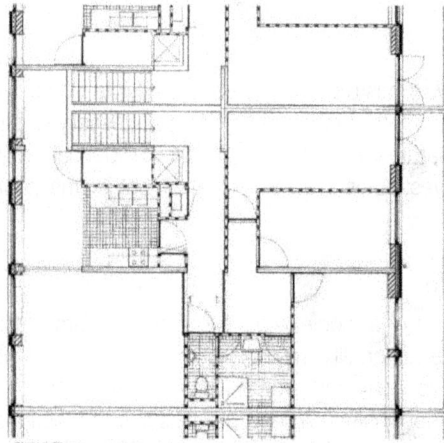

Figure 2. Gender and cultural adaptation policies in contemporary housing
Floorplan, left (housing in Barcelona, by C. Ferrater), the kitchen has been incorporated into the living room. (Montaner, J. M. y Muxí, Z. (2006), *Habitar el Presente. Vivienda en España: sociedad, ciudad, tecnología y recursos*, Madrid, Ministerio de Vivienda).
Floorplan, right (housing in The Hague, by A. Siza), has been subdivided into two halves which could be used as gender-specific spaces. (A+U (1989), *Alvaro Siza 1954-1988*, Tokyo, A+U Publishing).

segregation strategies which give preference to the role of men, and which relegate or exclude women, immigrants, young people, the elderly, are behind the spatial uniformity of these buildings[7]. This hypothesis has been of use in this study in analysing the qualitative aspects of the mismatch between the design of the polígonos and contemporary society.

---

7   Referencing cultural studies is justified by the commitment to incorporate this research within a system of socially engaged values. As applied to architecture, the starting point for cultural studies is faithful to the proposals of critical thinking: architectural space is not something neutral or objective, but rather a pre-established entity for power to dominate the lower classes. What is novel is the recognition that the logic underlying these imposition and subordination practices is not solely class-related. Segregationist strategies also revolve around race, sexuality, gender, age and illness.

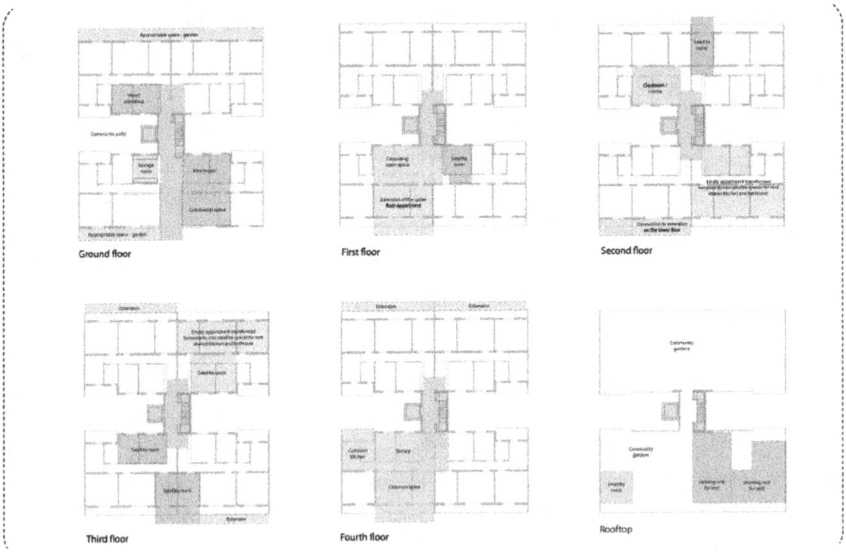

Figure 3. Reconversion into collective spaces of the common areas of an H-shaped block Competition UN-Hábitat for the revitalisation of social housing: Proposal for the neighbourhood of Orba, Valencia, by M. T. García and G. Navarrete. (http://masshousingcompetition.org/results/entry/578)

In the study upon which this chapter is based, the first of these issues we examined was gender. The polígonos built in the Franco era were designed for patriarchal families in which the father was sole breadwinner and the mother brought up the children. Public space belonged to men and the home was the 'woman's space' – a scenario not aimed at personal fulfilment, but rather to facilitate women's role as 'the managers of everyday family life'. In an extremely sexist society the woman's room was, by definition, the kitchen – which was conveniently separate from the rest of the residential unit and reduced to a minimum size. (The Technical Ordinances and Building Regulations of the Spanish National Institute for Housing recommended a floor area between 4 and 6 m^2, depending on whether the building had a utility room or not). In contrast, Montaner and Muxí suggest that in order to encourage sharing the workload, the kitchen must be generously sized and visible from the dining or living room.

Another issue analysed from the perspective of cultural studies was ethnic, national, and religious diversity. Given that 77.11% of Spanish demographic growth between 2001 and 2007 was the result of the arrival of foreign nationals – who account for the main demand for social housing – it is clear that this should be a priority for research. Modernist social housing followed eminently functionalist criteria. This poses a problem when they are occupied by people from non-western cultures, such as the Muslim community, for whom symbolic-religious issues can be extremely important.

In response to exactly these issues, trials in Holland have been carried out to divide housing into male and female areas which would permit the 'normal' use of domestic space during visits from people outside the family (Figure 2).

Finally, age is the third exclusionary factor identified by cultural studies which was considered important to our research. In this case, the most typical division and segregation between people is between the two extremes of the elderly and youth. Both are extremely important to the recovery of polígonos. The elderly represent the present, since they are the generation that moved into these areas in the 1960s and 1970s. Young people represent the future of the polígonos and they are a niche market that has increased exponentially in recent decades. The reasons for this are various: earlier emancipation from the family, an increase in geographic mobility, etc. Adapting polígono housing to the needs of these population groups has undeniable quantitative elements: solving mobility problems for the elderly; the flexibility necessary to permit sharing; and the adaptability needed to facilitate hybrid uses increasingly important to young people, such as live–work spaces. However, there are also qualitative elements to consider: how to permit collectivism through meeting rooms, community services, leisure spaces, co-working areas, sports areas, etc. (Figure 3).

Conclusions

This chapter has highlighted the mismatches between housing in residential polígonos and the requirements of contemporary Spain – the country in which the study was carried out. It suggests that these mismatches include limited space to live in, too many bedrooms, a rigid spatial distribution, mono-functionality, the unsuitability of spaces such as the kitchen, and cultural depersonalisation. Thinking more generally, it is arguable that these conflicts are primarily the result of two aspects of the architectural typology studied: floor area and room distribution. The obsolescence of the former is due to a greater demand for personal space, tied to an improvement in the standard of living. The 7–8 m² useable space per inhabitant of the 1950s is now approximately 13 m². It ranges from 9 m² in four-bedroom social housing, to 20 m² in one-bedroom housing.

With regard to spatial distribution, the mismatch is more irregular – given the distinction between theoretical and actual size. The former is to blame for a lack of flexibility. In terms of living space, issues such as the hierarchisation of bedrooms hinder the adaptation of the residential unit to changing personal or family circumstances. In functional terms, connecting living rooms and kitchens with the entrances limits the potential workspaces to the bedrooms, making it impossible to separate work and domestic areas. In addition, the strictly functionalist distribution of this type of housing makes it hard to accommodate the symbolic-representative needs of certain ethnic-religious communities. Division into male and female areas, requested by the Muslim community, would involve connecting the kitchens with the bedrooms and doubling the number of bathrooms to make them single-sex.

More specifically, the 'distribution crisis' in polígono housing can be emphasised by thinking about the obsolescence of two particular types of room: bedrooms and kitchens. In the case of bedrooms, there are too many and they are too small[8]. As a result, the 42 m² of useable floor area for three bedrooms is often transformed into a one-bedroom residential unit, which current regulations demand should be at least 40 m² in size. With regard to kitchens: these are too small and are separated from the living space[9].

The unsuitability of floor areas and spatial distributions obliges us to reconsider the utility and relevance of traditional architectural elements. Partition walls are the most problematic as they are difficult to move for various reasons. They often contain plumbing that is difficult to relocate, and the double-cavity and load-bearing wall constructions are extremely difficult to alter in any major way, resulting in layouts that are 'frozen in time'. Any proposed changes also mean that façades need to be reformulated because their openings are connected with rooms and because they limit the floor area available. To overcome these issues and still increase space, the typical proposal has usually been expanding the perimeter of the units with modules attached to the outside – a technique that involves a true transformation of the façade. A paradigmatic example of this was the intervention by Lacaton & Vassal in the Tour Bois-le-Prête, Paris, 2011.

Although they have many weaknesses the polígonos do have some strengths. There is an abundance of vacant space at the urban level, which currently takes the form of underused green areas and public spaces often only used for parking. (It should be noted that this is to be expected as, in some cases, there were distances of up to 40 metres between blocks). These large spaces can be occupied by collective services and activities, which potentially play a large and beneficial part in the lives of young people and the elderly. If it can be adapted in the ways outlined here, it is clearly possible for the social housing model discussed, and which is prevalent all over Europe, to recover the collectivist dimension that was so important at the time of its creation.

8   It should be noted that although this is true, the fact that the average number of bedrooms in polígono units is three, goes someway to compensating for increased size need – given that not all rooms are needed as bedrooms in most cases.

9   It should be noted that the fusion of living areas, dining room, and kitchen was laid down in proposals and regulations from the 1950s (Social Housing Plan, Law of Limited Income Housing, etc.).

Bibliography

Berland-Berthon, A. *Le démolition des immeubles de logements sociaux. Histoire urbaine d'une non-politique publique*, Paris: Certu, 2009.

Dhoquois, A. *Banlieues créatives en France. 150 actions dans les quartiers*, Autrement, 2007.

Druot, F.; Lacaton, A.; Vassal, J. P. *Plus: la vivienda colectiva. Territorio de excepción*, Barcelona: Gustavo Gili, 2007.

Eleb, M. 'Social, populaire, adapté? Le logement au XXe siècle'. In *Vers de nouveaux logements sociaux*. Milan: Silvana Editoriale, 2009.

Ferrer i Aixalà, A. *Els polígons de Barcelona*. Barcelona: Universitat Politècnica de Catalunya, 1996.

Hughes, J., Sandler S. *Non-plan: essays on freedom participation and change in modern architecture and urbanism*, London: Architectural Press, 2000.

Leupen, B. Frame and generic space. *A study into the changeable dwelling proceeding from the permanent*, Rotterdam: 010, 2006.

Montaner, J. M. y Muxí, Z. *Habitar el Presente. Vivienda en España: sociedad, ciudad, tecnología y recursos*, Madrid: Ministerio de Vivienda, 2006.

Monteys, X. Casa collage. *Un ensayo sobre la arquitectura de la casa*, Barcelona: Gustavo Gili, 2001.

Sambricio, C. (ed.) *Un siglo de vivienda social 1903-2003*, Madrid: Nerea, 2003.

Sambricio, C. and Sánchez Lampreave, R. (eds.) *100 años de historia de la intervención pública en la vivienda y la ciudad*, Madrid: AVS, 2008.

CHARLIE SMITH

CHASING THE GRAIL: RECONCILING PRIORITIES TO IMPROVE NEW HOUSING

Introduction

A raft of challenges face new housing design in the United Kingdom, at the forefront of which is a triumvirate of interrelated needs – to make dwellings more spacious, more affordable, and less damaging to the environment. Each of these is important in their own right, but are they reconcilable? Conventional thinking suggests larger dwellings cost more, as does increasing their environmental sustainability, so consequently they become less affordable.

This chapter explores these apparently conflicting priorities. It draws on a broad selection of research and argues that by thinking creatively it is possible to make advances in each of the separate needs to mutual advantage. In so doing, new housing can be created which is more spacious, sustainable, and affordable.

Space

The UK produces the smallest new housing in Western Europe – in Germany houses are 37 percent larger, in the Netherlands 40, and in Denmark 59 percent.[1] The issue of space was of course addressed by the Parker Morris Standards, introduced in 1967, but has become a subject of much debate once again. In 2010 the London Development Agency (LDA) introduced minimum space standards for new housing in the capital.[2] Potentially much more influential is the Government's proposal for a national space standard, which would enable local authorities to

---

1   Kees Dol and Marietta Haffner, eds., *Housing Statistics in the European Union* (The Hague: Ministry of the Interior and Kingdom Relations, 2010), 51.

2   Mayor of London, *London Housing Design Guide – Interim Edition* (London: London Development Agency, 2010).

demand that new housing developments meet minimum space requirements.[3]

The RIBA's *Case for Space* initiative studied space provision in private housing in the UK and compared it with that of Western Europe and it also highlighted that in extreme cases lack of space can detrimentally impact health and wellbeing.[4] The RIBA commissioned a survey in which almost a third of respondents cited lack of space as a cause of dissatisfaction with their homes.[5] The delightful airiness of a Georgian terrace stands in stark contrast to the underwhelming spatial experience of so many new housing projects. With this in mind it is perhaps unsurprising that 75 percent of people in the UK do not want to buy a newly built house.[6]

Affordability

There is a disturbing disparity between rising demand for housing and the number of new dwellings being built[7] which inevitably has an impact on affordability. Over a decade ago *The Barker Review* concluded that a dramatic increase in house building was needed to improve affordability, suggesting an additional 120,000 dwellings were required each year – almost doubling the existing provision to 245,000.[8] In 2014 just 141,000 dwellings were actually built.[9]

To meet today's demand in England alone, 240,000 new dwellings are required each year.[10] Yet fewer are being constructed than in any peacetime year since the First World War, even before accounting for a much larger population and smaller households.[11] The 'Homes for Britain' campaign is calling on all political parties to address this substantial shortfall and solve what it considers to be one of the biggest issues facing the country.[12] Unfortunately, the legacy left by years of disparity between need and provision leaves a Himalayan mountain to climb.

---

3   Department for Communities and Local Government, *Nationally Described Space Standard: Technical Requirements* (Consultation draft, 2014), 4.

4   Royal Institute of British Architects, *The Case for Space: The Size of England's New Homes* (London: RIBA, 2011).

5   Ipsos MORI, *Housing Standards and Satisfaction: What the Public Wants* (London: Ipsos MORI and RIBA, 2013), 3.

6   Future Homes Commission, *Building the Homes and Communities Britain Needs* (London: Future Homes Commission and RIBA, 2014), 31.

7   "Why Can't the UK Build 240,000 Houses a Year?" British Broadcasting Corporation, accessed January 13, 2015, http://www.bbc.co.uk/news/magazine-30776306.

8   Kate Barker, *Delivering Stability: Securing our Future Housing Needs* (London: HMSO, 2004), 5.

9   "Why Can't" British Broadcasting Corporation.

10   Confederation of British Industry, *Housing Britain: Building New Homes for Growth* (London: CBI, 2014), 9.

11   Matt Griffith and Pete Jefferys, *Solutions for the Housing Shortage* (London: Shelter, 2013), 3.

12   Jill Sherman, "Huge Rally Will Demand Surge in British Homebuilding," *The Times*, February 7, 2015: 18.

To find a solution to the situation whereby many people are unable to afford to buy or rent their own home means addressing the issue of cost. But how? In part this can be achieved through increasing supply, but balancing supply and demand will not in itself resolve the affordability crisis. Both the land costs and construction costs of providing dwellings must also be considered, and central to that discussion must be the financial implications of making new dwellings more environmentally sustainable.

Environmental Sustainability

Our climate is changing. 2014 was the UK's warmest year since records began over a hundred years ago.[13] It was also the planet's warmest since records began in 1880, with the ten warmest years occurring in the last two decades.[14] The Intergovernmental Panel on Climate Change (IPCC) contend that maintaining global warming below two degrees Centigrade demands reductions in anthropogenic greenhouse gas (GHG) emissions of 40 to 70 percent by 2050 and achieving near zero or below in 2100.[15]

Here is another Herculean challenge, but it would be wrongheaded not to make a serious attempt to solve it given that the consequences include rising sea levels, more incidences of extreme weather, and reduced crop yields to name but a few.[16] In 2009 housing accounted for one-quarter of UK GHG emissions,[17] almost four-fifths of which is attributable to space and water heating.[18] Furthermore, the environmental impact of new housing extends beyond GHG emissions, to include issues such as resource depletion and waste creation. Although politicians continue to prevaricate over the UK's commitment to zero carbon homes,[19] inaction is no longer an option.

13 "2014 Confirmed as UK's Warmest Year on Record," Meteorological Office, accessed January 7, 2015, http://www.metoffice.gov.uk/news/releases/archive/2015/Record-UK-temps-2014.

14 Jack Linshi, "2014 Was Officially the Hottest Year on Record," *Time*, January 6, 2015, accessed January 7, 2015, http://time.com/3656646/2014-hottest-year/, and "NASA, NOAA Find 2014 Warmest Year in Modern Record," National Aeronautics and Space Administration, accessed 19 January, 2015, http://www.nasa.gov/press/2015/january/nasa-determines-2014-warmest-year-in-modern-record/index.html.

15 Intergovernmental Panel on Climate Change, *Climate Change 2014 Synthesis Report – Summary for Policy Makers* (IPCC, 2014), 21.

16 Ibid. 13-15.

17 Department for Communities and Local Government, *Laying the Foundations: A Housing Strategy for England* (London: Communities and Local Government Publications, 2011), 4.

18 Jason Palmer and Ian Cooper, *United Kingdom Housing Energy Fact File 2012* (London: Department of Energy and Climate Change, 2012), 33-34.

19 "MPs Fail to Strengthen ZCH Standards," Buildings 4 Change, accessed February 17, 2015, http://www.building4change.com/article.jsp?id=2585#.VOMJDU0pWUI.

Unravelling the Priorities

These central challenges of space, affordability, and sustainability are all critical to new housing design and they are intrinsically linked. The cost of building a dwelling is related to its size – and both relate to the environmental impact that it will have – as illustrated in Figure 1.

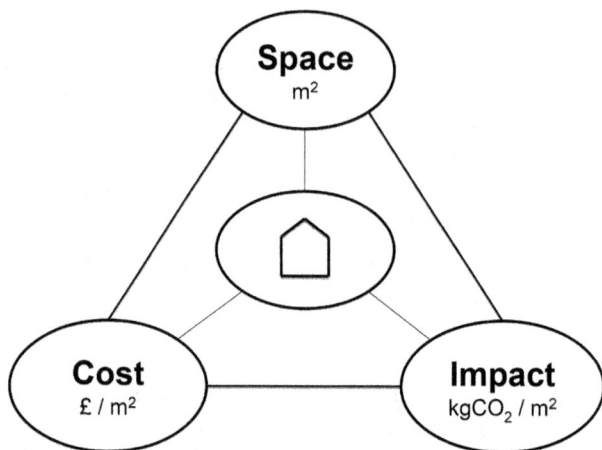

Figure 1. Cost, space and environmental impact are all interrelated.

Space and Cost

The Greater London Authority investigated the impact of increasing the size of new housing on construction costs when it first proposed minimum space standards. Their analysis showed that the additional costs incurred to achieve the new internal floor area ranged from one to ten percent of the original build-cost, averaging at four percent.[20] The Home Builders Federation also argues that increasing space standards will increase the cost of housing.[21]

In a disconcerting precedent, New York City's regulation for minimum apartment floor area (of 40 square metres) has recently been waived in the interest of creating more affordable housing. The My Micro NY project, due for completion in late 2015, will have

---

20   Greater London Authority, Homes and Communities Agency, and London Development Agency, *Draft London Housing Design Guide: Cost and Delivery Impact Assessment* (Pre-publication draft, 2010), 29.

21   Liam Kelly, "Should Minimum Space Standards Apply to Social and Private Housing?" *The Guardian*, April 19, 2013, accessed January 26, 2015, http://www.theguardian.com/housing-network/poll/2013/apr/19/minimum-space-standards-social-private.

dwellings with floor areas as small as 26 square metres.[22] In London, the developer Pocket sells housing 20 percent cheaper than the surrounding market rate, but which is up to 30 percent smaller than the *Case for Space* standard and that is required for affordable housing in the capital.[23] They contend that large windows, high ceilings, and extensive storage offset the smaller floor area.

Sustainability and Cost

Creating dramatically more sustainable buildings is vitally important, but it is not cheap. The Building Research Establishment (BRE) has estimated the additional costs incurred to meet the Code for Sustainable Homes (CfSH) compared to dwellings compliant with the Building Regulations. In 2011 the additional cost to meet Code Level Five was almost £20,000, and for Level Six almost £35,000.[24] A more recent study showed that the cost of meeting Level Five had fallen to a mean of £9,000, and for Level Six it had dropped to £21,000.[25] While this is a notable decrease – in a large part due to reductions in the cost of renewable energy technology – there remains significant additional expense in building sustainable housing. Research indicates that a 25 percent premium is added to standard build costs to meet Level Six.[26] There is a strong body of research that suggests a large proportion of the most cost-effective measures for increasing the sustainability of new housing have already been undertaken,[27] leaving more expensive options for any further improvements.

So how can dwellings be made larger, but at the same time more affordable? How can environmental impact be significantly reduced without increasing cost? Are these ambitions of space, affordability, and sustainability mutually exclusive? Creating more sustainable buildings is crucial for the wellbeing of the planet, but space can affect the health and wellbeing of a dwelling's occupants. How do we balance the need to reduce environmental impact and improve space without compounding the pervasive unaffordability that exists in housing? Is this seeking some kind of Housing Grail?

---

22   Patricia Arcilla, "New York to Complete First Prefabricated "Micro-Apartments" this Year," *ArchDaily*, February 24, 2015, accessed February 26, 2015, http://www. archdaily.com/?p=602157.

23   Martina Lees, "Talk is Cheap," *The Sunday Times – Home*, April 19, 2015.

24   Building Research Establishment, *The Future of Sustainable Housing* (Watford: BRE Global, 2013), 6.

25   "Costs of Building to the Code for Sustainable Homes," Element Energy and David Langdon, accessed January 16, 2015, http://www.brighton-hove.gov.uk/content/ planning/local-development-framework/ldf-background-studies.

26   Ibid.

27   Robert Lowe and Tadj Oreszczyn, "Regulatory Standards and Barriers to Improved Performance for Housing," *Energy Policy* 36 (2008): 4479, accessed January 26, 2015, doi:10.1016/j.enpol.2008.09.024.

Reconciling the Three Priorities

Proposed by Weizsäcker et al., 'Factor Four' is an innovative but simple concept which suggests that the standard of living extracted from one unit of natural resource can be quadrupled, allowing people to live twice as well while using half as much.[28] A central principle is that the individual benefits of making improvements can be utilised to mutual advantage, setting out a new way of thinking about what is meant by 'efficiency.' It is argued that advanced efficiency can be achieved through integration – thinking about a design challenge as a whole, not as disjointed pieces.[29] That way, savings achieved in one place can be utilised in another. Such principles need to be applied to the way housing is conceptualised to enable dwellings to become more spacious, whilst costing and consuming less.

Redefining the Notion of 'Cost' and Affordability

There is an assumption that sustainable housing costs more. But surely this depends on how 'cost' is defined and how increased efficiency is evaluated? Traditionally the cost of housing is fragmented between build cost and living cost. An alternative would be to monetise the environmental saving of consuming less. For example, The Stern Review concluded that, if no action is taken, the costs of climate change will be equivalent to losing at least five percent of global GDP each year, while the costs of taking measures to avoid its worst effects would be one percent.[30] Another approach would be to consider lifecycle cost as opposed to capital outlay, because the traditional disjuncture prohibits the true saving of increased efficiency to be evaluated.

In their winning submission to the *Wolfsen Economics Prize* URBED described creating a Garden City extension with a funding model similar to those used in Germany and Holland – where housing is so often held up as a model of quality, space, and sustainability. They suggest an approach that directs the 'unearned increment' in land value (that between the cost of acquiring land and its future value when sold for development) to be invested in the creation of widespread infrastructure and, of particular note, higher quality housing.[31] Their model rethinks the funding of housing on a large scale – that of a substantial city extension – but it could be applied to smaller scale projects too.

More enlightened models of housing finance should address long-term rather than short-term views. Consider the current funding model for house purchases; mortgage lenders base their affordability assessment on prospective buyers' existing incomes,

---

28   Ernst von Weizsäcker, Amory B. Lovins and L. Hunter Lovins, *Factor Four: Doubling Wealth – Halving Resource Use* (London: Earthscan, 1998), xviii.

29   Ibid. xxiv.

30   Sir Nicholas Stern, *The Stern Review: The Economics of Climate Change – Executive Summary* (Cambridge: Cambridge University Press, 2006), ix and xii.

31   David Rudlin and Nicholas Falk, *Uxcester Garden City – Second Stage Submission for the 2014 Wolfson Economics Prize* (Manchester: URBED, 2014), 16.

instead of the running cost of the house they are trying to buy. With utility price rises showing little sign of abating, this becomes increasingly nonsensical. The average annual cost of utilities in England and Wales is £1,637 for both fuel and water.[32] If the energy and water costs for a new house were a fraction of this – as would be the case in Code Level Six dwellings – does that not become a much more affordable property to live in?

In Freiburg – another model of exemplary housing – it has been found that although higher quality design, construction, and space provision added around ten percent to the cost of new dwellings, this was more than recouped through energy savings.[33] The Solcer House in Wales, completed in 2015, is the UK's first low cost energy positive dwelling; it demonstrates that housing can built affordably, to good space standards, and generate more energy than it consumes – enabling the excess to be sold.[34] These examples reinforce the 'Factor Four' concept, of utilising mutual advantages. When viewed in lifecycle terms the priorities become achievable at an overall cost saving.

Alternative ways of house building

It has been argued that the contemporary house building industry is almost perfectly configured not to solve the housing crisis, not least because volume house builders see issues such as quality, affordability, and sustainability as additional costs rather than added value.[35] What alternatives are there?

There are more cost-efficient ways to construct housing than the traditional methods used by UK house builders. Prefabricated systems – now rebranded 'advanced housing manufacture' or less alarmingly 'modern methods of construction' – have long been available. The 2005 Design for Manufacture competition aimed to address major increases in construction cost. It concluded that factory based production reduces build costs; furthermore, improved quality control means elements fit together better

---

32   "Annual Domestic Energy Charges," Department of Energy and Climate Change, accessed January 28, 2015, https://www.gov.uk/government/statistical-data-sets/annual-domestic-energy-price-statistics, and "PN 03/13 Water and Sewerage Bills to Increase," The Water Services Regulation Authority (Ofwat), accessed January 28, 2015, http://www.ofwat.gov.uk/mediacentre/pressnotices2008/prs_pn0313bills.

33   Peter Hall, Good Cities, Better Living – How Europe Discovered the Lost Art of Urbanism (Abingdon: Routledge, 2014), 265.

34   John Vidal, "Britain's First 'Energy Positive' House Opens in Wales," The Guardian, July 16, 2015, accessed July 29, 2015, www.theguardian.com/environment/2015/jul/15/britains-first-energy-positive-house-opens-in-wales.

35   Alastair Parvin, "How 3D Printing and Land Reform Could Help to Solve the Housing Crisis," The Guardian, January 20, 2015, accessed February 26, 2015, http://www.theguardian.com/society/2015/jan/20/3d-printing-land-reform-solve-housing-crisis.

so there is less heat loss and infiltration.[36] Cost reductions achieved through increased production efficiency can then be invested back into increasing the environmental performance of the envelope, and the space contained within it.

Modern methods of construction also reduce environmental impact by minimising the amount of material used and wastage created. These approaches could be combined with highly efficient building fabrics. Not only should buildings be super insulated and as airtight as feasible, they should facilitate reducing energy use in other ways. For example, prefabricated systems must be flexible enough to enable designers to address orientation, utilising passive heat gains in southerly directions whilst reducing heat loss in northerly facing elevations. A 'one size fits all' systems approach is clearly unacceptable. Prefabrication is gaining traction, but its use is limited, and it is still widely perceived as innovative.[37] The Homes and Communities Agency has highlighted the reluctance of house builders to adopt prefabrication, which is ironic considering that they produce such a limited range of standardised house types.

Zogolovitch and Zogolovitch propose new procurement routes as a way to reconcile issues of cost and space, suggesting that custom-build approaches using prefabrication can create cost efficiencies which can be spent on more space.[38] They also highlight that in self-build models the profit incentive of the commercial house builder is negated. Custom- and self-build methods mean that occupancy savings, such as reductions in utilities use, are rewarded to the dwellings' builders. They offer the opportunity to close the fractured loop between construction and occupation costs, enabling savings made in construction to be vested in larger and more energy-efficient dwellings. It is a method through which the 'Factor Four' model of using mutual advantages to achieve more for less can be realised.

The UK has a much lower rate of self-building than other European countries at less than ten percent; in Austria it accounts for around 80 percent of completions, and in France 60 percent.[39] Self-build can be cost effective, typically saving 20 to 40 percent.[40] In Berlin, for example, custom-build housing has resulted in savings of 25 percent over conventional market-built dwellings.[41] It is noteworthy that URBED championed the adoption of more diverse housing procurement routes, including

---

36 Homes and Communities Agency, *Designed for Manufacture – Lessons Learnt 2* (London: Homes and Communities Agency, 2010), 87.

37 Ibid, 88.

38 Gus Zogolovitch and Roger Zogolovitch, "Solidspace," *Blueprint* 332 (2014): 95.

39 Wendy Wilson, and Sarah Heath, "Self-build and Custom Build Housing Sector," accessed February 5, 2015, www.parliament.uk/briefing-papers/SN06784.pdf.

40 "Self Build One-off Home," The Self Build Portal, accessed February 5, 2015, http://www.selfbuildportal.org.uk/self-build-one-off-home.

41 "Research and Development Programme," National Custom and Self Build Association, accessed February 5, 2015, http://www.nacsba.org.uk/researchdevelopment.

self- and custom-build.[42] The charity Shelter also advocates more innovative models of housing development, including custom-build, to address the housing shortage.[43]

An 'Open' Approach to Space

The RIBA's *Case for Space* argued more research is needed into what constitutes adequate space to suit contemporary living. One option is to be less preoccupied with numbers of bedrooms and bathrooms, and pay more attention to the overall space dwellings contain and – crucially – the ways in which it can be meaningfully utilised for the rituals of modern 'dwelling.' It has been suggested, perhaps optimistically, that a move away from choosing dwellings primarily on the number of bedrooms would be facilitated by providing accessible information about energy efficiency.[44]

Addressing space provision may also include rethinking how space is utilised. Steven Holl's 1991 Void Space / Hinge Space project embodies a contemporary interpretation of the traditional Japanese concept of 'fusuma.' Conceptualised as 'hinged space,' dwellings can be adapted to suit their occupants' requirements at different times of the day; this diurnal adaptation allows expansion of living areas during the day, which is then reclaimed by bedrooms at night.[45]

The proposed national space standard for England mostly replicates the LDA's standards for London. Whilst the RIBA largely support these proposals, they are still up to 20 percent smaller than their German equivalents – so there is still much room for improvement. Furthermore, it is argued here that space must be considered three-dimensionally, in terms of volume and not just area, to alleviate claustrophobic minimal ceiling heights so common across new housing. It is encouraging that the proposed national space standard incorporates a minimum ceiling height of two and a half metres across the main living spaces.[46] But this still falls far short of the traditional Georgian terrace – so desired for it spatial qualities and consequent benefits to natural light – where ceiling heights are three metres or more.

42   Rudlin and Falk, *Uxcester Garden City*, 65.

43   Peter Jefferys et al., *Building the Homes We Need – A Programme for the 2015 Government* (KPMG, 2014), 69.

44   Simon Baker, "Too Quiet on the Home Front," *The RIBA Journal* 121(2) (2014): 44.

45   "Void Space/Hinge Space Housing," Steven Holl Architects, accessed January 19, 2015, http://www.stevenholl.com/project-detail.php?id=36&.

46   DCLG, *Nationally Described Space Standard*, 4.

What Are the Drivers and Barriers to Change?

House builders view legislation as the most effective way to increase the sustainability of new housing.[47] Enshrining carbon reduction and increased space provision within the Building Regulations is, therefore, a logical strategy; but how can such targets be achieved whilst guarding against spiraling costs, and without wider environmental considerations being sacrificed? After all, the integration of the CFSH into the Building Regulations is at the expense of many of the other environmental impacts that the Code evaluated.

Although there is end user demand for increasing space, house builders rate customer demand as a lesser driver for providing very sustainable housing.[48] It will be interesting to see if the BRE's new Home Quality Mark, launched in March 2015,[49] reflects changing customer attitudes. It has also been suggested that widespread adoption of dramatically more sustainable housing would necessitate radical changes in construction methods and practices, leading to a new architectural vernacular with an associated cultural backlash[50] – a consequence of pervasive distrust of the new.

Weizsäcker et al. make the interesting observation that architects are traditionally paid on a percentage of a project's cost; therefore achieving reduced build costs could make them work for a smaller fee rather than incentivising them through what they save.[51] There is also a chronic shortage of knowledge and skills in the construction industry required to achieve dramatic improvements in the sustainability of housing.[52] Evidently many challenges still lie ahead.

Exploring the Priorities in Student Projects

Students studying the MArch Architecture programme at Liverpool John Moores University have designed housing projects for sites in Liverpool, choosing between one of three typical UK types: an urban block, terraced housing, or detached / semi-detached. They were challenged to translate the three priorities into their design proposals. As theoretical projects they were permitted a high degree of intellectual and creative freedom, and as a result these designs push boundaries in exploring what housing could be.

---

47 Mohamed Osmani and Alistair O'Reilly, "Feasibility of Zero Carbon Homes in England by 2016: A House Builder's Perspective," *Building and Environment* 4 (2009): 1920, accessed January 26, 2015, doi:10.1016/j.buildenv.2009.01.005.

48 Ibid. 1922.

49 "Why a Home Quality Mark?" Building Research Establishment, accessed March 12, 2015, http://www.homequalitymark.com/why_home_quality_mark.html.

50 P.F.G. Banfill and A.D. Peacock, "Energy-efficient New Housing – The UK Reaches for Sustainability," *Building Research and Information* 35:4 (2007): 434, accessed January 26, 2015, doi: 10.1080/09613210701339454.

51 Weizsäcker, Lovins and Lovins, *Factor Four*, xxv.

52 Lowe and Oreszczyn, "Regulatory Standards," 4478.

Many students embraced the space standards proposed by the RIBA. Interestingly, a prominent theme was to start from that quantitative figure and explore it qualitatively; they considered how space could be used most effectively, often developing alternative scenarios for different potential occupants. This led to thinking beyond conventional dwelling spaces, and to questioning what modern patterns of living actually demand. Some commonalities emerged, such as dedicated spaces to work from home or to enable adult offspring (unable to afford their own dwelling) or elderly relatives to live as part of an extended family. As such, the 'family unit' became a plastic concept which the students perceived as flexible and changing significantly over time. Some proposed multiple living rooms so that occupants could relax in different ways at the same time – suggesting the notion of the whole family gathering around one television is an outdated one. This starts to address the RIBA's call for more consideration about what space is adequate to suit contemporary living.

Students looked at other ways in which the design of dwellings could respond to changing circumstances. Like Holl's Void Space / Hinge Space and Gerrit Rietveld's 1924 Schröder House, some of the projects incorporated sliding or folding screens so that rooms could be easily reconfigured throughout the day – subdivided when different activities had conflicting needs, and then recombined to create an open plan.

Whilst it might seem fanciful to imagine that people would substantially adapt their homes instead of moving, increasing unaffordability to upsize means that moving is not an option open to all. Much of the media coverage about the UK housing crisis focuses on those unable to buy or rent their first home, and its effects on those unable to move up the housing ladder as their circumstances change are often overlooked.[53] Some students looked at how additional space would be added by building upwards or outwards – as an integral design feature and not an ad hoc extension. A contemporary 'outhouse' in the gardens of several projects provides a sense of separation between the main dwelling and a workspace, or gives elderly relatives or adult offspring a degree of independence.

It could be argued that space standards defined by area will promote two-dimensional responses. Encouragingly, thinking about internal space three-dimensionally – as opposed to just in terms of square metres – was another common theme; many projects proposed higher than average ceilings, variation across the section and double height spaces to maximise the quality of internal spaces.

Studying architecture, these students were not in a position to accurately evaluate the cost of their proposals in detail. However, when considering the structure and fabric of their projects many turned to advanced housing manufacture to minimise building costs and increase affordability. Their strategies include standardisation and prefabrication – which have both been cited by policy makers as a way to reduce construction costs. Students studied how their designs could be panelised to facilitate prefabrication offsite, and how traditional materials such as brick could be used in modern methods

53   Martina Lees, "Home Truths," *The Sunday Times – Home*, April 19, 2015.

of construction. Some also made a correlation between affordability and occupancy costs by dramatically reducing utility use – reconciling affordability and sustainability.

When considering the environmental performance of their dwellings many students referred to the Passivhaus energy performance standard, perceiving this as an industry benchmark for achieving high levels of sustainability. Passivhaus works on the principles of good thermal insulation, passive solar gains, excellent airtightness, and mechanical ventilation with heat recovery.[54] Interestingly, concern has recently been raised over Passivhaus dwellings overheating in summer; some reports have suggested that the high levels of insulation mean that peak temperatures in summer would be uncomfortably high, which could be exacerbated if the climate warms as predicted.[55]

Lack of natural light is a significant cause of dissatisfaction with housing in the UK.[56] A number of the projects addressed this issue and maximised daylight provision. In some instances this was achieved with courtyards or skylights and light wells, as well as large windows. Other methods proposed for minimising environmental impact include rainwater harvesting, renewable energy generation, and using reclaimed materials. These are not innovative techniques, demonstrating that achieving dramatic improvements in the sustainability of housing is not dependent on discovering the means by which to do so, but on finding ways to implement these techniques as a matter of course.

Concluding Remarks

There is a desperate urgency to increase the provision of new housing in the UK, with an accumulating shortfall between the dwellings needed and those being built of 100,000 to 150,000 a year.[57] Put starkly, since 2010 six babies have been born for every new home built.[58]

In the necessary drive to increase the provision of housing it is absolutely vital that the space within those dwellings is generous, that the impact they will have on the planet's environment is minimised, and that their cost is affordable. However, time is ticking by. As it does the housing shortage grows increasingly acute, more people are priced out of the market, and opportunities to address climate change slip away.

---

54 Building Research Establishment, "Passivhaus – Basic Principles," accessed July 1, 2015, http://www.passivhaus.org.uk/page.jsp?id=17.

55 Jonathan Leake, "Residents Roast in Eco-Homes' Greenhouse Effect," *The Sunday Times*, May 10, 2015.

56 Ipsos MORI, *Housing Standards*, 3.

57 Griffith and Jefferys, *Solutions for the Housing*, 3.

58 Tom Ough, "Six Babies for Each New Home Since 2010," *The Times*, December 30, 2014.

No single strategy will solve the UK's housing crisis.[59] Funding and planning legislation should be changed to promote more small- and medium-sized house builders, and more self- and custom-builds; larger house builders should embrace prefabrication and reinvest cost savings in greater space and sustainability; training and apprenticeships must educate in both modern methods of construction and sustainability; mortgages should promote highly sustainable housing and offset their dramatically reduced running costs in affordability assessments. The list goes on.

The Factor Four concept argues that all strategies – policy, procurement, and design – must be thoroughly integrated to maximise their effect. Approaches are desperately needed that embrace diverse ways of both procuring and constructing housing and which reconceptualise funding so that the benefits of advanced efficiencies and the substantial reductions in occupation costs can be reinvested in providing more space and much improved environmental performance. Good design should maximise the quality of space, the use of space, and improve sustainability.

By thinking creatively and holistically it is possible to utilise the individual benefits of these improvements for mutual advantage, but this is not the case at present. In so doing, new housing can be created which is more spacious, sustainable, and affordable. The architect Mies van der Rohe said, 'Less is more.' Doing 'more with less' must be applied to new housing design and construction.

Bibliography

Arcilla, Patricia. 'New York to Complete First Prefabricated 'Micro-Apartments' this Year.' *ArchDaily.* February 24, 2015. Accessed February 26, 2015, http://www.archdaily. com/?p=602157.

Baker, Simon. 'Too Quiet on the Home Front.' *The RIBA Journal* 121(2) (2014): 43-44.

Banfill, P.F.G. and A.D. Peacock. 'Energy-efficient New Housing – The UK Reaches for Sustainability.' *Building Research and Information* 35:4 (2007): 426-36. Accessed January 26, 2015, doi:10.1080/0913210701339454.

Barker, Kate. *Delivering Stability: Securing our Future Housing Needs.* London: HMSO, 2004.

British Broadcasting Corporation. 'Why Can't the UK Build 240,000 Houses a Year?' Accessed January 13, 2015. http://www.bbc.co.uk/news/magazine-30776306.

Building Research Establishment. 'Passivhaus – Basic Principles.' Accessed July 1, 2015, http://www.passivhaus.org.uk/page.jsp?id=17.

Building Research Establishment. 'Why a Home Quality Mark?' Accessed March 12, 2015. http://www.homequalitymark.com/why_home_quality_mark.html.

Building Research Establishment. *The Future of Sustainable Housing.* Watford: BRE Global, 2013.

Buildings 4 Change. 'MPs Fail to Strengthen ZCH Standards.' Accessed February 17, 2015. http://www.building4change.com/article.jsp?id=2585#.VOMJDU0pWUI.

---

59 Martina Lees, "A New Dawn," *The Sunday Times – Home*, April 19, 2015.

Confederation of British Industry. *Housing Britain: Building New Homes for Growth*. London: CBI, 2014.

Department for Communities and Local Government. *Nationally Described Space Standard: Technical Requirements*. Consultation draft, 2014.

Department for Communities and Local Government. *Laying the Foundations: A Housing Strategy for England*. London: Communities and Local Government Publications, 2011.

Department of Energy and Climate Change. 'Annual Domestic Energy Charges.' Accessed January 28, 2015. https://www.gov.uk/government/statistical-data-sets/annual-domestic-energy-price-statistics.

DoI, Kees and Marietta Haffner, eds. *Housing Statistics in the European Union*. The Hague: Ministry of the Interior and Kingdom Relations, 2010.

Element Energy and David Langdon. 'Costs of Building to the Code for Sustainable Homes.' Accessed January 16, 2015. http://www.brighton-hove.gov.uk/content/planning/local-development-framework/ldf-background-studies.

Future Homes Commission. *Building the Homes and Communities Britain Needs*. London: Future Homes Commission and RIBA, 2014.

Greater London Authority, Homes and Communities Agency, and London Development Agency. *Draft London Housing Design Guide: Cost and Delivery Impact Assessment*. Pre-publication draft, 2010.

Griffith, Matt and Pete Jefferys. *Solutions for the Housing Shortage*. London: Shelter, 2013.

Hall, Peter. *Good Cities, Better Living – How Europe Discovered the Lost Art of Urbanism*. Abingdon: Routledge, 2014.

Steven Holl Architects. 'Void Space/Hinge Space Housing.' Accessed January 19, 2015. http://www.stevenholl.com/project-detail.php?id=36&.

Homes and Communities Agency. *Designed for Manufacture – Lessons Learnt 2*. London: Homes and Communities Agency, 2010.

Intergovernmental Panel on Climate Change. *Climate Change 2014 Synthesis Report – Summary for Policy Makers*. IPCC, 2014.

Ipsos MORI. *Housing Standards and Satisfaction: What the Public Wants*. London: Ipsos MORI and RIBA, 2013.

Jefferys, Peter et al. *Building the Homes We Need – A Programme for the 2015 Government*. KPMG, 2014.

Kelly, Liam. 'Should Minimum Space Standards Apply to Social and Private Housing?' *The Guardian*, April 19, 2013. Accessed January 26, 2015, http://www.theguardian.com/housing-network/poll/2013/apr/19/minimum-space-standards-social-private.

Leake, Jonathan. 'Residents Roast in Eco-Homes' Greenhouse Effect.' *The Sunday Times*. May 10, 2015.

Lees, Martina. 'A New Dawn.' *The Sunday Times – Home*. April 19, 2015.

Lees, Martina. 'Home Truths.' *The Sunday Times – Home*. April 19, 2015.

Lees, Martina. 'Talk is Cheap.' *The Sunday Times – Home*. April 19, 2015.

Linshi, Jack. '2014 Was Officially the Hottest Year on Record.' *Time*, January 6, 2015. Accessed January 7, 2015. http://time.com/3656646/2014-hottest-year/.

Lowe, Robert and Tadj Oreszczyn. 'Regulatory Standards and Barriers to Improved Performance for Housing.' *Energy Policy* 36 (2008): 4475-81. Accessed January 26, 2015. doi:10.1016/j.enpol.2008.09.024.

Mayor of London. *London Housing Design Guide – Interim Edition*. London: London Development Agency, 2010.

Meteorological Office. '2014 Confirmed as UK's Warmest Year on Record.' Accessed January 7, 2015. http://www.metoffice.gov.uk/news/releases/archive/2015/Record-UK-temps-2014.

National Aeronautics and Space Administration. 'NASA, NOAA Find 2014 Warmest Year in Modern Record.' Accessed 19 January, 2015. http://www.nasa.gov/press/2015/january/nasa-determines-2014-warmest-year-in-modern-record/index.html.

National Custom and Self Build Association. 'Research and Development Programme.' Accessed February 5, 2015. http://www.nacsba.org.uk/researchdevelopment.

The Water Services Regulation Authority (Ofwat). 'PN 03/13 Water and Sewerage Bills to Increase.' Accessed January 28, 2015. http://www.ofwat.gov.uk/mediacentre/pressnotices2008/prs_pn0313bills.

Osmani, Mohamed and Alistair O'Reilly. 'Feasibility of Zero Carbon Homes in England by 2016: A House Builder's Perspective.' *Building and Environment* 4 (2009): 1917-24. Accessed January 26, 2015. doi:10.1016/j.buildenv.2009.01.005.

Ough, Tom. 'Six Babies for Each New Home Since 2010.' *The Times*, December 30, 2014.

Palmer, Jason and Ian Cooper. *United Kingdom Housing Energy Fact File 2012*. London: Department of Energy and Climate Change, 2012.

Parvin, Alastair. 'How 3D Printing and Land Reform Could Help to Solve the Housing Crisis.' *The Guardian*, January 20, 2015. Accessed February 26, 2015. http://www.theguardian.com/society/2015/jan/20/3d-printing-land-reform-solve-housing-crisis.

Royal Institute of British Architects. *The Case for Space: The Size of England's New Homes*. London: RIBA, 2011.

Rudlin, David and Nicholas Falk. *Uxcester Garden City – Second Stage Submission for the 2014 Wolfson Economics Prize*. Manchester: URBED, 2014.

The Self Build Portal. 'Self Build One-off Home.' Accessed February 5, 2015. http://www.selfbuildportal.org.uk/self-build-one-off-home.

Sherman, Jill. 'Huge Rally Will Demand Surge in British Homebuilding.' *The Times*, February 7, 2015.

Stern, Sir Nicholas. *The Stern Review: The Economics of Climate Change – Executive Summary*. Cambridge: Cambridge University Press, 2006.

Vidal, John. 'Britain's First 'Energy Positive' House Opens in Wales.' *The Guardian*, July 16, 2015. Accessed July 29, 2015. www.theguardian.com/environment/2015/jul/15/britains-first-energy-positive-house-opens-in-wales.

Weizsäcker, Ernst von, Amory B. Lovins and L. Hunter Lovins. *Factor Four: Doubling Wealth – Halving Resource Use*. London: Earthscan, 1998.

Wilson, Wendy and Sarah Heath. 'Self-build and Custom Build Housing Sector.' Accessed February 5, 2015. www.parliament.uk/briefing-papers/SN06784.pdf.

Zogolovitch, Gus and Roger Zogolovitch. 'Solidspace.' *Blueprint* 332 (2014): 92-6.

EUSEBIO ALONSO GARCÍA

ACTIONS TO RECOVER THE ABSENT CITY – SIMULTANEITY AND HYPER SOCIALIZATION – STRATEGIES OF INTERVENTION IN A NEIGHBOURHOOD ON THE PERIPHERY

Introduction

This chapter explores intervention projects aimed at recovering the quality of public space and the private living conditions of residents in a typical Spanish neighbourhood, La Rondilla, on the periphery of Valladolid, Spain. La Rondilla (Figure 1) was developed in the 1960s on the formerly agricultural periphery of Valladolid which, at the time, was composed of new working-class neighbourhoods built by privately funded speculative construction. It is a dormitory town, dense and compact, but it lacks infrastructure and public spaces. It is composed of a succession of parallel six-storey blocks, separated by narrow streets. Its density of dwellings makes it desirable from the perspective of the *market*, but its minimum public spaces make it a place that is not so desirable for *living*.

In July 2013 La Rondilla was the subject of an international workshop, 'Accommodation for Other Ways of Life', in which twenty-two students of architecture from Valladolid, Madrid, Porto, and Rome, worked for ten days. The workshop analysed the urban space of this populous neighbourhood and developed design proposals at different scales – the neighbourhood as a whole, neighbourhood blocks, and housing. The aim was to increase the complexity of social spaces and improve the everyday lives of residents. Within the framework of this workshop contemporary social and urban theories were continually referenced to give the participants working models of intervention in the inherited city. This involved the re-appropriation of the roofs, lower floors, and the interstitial spaces of the housing blocks for collective enjoyment. These

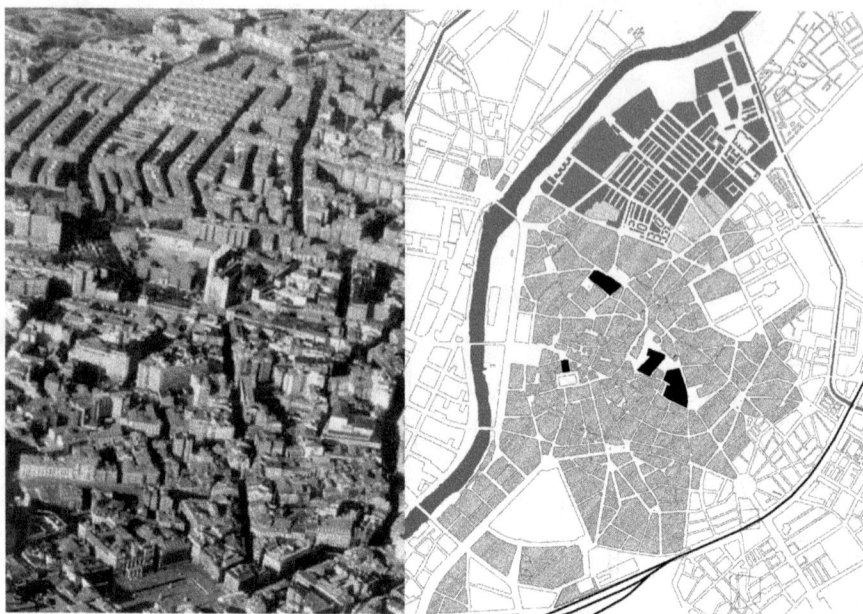

Figure 1. District of La Rondilla, Valladolid.

are models premised on recovering relational and meeting spaces and restoring the right to the city in the 21st century.

The workshop led to the development of four thematic approaches: 1. Break, free, recover; 2. Inhabited roofs; 3. The inclusion of new building benchmarks; and 4. The street belongs to everybody. These approaches tested different mechanisms of appropriation which were defined as *Spacing the House, Inhabiting the city, Inhabiting the sky*, and *Recovering the absent city*. The need to reorganise planning, financial, legal, institutional, and private agreements so as to implement these ideas does not invalidate their capacity to improve the quality of residential construction and life. Such changes are needed and, as a result, proposed.

Simultaneity and Hyper-Socialization

Without streets

In the iconic Neorealist film *The Bicycle Thief* (Vittorio de Sica, 1948), we see a new neighbourhood at the beginning of its life. It is devoid of infrastructures and has mud streets. People take water from a fountain and fill their buckets with it in order to bring it to their houses. One of the first scenes shows the lead couple talking about their problems while they walk from the fountain to their house, located in the one of the blocks in the new district. It is a scene reminiscent of La Rondilla. Developed some years later, La Rondilla had, by the 1970s, become denser and more compact than the district shown in de Sica's film, but similarities remained. The *Ribera de Castilla* was a large area between the district and the Pisuerga River devoid of infrastructure, such as parks and other public facilities, which were located there after many civic protests.

Neighbourhoods and mud

La Rondilla then, was born disconnected from the traditional city and lacked the appropriate public services and spaces. It was also built without the minimum spaces needed for the development of modern urban life and lacked a variety of scales and functions – streets, squares, parks, etc. – which could have served as a support for social relations. The architecture also reflects a lack of sensitivity to the environment, an incapacity to articulate diverse urban spaces, and the formal automatism of its volumes which, repeated over and over again, produce monotony in height and volume. This contrasts with the vibrant harmony of Valladolid's older buildings whose towers and churches reveal the former economic and territorial power of the city.

There are several paradoxes that accompanied the urbanization process of this district. Before its construction, there was a landscape of orchards which surrounded the historical centre of Valladolid. As a result of the industrialization of the 1960s, immigration from the small rural areas of the province and the region took place. A significant number of the workers in this new industrial city became the buyers and inhabitants of the new buildings. This district was called *dormitory town* because this was virtually the only necessity that it provided. Initially, there were no other services such as parks and schools, but after a decade of social and political wranglings these were added. However, the absence of free space in the city's interior meant they were located in the periphery which was an illegal garbage dump.

From the three fields, or layers, that Lefebvre[1] identified – *the rural, the industrial, the urban* – the urban was put at risk in La Rondilla due to the absence of appropriate spaces for community for development of the everyday in the city and the places of encounter between citizens, for example. The disposition of blocks also favoured the isolation of its few public spaces. The streets did not find a continuity that could promote the diversity of moving and crossing of the urban.[2]

House and city

Reflecting on the problem of housing leads to the reflection on the idea of the city. Aldo van Eyck expressed this duality, comparing it with the one existing between the leaf

---

1   Henri Lefebvre, *La revolución urbana*, Madrid, Alianza Editorial, 1983 (*1970*), 34-35.
2   In her analysis of the Rockefeller Center Jane Jacobs demanded the convenience of an alternative street to mitigate the excessive length of the blocks: '...can be compared the decay of these long blocks with the use fluidity that an extra street is able to produce'. Jane Jacobs, *Muerte y vida de las grandes ciudades*, Madrid, Capitán Swing, 2011 (1961), 214.

and the tree [3]. He expressed a fractal conception of the issue by interpreting the self-similarity of different structures at different scales.[4] In this conceptualization, the level of complexity continued independently of the size of the social group and, ultimately, the different scales in which our lives develop – from the most private, to the most collective and social.[5]

House and city are two different scales of our way of inhabiting the two extremes of the problem, and this inhabiting lies at the heart of our relationship with the world and our relationship with other people. So, when we talk about the concepts of intimacy, privacy, collectivity and community[6] we are discussing historical evolutions that have accompanied social ups and downs which, at times, have been very convulsive. The architecture of the house and the architecture of the city necessarily involve this relationship between humans and place – offering spaces of different degrees of privacy and public spaces for meeting.

The *everyday* of the human is, then, constructed at different scales or, as Lefebvre affirms, at *multiple levels*. In dealing with this phenomenon we are faced the inevitable fragmentation of the urban. In other words, in our desire to understand the problem we break up knowledge, short-circuiting its necessary interrelations and thus put a more agreed and coherent solution at risk.[7] From the house to the city, from the room to the metropolis, we construct spaces at different scales (district, neighbourhood, street, etc.) for the satisfaction of our individual and urban necessities. We do this through creative activity.[8]

---

3   Aldo van Eyck expressed his ideas in the Forum magazine (1962-63) thus: 'tree is leaf and leaf is tree – house is city and city is house – a tree is a tree but it is also a huge leaf – a leaf is a leaf but it is also a tiny tree – a city is not a city unless it is a huge house – a house is a house only if it is also a tiny city'. Aldo van Eyck, Building a house, in VV.AA., Aldo van Eyck, Amsterdam, Stichting Wonen, 1982, 44-45.

4   Benoît Mandelbrot, Los objetos fractales. Forma, azar y dimensión, Barcelona, Tusquets, 1996 (1975).

5   Science offers this global conception through the concept of Gaia – according to which the earth behaves like a self-regulating system that tends towards balance. The theory of 'Gaia' was first elucidated in 1969 by James Lovelock.

6   Christopher Alexander and Serge Chermayeff, Comunity and Privacy, New York, Doubleday, 1963

7   According to Manuel Delgado, the social space of Lefebvre has a hydrostatic and hypercomplex condition '... dominated by relative fixations, movements, flows, waves and understanding'. Manuel Delgado, El animal público, Barcelona, Anagrama, 1999, 38.

8   Reflecting these ideas, Bernard Waldenfels states: '...everydayness constitutes the intersection of social conditions and individual necessities'. Bernard Waldenfels, De Husserl a Derrida, Barcelona, Paidós, 1997 (1992), 139.

Strategies of Intervention in a Neighbourhood on the Periphery

Actions

Within the framework of the workshop discussed here, we analysed the *production of the space*, and examined the possibilities of intervention for change and regeneration. In order to engage in this inherited urban form we have to deal with interrelating levels of a complex social space that range from the house to the city scale. It is important to realize this, as our ability to transform it depends on the ability to read it. The district of Rondilla in Valladolid suffers major deficiencies and what is needed to make it a good contemporary urban and domestic space is significant.[9]

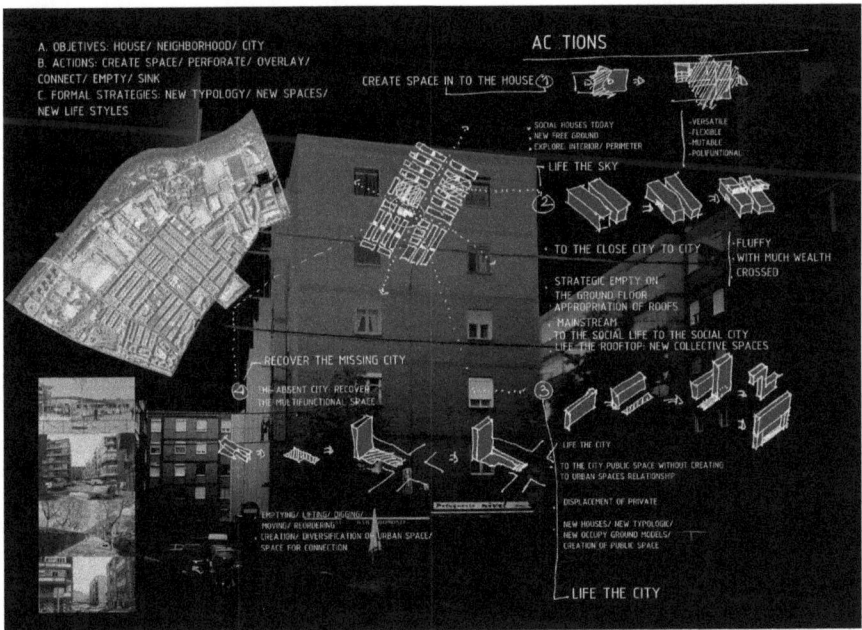

Figure 2. Concept ideas proposed include: Spacing the house; Inhabiting the sky; Inhabiting the city; Recovering the absent city.

---

9   In The Production of the Space, Lefebvre promises to demonstrate: 'the active – the operational or instrumental – role of space, as knowledge and action, in the existing mode of production. Henri Lefebvre, The Production of Space, Oxford, UK, Blackwell Publishing, 1991 (1974), 11.

The workshop, 'Accommodation for other Ways of Life', critically analyzed the situation at hand so as to contribute intervention proposals that would put the resilience of its urban and architectonic conditions to the test. It was a process that allowed us to think about the contemporary city more generally, and propose intervention strategies that are at once specific and, potentially, generic. These strategies deal with different scales: the housing unit, its mechanisms of grouping, the existing construction typologies, and those which would result from the intervention proposals. It also allowed us to look at the collective spaces, the resulting new spaces, and the relationships between them that are the result of this initial phase of theory and practical analysis. Four topics were proposed at the outset: *Spacing the house; Inhabiting the sky; Inhabiting the city; Recovering the absent city.* These strategies, or creative actions (Figures 2–5) were all intended to update the inherited city. Each strategy implies a dialectic relationship with reality, the will to transform it, and the application of a highly contingent process. [10]

Some of the categories that Lefebvre identified in the urban form are useful to conceive these intervention strategies that allow the overlapping of new and old systems of spatial organization in the neighbourhood: *multiplicity*[11], *simultaneity*[12], *updating*[13].

Spacing the house

Modern architecture has widely explored the quality of space and, in particular, the relations that can exist between the interior and exterior, and the spatial richness that this implies. In this context, space is configured by light and views which, if absent, mean that we cannot consider the space in question as habitable. By way of example, consider a photograph of the architect Herman Hertzberger. In it, an elderly couple is sitting having something to eat on the boot of a car, which is open. Not intended to be a habitable space, the boot becomes a living space with the aid of light, privacy, and the views – even if only momentarily. It is a good example of the concept of *appropriation*.[14]

The cinema director Jacques Tati, identified the obsession of modern architecture with the relations between interior and exterior and its yearning for the house to enjoy the outside space. In a scene of *Mon Oncle* (1958), Monsieur and Madame Arpel, proud of their modern house with a garden, are sitting right outside the house, looking towards

---

10   These notions are all inspired by the work of Arendt: Hanna Arendt, La condición humana, Barcelona, Paidós, 1993 (1958).

11   'Social spaces interpenetrate one another and/or superimpose themselves upon one another'. H. Lefebvre, The production of space, op. cit. 86.

12   'The form of social space is encounter, assembly, simultaneity'. H. Lefebvre, The production of space, op. cit. 101.

13   'Every social space is the outcome of a process with many aspects and many contributing currents, signifying and non-signifying, perceived and directly experienced, practical and theoretical'. H. Lefebvre, Ibid, 110.

14   The appropriation, as Lefebvre clarifies, does not allude to the property, but rather time and space. Henri Lefebvre, De lo rural a lo urbano, Barcelona, Editorial Peninsula, 1978 (1970), 186.

the inside to watch the TV, which is in the living room. In this example, the exterior space of the garden is a complementary support of everyday domestic life. In both cases, inside and outside coexist and this reminds us of Lefebvre for whom a project that approaches Hölderlin´s poetic living must aspire to synthesise two opposed principles: *utopia* and *pragmatism*.[15] To this, we could add, inside and outside.

Inhabiting the city

The city is the space that people have created to establish relations.[16] The diversity of relationship has shaped different typologies of urban spaces and these, in turn, tell us about the idiosyncrasy of each community – about the way in which people develop their existence. When approaching an apparently technical problem, like the organization of the traffic in Philadelphia, Louis Kahn (1954) analyzed the flow and circulation of traffic, identifying different situations (road, pedestrian, crossing, intersection, access to parking, etc.). He reflected the graphic coding of these onto maps, making an existential interpretation of the system of relations that arose from urban traffic. Situationists raised the system of urban relations to another level still, redrawing the map of Paris as a psychogeographic cartography in which the city appeared fragmented and recomposed, according to its affective drift – *détournement* – its existential and random wandering. However, they also proposed a review of our understanding of the city as a mere market for goods and a place of objects (buildings).[17] Both cases are alternatives to implosive developments that allow us to articulate different urban structures from inherited ones, making *spacing the city* a possibility.[18]

Instead of the current rigid layouts of the neighbourhood, with their clear distinctions between what is private and what is not, this workshop looked to suppress the borders, *crossing them*, by using the techniques of *appropriation* and *détournement*[19]. *Détournement* consists of the appropriation and creative reorganization of existing elements.

---

15   These dichotomies are reflected in Lefebvre in his thoughts on place, practice and living. H. Lefebvre, La revolución urbana, op. cit. 187.

16   This notion reflects the thoughts of Saskia Sassen. See: Saskia Sassen, La ciudad global, Buenos Aires, 1999, p. 42

17   L. Andreoti et altri, Situacionistas: arte, política y urbanismo, Barcelona, Actar, 1996.

18   Post World War Two precedents for this include: designs for the Centre of Frankfurt by Candilis, Josics and Woods (1963); the extension of the Camera of Representatives in Rome by Giuseppe and Alberto Samonà (1967); and the competition for the Centre Pompidou in Paris (1970).

19   Lefebvre favours appropriation over domination. See: H. Lefebvre, The production of space, op. cit. 164-168.

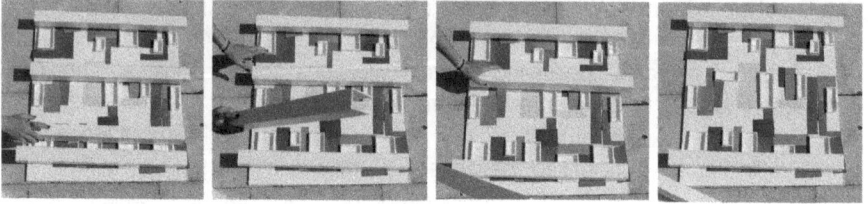

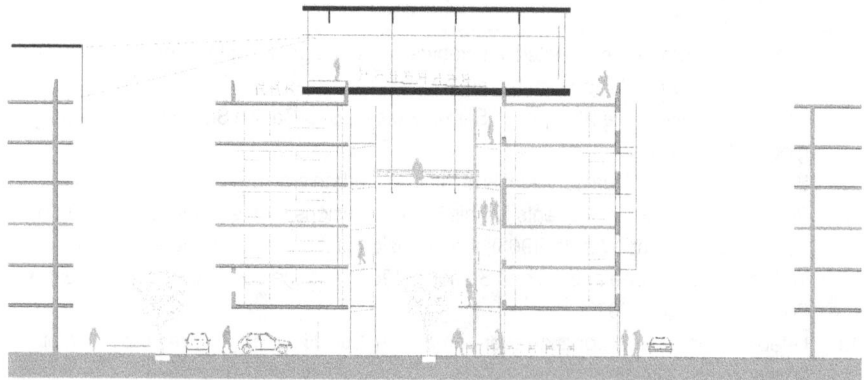

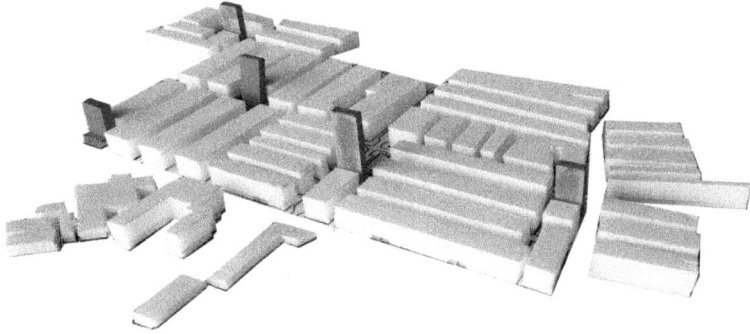

Figure 3. Scale model and exterior perspective. Concept ideas proposed include: Finding voids in the ground floor; to use as social space; regrouping of the interstitial spaces between blocks and old streets; crossing circulation; locating houses at high levels.

Figure 4. External perceptive and section. Concepts proposed: use roofs as new social space; use the inner courtyards as 'sponge spaces'; create new accesses the houses; ensure the visibility of collective spaces.

Figure 5. Site section and model. Concepts proposed: create a new skyline for the neighbourhood; create new squares; ensure the legibility of the structure of social spaces

Inhabiting the sky

We have mentioned some projects in which the relation between the building and public space is no longer conventional. The same applies to their relation with the land. These projects explored the possibilities of public spaces not being located exclusively on the ground. Instead, they were to be located on the roofs which ceased to be the end of the building and were transformed into the beginning of new relationships in the community[20] – a spontaneous theatre.[21]

In the 1960s, some experiences linked to art and pop culture questioned, in a brilliant and audacious way, what and where the public space of collective action and representation could be.[22] Trisha Brown, in her performance *'Man Walking down the Side of a Building'* (1970), in which the facade of a building was used as the stage along which a man descended, moved the traditional theatrical space into the city itself.[23] This reflected ideas that were emerging in the 1960s, when contemporary dance and music went out to the streets and explored interactive relationships with public space. For example, on 30th January 1969 people stopped in the street, amazed by the sound that came from the roof of number 3 Savile Row in London. While the police tried to keep order, The Beatles were giving a live concert on the roof of the Apple Records building.[24]

Conclusions: to Recover the Absent City and the Right to the City

In an engraving of Valladolid from the 16th century (Braun and Hogenberg, Valladolid 1574), the city was silhouetted against the sky. In the foreground is the cultivated land. Behind that, the low and extensive buildings of the urban centre of the small town – the vibrant sequence of towers and churches that together made up the districts, parishes, and convents of the city. This vibrant image, plastically active and eloquently revealing the crucial areas of the city, is clearly different and distant from the dull and excessively

---

20 A contemporary precedent for this includes The High Line, Diller and Scofidio + Renfo. More historical precedents can be found in the work of Hannes Meyer and Ludwig Hilberseimer and Peter and Alison Smithson. For comments on Le Corbusier in this regard, see: Eusebio Alonso, Estrategias alucinatorias en el ultimo Le Corbusier, in VV. AA., Critic/All Actas, Madrid, critic/All Press, 2014, 55-73; Eusebio Alonso, De Ronchamp al Hospital de Venecia. Mito religioso y memoria colectiva en el último Le Corbusier, in VV. AA., Arquitectura, símbolo y modernidad, Valladolid, Universidad, 2014, 349-366.

21 Again, for ideas on this imn the writing of Lefebvre see: Henri Lefebvre, El derecho a la ciudad, op. cit. 100.

22 These activities find echoes in Arendt. See: H. Arendt, op. cit. 21-22.

23 Victoria Perez, ¡A bailar a la calle! Danza contemporánea, espacio público y arquitectura, Salamanca, Universidad, 2009.

24 For relevant commenst by Lefevre of the ideas and issues underlying such pop-culture phenamona, see: H. Lefebvre, El derecho a la ciudad, op. cit. 68.

horizontal image of the neighbourhood of La Rondilla. It is an image we see as a precedent for our proposals (Figures 3–5).

In the film with which we started this chapter with, Sica's *The Bicycle Thief*, after the many ups and downs, the protagonist (and us, as sympathetic spectators) realizes that his difficulties are the same as those of his fellow citizens. When his son lends him a hand and he seems to have overcome his desperation, the camera moves away and lets us see that they walk together, but also next to so many others in the city, also struggling to overcome their difficulties. It coincides with the voice-over of a hopeful narrative.[25] It is not only buildings that overlay our cities, but our lives as well. This too is something we need to remember in our interventions with the city and, in particular, its housing.

The work carried out in the workshop 'Accommodation for Other Ways of Life', taught us lessons. These contributed, in the first place, to developing specific strategies of intervention in a residential piece of an inherited city. These strategies, we suggest, allowed the development of design proposals that update the neighbourhood's urban conditions and the quality of its social space. We also suggest that the critical analytical tools developed are applicable beyond this particular case study and that the theoretical social and urban concepts employed in the initial part of the process gave us the creative and intellectual tools needed to discuss space, urban society, and alternative design approaches

Bibliography

Andreoti, L., Costa, X et al. Situacionistas: arte, política, urbanismo. Barcelona: Actar, 1996.

Alexander, C., Chermayeff, S., Comunity and Privacy, New York: Doubleday, 1963.

Alonso, E., De Ronchamp al Hospital de Venecia. Mito religioso y memoria colectiva en el último Le Corbusier, 349-366, in VV. AA., Arquitectura, símbolo y modernidad, Valladolid: Universidad, 2014.

Alonso, E., Estrategias alucinatorias en el último Le Corbusier, 55-73, in VV. AA., Critic/All Actas, Madrid: Critic/All Press, 2014.

Alonso, E., Mario Ridolfi. Arquitectura, contingencia y proceso, Valladolid: Universidad, 2014.

Alonso, E., Paulo Mendes da Rocha. Constructor de horizontales en el aire, DPA 30: Barcelona, 2014.

Arendt, H., La condición humana. Barcelona: Paidós, 1993.

Calvino, I., Seis propuestas para el próximo milenio, Madrid: Siruela, 1990.

Delgado, M., El animal público, Barcelona: Anagrama, 1999.

Eyck, A. van, Building a house, in VV. AA., Aldo van Eyck, Amsterdam: Stichting Wonen, 1982.

---

25 Arguments on the relevance of these ideas to the perception of architecture in this context see: Eusebio Alonso, Mario Ridolfi. Arquitectura, contingencia y proceso, Valladolid, Universidad, 2014 (2007).

Gonzalo, Constantino, Democracia y barrio. El movimiento vecinal en Valladolid, 1964-1986, Valladolid: Universidad, 2013.

Hertzberger, H., Lessons for students in Architecture, Rotterdam: 010 Publishers, 2005.

Jacobs, J., Muerte y vida de las grandes ciudades, Madrid: Capitán Swing, 2011.

Lefebvre, H., El derecho a la ciudad Barcelona: Editorial Península, 1978.

---.La vida cotidiana en el mundo moderno, Madrid: Alianza Editorial, 1972.

---.De lo rural a lo urbano, Barcelona: Editorial Península, 1978.

---.La revolución urbana, Madrid: Alianza Editorial, 1983.

---. The production of space, Oxford: Blackwell Publishing, 1991.

Mandelbrot, B., Los objetos fractales. Forma, azar y dimensión, Barcelona: Tusquets, 1996.

Pérez, V., ¡A bailar a la calle! Danza contemporánea, espacio público y arquitectura, Salamanca: Universidad, 2009.

Sassen, S., La ciudad global, Buenos Aires, 1999.

Waldenfels, B., De Husserl a Derrida, Barcelona: Paidós. 1997.

GEORGIOS ARTOPOULOS AND IOANNIS A. PISSOURIOS

DWELLING IN PERMANENT EPHEMERALITY: THE RESIDENTIAL AREAS OF PAPHOS

Introduction

In Cyprus, contemporary affordable housing, mostly led by developers, promises an antidote to the small spaces, small windows, lack of storage spaces, and the reduction of common spaces to a circulatory minimal found in most contemporary residential blocks in urban environments. In Eastern Europe and the Eastern Mediterranean region, housing blocks for low-income families, workers, and refugees[1] have been criticised in the past as stark, dehumanizing, universal, sterile, and mechanistic, and were held responsible for many social problems, like social disintegration. The purpose of the Design Studio in Urban Design and Housing (ARCH S05), which is one of the requirements of the BA course in Architecture at Neapolis University (2nd year), is to understand the design idioms and special conditions of mobility in Cyprus, and its aim is a closer study of the architectural and social value of common spaces in housing projects located in challenged urban environments. Today, the development and establishment of processes that generate shared identities based on the use of common spaces is an important issue in contemporary architectural discourse about equal opportunities and the sustainable interaction of multicultural societies in European cities.

In this project we focused on the design of inclusive communal spaces in housing, and our agenda looked at human association and place-making. The communal spaces in housing complexes are of varied typologies: they can be open, closed, or permeable,

---

1   Cf. *Open Debate and Exhibition* on 'The refugee neighbourhoods under threat from the projects of 'development' and 'refurbishment',' organized at the National Technical University of Athens (30-10-2000).

and have the form of courtyards, landscaped gardens, or amplified landings. They are perceived, sometimes successfully, and at other times unsuccessfully, as spaces of social interaction, association, and identification. In this context we read open spaces in housing projects – beyond their primary function as circulation plateaus – not through the Modernist notion of public space (e.g., generic, empty space that is 'flexible' enough to accommodate variable uses), but rather as non-pre-programmed spaces; spaces that are 'unstable' and can be transformed by users.

Background

The city of Paphos has a remarkable history which can be traced back 2,300 years. The ancient town of Paphos was founded in the late 4th century BC by the last King of PalaiPaphos, Nicocles. PalaiPaphos was one of the most famous places of pilgrimage for the ancient Greeks, and one of the city-kingdoms of ancient Cyprus (Hadjidemetriou, 2007). New Paphos was such an important town that by the late 2nd century BC it became the capital of the island. During medieval times, New Paphos was reduced in size and its inhabitants gradually moved to a new residential area, the Ktima district.

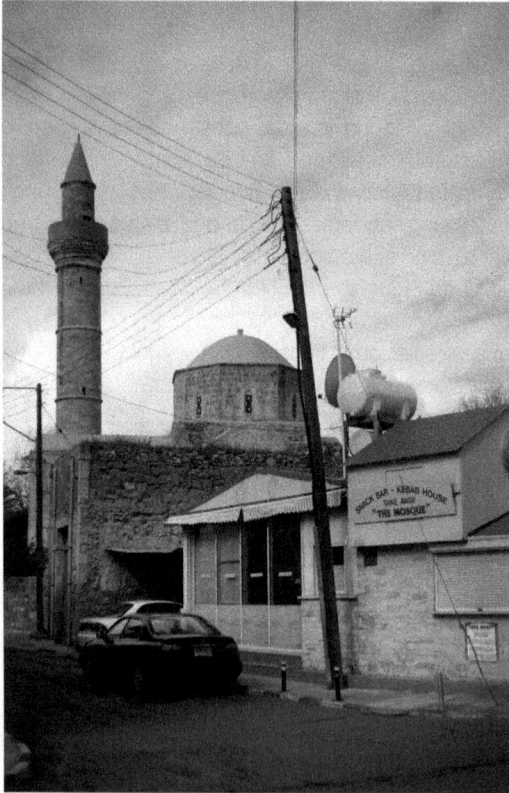

Figure 1. The Mosque Hagia Sophia in Mouttalos quarter with ephemeral constructions in front

Figure 2. A typical dwelling condition in Mouttalos: ephemerally fixing construction issues since 1974

Ktima, which is today the centre of the city, soon became the administrative centre of the town. Its name, Ktima (engl. trans. *field*) refers to the Royal Acquisition, suggesting the existence in the area of a royal field or estate, which belonged to a knight during the Lusignan period (1192–1489). Since Ottoman rule (1571–1878), Paphos has had a Muslim community living together with the Greek-Orthodox community. The city of Paphos played an important role during the 1955–1959 struggles against the then British rulers, at the end of which Cyprus became an independent Republic. Three years later there were inter-communal riots all over Cyprus, and Mouttalos, the Muslim quarter of the city, was separated from the town centre of Paphos (Ktima) (Maragou, 2003).

The quarter of Mouttalos stretches geographically westward to Fellahoglou Street, the major shopping street of the city, which was once the commercial zone where Turkish-Cypriots and Greek-Cypriots from the nearby villages traded, and thus operated as a common ground for the two communities. An important social centre for both Muslim and Orthodox Christian residents, Ottoman baths built in 1592 by the commander of Paphos, Mehmet Bey Empoumpekir, are located in the south-eastern side of

Mouttalos. Another important nearby site of interaction between the two communities is the Municipal Market, built in 1920, which was once a meat, fish, and vegetable market.

After the 1974 war and the division of the island, Greek-Cypriots fled to the south, and the Turkish-Cypriots settled in the north, including the Turkish-Cypriots who lived in Paphos. The population transfer left Mouttalos empty of life; an abandoned built environment that was shaped by the everyday lives, habits, rituals, and the social behaviour of an absent community. The Mosque Hagia Sophia, exhibiting a combination of medieval and Ottoman architectural elements, the local square with its form typical of the Eastern Mediterranean region, along with other amenities of the area, were originally created in response to the cultural and social needs of the Turkish-Cypriot community. However, the violent exchange of populations between the North and South parts of the island led Greek-Cypriot refugees to settle in the quarter and forced them to (according to the official state wording) 'provisionally' dwell in the historically produced aggregate of the existing urban fabric that is still legally owned by its previous inhabitants (Figure 1). For its new inhabitants, this confined, complex, almost medieval form of built environment resonated its cultural production by the 'other' community.

According to the findings of a survey[2] about environmental comfort and the building conditions of the settlement, this latent identity of the place – along with the yet-to-be-realised intention of the Greek-Cypriot refugees to return to their houses in Northern Cyprus, in the event of a resolution of the division – are the main reasons for both the limited adaptation of the quarter to the social and cultural characteristics and everyday activities of its new users, and the lack of any significant rehabilitation work. This approach of *permanent ephemerality* to dwelling has generated a quasi-space that remains in limbo even today – existing in-between the uncertain formation of a place and a *non-place* (Augé, 2009) (Figure 2). This hybrid condition has arguably traumatized the civic identity of one of the very few historic quarters of a city that is topographically and socially divided in two plateaus.

Paphos

Unlike other Cypriot cities, Paphos spreads across two distinct geographic areas, which were developed in different chronological phases: the new Paphos, and Paphos town centre (Ktima), commonly referred to as Kato (Lower) and Upper Paphos. Based on tourism and the construction sector, mainly operating in Kato Paphos and the nearby areas, the economy of the city has grown rapidly since 1974. During the last four decades Cyprus has been transformed from an agriculture-based economy into an international provider of economic services. Significantly, together with the sector of economic services, the construction sector and tourism benefited the economic

---

2   The survey was conducted in the context of The Cyprus Institute's collaboration with Neapolis University (PI: Professor Mattheos Santamouris), with the assistance of a team of NUP students of architecture, cf. Pignatta *et al.*, 2016.

Figure 3. Aerial view of Paphos that highlights the location of the two sites of study and the geological rim that separates the old part of the city from its Port and Kato Paphos

growth of the country: tourist numbers have increased from 353,375 arrivals in 1980 to 2,069,000 in 1994 – an increase of almost 600% in a decade and a half. Similarly, there was a threefold increase in building by the construction sector – from 6,891 new dwellings delivered in 1995 to 18,195 dwellings in 2008 (Statistical Service of the Republic of Cyprus, 2015).

This proliferation of the construction sector should not be regarded as irrelevant to tourist growth, as Cyprus gradually became an international provider of holiday houses. The mild climate of the island and the low cost of living, as well as the low taxation and aggressive incentives for property ownership significantly benefited the real estate market. The growth of the construction sector is best illustrated in the following statistics: in 2000, 12,664 houses were sold, 12,214 (96.4%) of which sold in the domestic market and 450 (3.6%) in the overseas market. Seven years later, in 2007, the total production of houses increased to 21,245 houses, from which 9,964 (46.9%) were sold in the domestic market and 11,281 (53.1%) in the overseas market (Cyprus Property News, 2014). This transition had a striking effect on the real estate market, as the average prices of dwellings (euro per square meter) increased annually by 15% between 2000 and 2008 (Pashardes and Savva, 2009). As a result, house ownership has been rapidly transformed from a social necessity of the local market to a commodity of the international real estate market. The impact of this change was severe, not only on the architectural quality of dwellings, but most importantly on the quality of the built environment.

Of all Cypriot cities, this spatial transformation had the greatest impact on the urban space of Paphos. The seaside area developed for the 2017 Cultural Capital of Europe is considered among the most contested urban environments – having historically layered pasts yet perplexing present-day realities. The distinction between the old town and the UNESCO World Heritage Site in Kato Paphos (the social and spatial coherence of which is currently challenged by unplanned touristic developments) has created a sharp division in the city that is also reflected in their inhabitants' demographics – with local residents living in the old town, and tourists being secluded in the sea front. The impact of this invisible division on the lived experience of the city is intensified by the topography of the landscape, with the old town stretching atop the hill while being separated from the World Heritage Site by means of the geological rim (Figure 3).

Socio-Economic Problems – Design Studios

The impact of this division on the sustainable development of the city, together with the contemporary challenges of the Cypriot city planning schemes, like the loosely defined built-up spaces and the scarcity of public spaces, have led to a study of two sites by the authors. The sites are used for Design Studio projects presented in Section Three of this volume the brief of which focuses on the analysis of two sites: one located in the historic core of the city, in Mouttalos, and the other in the Universal area, which exhibits all the typical characteristics of newly (after 1990s) built-up areas in most Cypriot cities (Figure 3). Through these two case studies, students are introduced to the discourse about the politics of common resources, in the context of the contemporary fragmented and multicultural cityscape. In particular, the Design Studio rethinks the relationship between the challenged built environment of Paphos and the complexity of its cultural landscape (home to British expats, Cypriots, Chinese, Russians, Georgians, Greeks, and others).

Both the central government and land developers regarded the popularity of Paphos as a tourist destination to be a great opportunity to enter the international market of holiday residences. To this end, successive, large-scale expansions of the city planning scheme were executed, which were highly disproportionate to the real needs of the local communities, in order for land (and housing) prices to stay low and be competitive in the international real estate market. The production of urban space was restricted by the design of these housing developments, which were planned as low density residential areas with typical, universally appealing amenities and communal facilities that respond to the lifestyle of summer dwellers and their ephemeral stay on the island. Today, these areas of the city are inhabited by even fewer residents than the low density city plans were originally intended for as the oversupply of built up urban areas has led to their only partial development, and only a fraction of their inhabitants are permanent.

Arguably, these conditions of the built environment defy the already challenged identity narrative and lived experience of Paphos. First, these residential areas became mono-functional as a direct result of the inability of non-residential (i.e., central) uses to emerge in areas with low density permanent populations. Second, the existence of numerous undeveloped areas fragments the continuity of the urban space. As stipulated in the relevant planning legislation (*Town and Country Planning Law*), the construction of public amenities (including roads and open green spaces) is a responsibility of each private landlord and is a prerequisite for the acquisition of planning permission. Thus, public amenities are constructed only after a landlord decides to develop the land.

In the context of this kind of incremental procedure of urban space production, roads and pedestrian routes (that have been designed by the central planning authority to connect to the existing circulation network) frequently lead to dead-ends, while open green spaces remain incomplete, reinforcing the fragmented hypostasis of the urban space. In addition to this, the common use of a tree-structured network pattern – to achieve low noise pollution and pedestrian-friendly design – impacts the overall accessibility of built space. Significantly, these design-led decisions limit daily transportation means to private vehicles. Third, and most important, social interaction

Figure 4. Aerial view of the Universal quarter

and socialisation processes in these residential areas has been reduced to a bare minimum. This is the result of the cumulative influence of low population densities, extensive use of private means of transportation, limited accessibility, and incomplete open green spaces – all characteristics reflected in the second site of the Design Studio, the Universal quarter (Figure 4).

Together with the challenged and fragmented structure of the urban space, the business model of these housing projects also affects the architectural qualities of the built up areas of the city. This is because these housing projects are usually designed to be attractive to a *statistical mean*, as they are addressed to a universal clientele that comprises the potential market of buyers. The attributes of this market, and the reasons for real estate investment in this case, are convoluted. First, the buyers of these properties may never live in Cyprus – a great deal of sales are taking place for citizenship and visa acquisition purposes only. Among other EU member states, Cyprus offers one of the most attractive and flexible citizenship and visa programs in Europe, which allows non-European people to work, travel, study, and live anywhere within the European Union. Second, the socio-cultural characteristics of this target group are mixed and varied, and Paphos is already a multicultural place: 64% of the population is Cypriots, 28% are EU citizens, and 8% are non-EU citizens (Statistical Service of the Republic of Cyprus, 2014).

Ubiquity and Uniformity

Products of these socio-economic particularities, the housing developments in Paphos are characterised by *ubiquity* and *uniformity* as they are designed and built to attract as wide an audience as possible. These design preferences are applied ignoring the social and cultural sustainability of the city as a whole, and without respecting the identity of the place (Figure 5). In areas like the Universal quarter the dominant housing pattern is a particular type of housing complex – preferred due to its low construction cost and its capacity for accommodating amenities like communal pools and small gardens, which support the function of the dwellings as summer houses. This approach to integrating communal spaces in housing has a negative impact on the intensity of social interaction and opportunities for the occupation of shared spaces, as it provokes the fragmentation and clustering of the latter into smaller, more private pockets of social interaction. The owner controls the social interaction that is taking place on these private green spaces and consequently they do not offer opportunities for surprise and unexpected encounters, an abundance of sensual stimuli, or any of the events that happen in a vivid urban space.

In developing the Studio research, the interplay of the different spatial conditions in the two selected sites generated constructive dialogue and conversation between student teams. Unlike historic cities, contemporary housing developments (residential or ubiquitous city-centres) lack the capacity of social adaptation and change. Fragmented territories contested by rapid growth and unplanned tourist developments, like in the Universal quarter, offer no alternatives to the historic parts of the city, like Mouttalos.

Figure 5. New and old housing projects at the Universal quarter defy the context and identity of the place

On the contrary, the lack of continuity and organization in the urban fabric weakens the relationship of new and old. This fragmentation challenges the operation, and support, of cultural activities and the sharing of the *common resources* of the city, such as the networks of built and open spaces (e.g., roofs, courtyards, arcades, patios, pavements, squares, and landscape), as well as networks of ventilation, natural lighting, shade, odours, and general microclimates. As these space-resources are scattered in the urban landscape, unassociated and inaccessible, they prevent their users (i.e., inhabitants and visitors) from orienting themselves, from reading the organization of public and open space (via cognitive structures) and eventually from 'making sense' of their environment. Therefore, collective uses of common resources potentially become an interface for communication and shared activities that may form a new narrative-idiom for the communities that use the two sites of study.

How could heterogeneous groups of individuals share the space of the city and co-occupy public space? How could the existing common resources, like landmarks, monuments of cultural heritage, points of stasis, etc., act as a catalyst to the establishment of new relations between citizens, local residents, and passers-by/ tourists? How could we design for rootedness that offers opportunities to establish relationships with a non-place? And finally, in the Design Studio we asked about architecture can deal with the societal impact of historic places that are associated with the 'other'? One simple starting point, if not answer, is walking. Walking can function as a parallel performance of past, present, and future times, and its stage is the urban landscape; in so doing, users of the city embody a distinctive relationship with their surroundings. When users of a city explore the built environment, places are 'actualized' (e.g., becoming; cf. Foucault's concept of *heterotopias*) like nodes in a network, a territory that emerges out of the synthesis of their paths. This context framed many of the student projects, which used everyday activities, cultural exchange, and the action of walking as a starting point for developing their concepts.

Conclusions and Beginnings

The city offers a rich experience with its complexities, indeterminacy, and abundance of possible interactions accessible by the wanderer, local, or tourist. Through walking individuals interfere with physical constructions, points of interest, points of stasis, complex situations of interaction, the communication and exchange of information, the structured or sensual, and the uncertain; *thick* moments that alert or relax the body, distract the senses, and disrupt continuity of movement. All these situations are socially defined by each individual actor's narrative and depend on their agency. How can design interfere with these constantly changing relations and spatially-distributed associative conditions and also intensify opportunities for their actualisation?

The objective of the research done through this Studio was to provoke and facilitate the situated action of a group of people, be it locals or tourists, based on the assumption that any community requires some sort of common goal, understanding, condition, or identity. Actualising this congregation intensifies the interaction of individuals towards the convergence of their passages through the city to the ephemeral occupation of a common place. Spatial agency and geometric configuration of the city can promote and facilitate, or disrupt and limit, opportunities for the emergence and continuous reconfiguration of these experiences by means of the cognitive activities that are triggered by each individual's passage through the cityscape.

Human actions are socially and historically defined and thus are associated with identity. However, cultural and social systems traditionally operate by imposing binary distinctions (e.g., 'us' and the 'others') between generalized cases and normative behaviours in everyday interactions. It is thus imperative for design to accommodate irregularity and difference, and offer new opportunities for the emergence of associations with a place (with its unique, singular characteristics) that can act as a transformational motive in cultural and social systems. Our research and associated Design Studio projects, focused on spatial irregularities and social associations emerging in everyday activities in order to approach the challenged identity of the quarter of Mouttalos, and the ubiquitous urban fabric of the Universal, as unique parts of the city that negotiate interaction opportunities, rather than as areas that define boundaries in the daily experience of the city, performing as borders of 'otherness' (Hirst and Vadeboncoeur, 2006). And finally, in the Design Studio we sought for concepts that will enable architects to deal with the societal impact of historic places that are associated with the 'other.'

Bibliography

Augé, Marc. *Non-Places: An Introduction to Supermodernity* (2nd edition). Verso, 2009.

Binnie, John, Holloway, J., Millington, S. and Young, C., eds. *Cosmopolitan Urbanism.* London: Routledge, 2006.

Browning, Gary. *Understanding Contemporary Society: Theories of the Present.* Sage, 2000.

Cilliers, Paul. *Complexity and postmodernism: understanding complex systems.* London: Routledge, 1998.

Connerton, Paul. *How Societies Remember.* Cambridge, 1989.

Cyprus Property News. 'Cyprus property sales hit new record low in 2013.' Accessed August 10, 2015. http://www.news.cyprus-property-buyers.com/2014/01/09/cyprus-property-sales-record-low/id=0016577.

Gaffikin, Frank, Malachy Mceldowney and Ken Sterrett. 'Creating Shared Public Space in the Contested City: The Role of Urban Design.' *Journal of Urban Design* 15 (4) (2010): 493–513.

Hadjidemetriou, Katia. *A History of Cyprus* (2nd edition). Nicosia: 2007.

Hall, Suzanne. *City, Street and Citizen.* Routledge, 2012.

Hirst, Elizabeth and Vadeboncoeur, Jennifer A. 'Patrolling the Borders of Otherness: Dis/placed Identity Positions for Teachers and Students in Schooled Spaces.' *Mind, Culture, and Activity* 13 (2006): 205–27.

Maragou, Anna. *Paphos: Myth/Time/Place/People.* Nicosia: Municipality of Paphos, 2003.

Mitleton-Kelly, E. 'A Complexity Approach to Co-creating an Innovative Environment.' *World Futures: The Journal of General Evolution* 62 (3) (2006): 223-239.

Neelam C. Poudyal, Donald G. Hodges, Bruce Tonn and Seong-Hoon Cho. 'Valuing diversity and spatial pattern of open space plots in urban neighbourhoods.' *Forest Policy and Economics* 11 (3) (2009): 194-201.

Neill, William J. V. *Urban Planning and Cultural Identity.* London: Routledge, 2004.

Pashardes, Panos and Savva, Christos S. 'Factors Affecting House Prices in Cyprus: 1988-2008.' *Cyprus Economic Policy Review* 3 (2009): 3-25.

Pignatta, Gloria, Chatzinikola, C., Artopoulos, G., Papanicolas, C.N., Serghides, D. K. and Santamouris, M. 'Winter survey on the indoor environmental quality in low and very low income households in Cyprus.' *4th International Conference on Countermeasures to Urban Heat Islands* (IC2UHI). Singapore: 2016.

Sorkin, Michael (ed.). *Variations on a Theme Park.* New York: Noonday, 1992.

Statistical Service of the Republic of Cyprus. 'Construction and Housing.' Accessed August 10, 2015. http://www.mof.gov.cy/mof/cystat/statistics.nsf/industry_construction_62main_en/industry_construction_62main_en?OpenForm&sub=2&sel=2.

Statistical Service of the Republic of Cyprus. 'Table B7: Population enumerated by citizenship, sex, district and urban/rural area.' Accessed August 10, 2015. http://www.cystat.gov.cy/mof/cystat/statistics.nsf/populationcondition_22main_en/populationcondition_22main_en?OpenForm&sub=2&sel=2.

AVI FRIEDMAN

ARCHITECTURAL FLEXIBILITY AND AFFORDABILITY IN HOUSING

Introduction

Homes can be designed and marketed to provide buyers with choice as to the amount of space purchased and the contents of their home. This choice will enable families with modest means to have a better fit between their dwelling, household composition, lifestyle, and resources. In addition, rather than buying a fully finished unit, their home's flexible design should enable them to house themselves progressively as means become available.

The Next Home, was a prototype design based on these strategies that was constructed at McGill University as a demonstration and later adopted by private sector builders. This chapter explains the rationale for such an approach, the design principles of the Next Home, and the application of the concept in the marketplace.

A Need for a New Paradigm

The Next Home demonstration project was proposed as a direct response to contemporary North American households with their diversity of interior design needs and affordability constraints (Figure 1). The project extends the research undertaken by the author on the Grow Home project: an affordable, narrow-front, rowhouse prototype of which over 10,000 units were subsequently built in Canada[1]. A primary consideration in the approach of these prototypes is the economic and demographic changes that have rendered many notions inherent in the traditional design and marketing of housing obsolete.

Old home ownership models are weakening. The traditional mortgage system requires

---

1   W. Rybczynski, et al. *The Grow Home* (Montreal: McGill School of Architecture Affordable Homes Program, 1990).

Figure 1. The Next Home: full-scale prototype was constructed on the campus of McGill University

the borrower to possess a long-term job – a basic security which many people no longer have. Rising costs for land and urban infrastructure justify the building of houses on smaller plots of land in denser communities, while financial insecurity on the part of the homeowners validates a need to purchase an affordable and compact housing unit and consider other paradigms on offer for housing design and marketing.

For many first time buyers, affordability is a major – if not the only – impediment to home-ownership, since the relative cost of housing has doubled in recent decades[2]. In a situation where housing prices rise much more steeply than household earnings, purchasing a compact amount of space at a relatively low cost is a means of coping with the housing affordability crisis[3].

---

2   P. Filion and T.E. Bunting, *Affordability of Housing in Canada* (Ottawa: Supply and Services Canada, 1990).

3   The 'affordability gap' – a much-used phrase with regard to contemporary housing – refers to a situation where the rate of increase of shelter costs far outstrips the rate of increase of income: in the U.S. during the 1980s, the median price of a new home rose by over 23% while median income went up by only 8%; gross rents increased by 14% while renters' income rose by only 5%.

Under strained conditions – both global and personal – potential homeowners are finding that committing a smaller portion of their earnings to housing is a distinctly desirable, if not unavoidable, option. Therefore, buying unpartitioned and unfinished space, with the intention to upgrade and expand at a later date when finances permit, is another affordability strategy that was used in the past and is currently considered by wary homeowners. A parallel, increasingly popular trend has been the opening of home renovation 'supermarkets' where homeowners are able to select from a wide range of tools and products that are easy to use and install. It enables them to renovate and expand their homes: a trend that directly complements the idea of user involvement in their unit design.

The new economic landscape has similarly led to dramatic demographic responses. Significantly, while the number of families and households in Canada (and similarly in the US) is increasing, the size of these domestic arrangements is decreasing. This trend towards greater numbers of households is relevant not only to the family dynamic but to an additional noteworthy phenomenon: fewer people are living within families[4] [5]. The effect of these demographics is found in the need for homes that are designed flexibly to reflect the changing nature of a diverse range of occupant groups. At the same time, baby boomers are continuing to have the largest impact on the age structure of the population. Inevitably, fewer numbers of young people will be 'supporting' a greater number of older people, a prospect which creates incentives for the elderly to take active measures to safeguard against a precarious future of insufficient or non-existent government pensions, and shortages of suitable institutional care housing.

Furthermore, another household type which has gained in numbers over the years is the household composed of only one person. In previous years young, single people were not considered potential homebuyers. Nowadays, there are not only many young male and female singles who purchase homes on their own before marriage, but many who buy homes without the specific intention of marrying in the near future[6] [7]. Homebuilders who neglect to market their products to single people are sacrificing a considerable portion of first-time buyers, as are architects and planners who fail to design housing units and communities with single owners in mind. Flexible design strategies, whereby both traditional and non-traditional households may reside in the very same structure need, therefore, to be considered.

---

4   Statistics Canada, *Annual Demographic Statistics, 2001* (Ottawa: Statistics Canada. Catalogue no. 91-213, 1990).

5   In the U.S., married couples with children make up less than one quarter of all households, a significant drop from almost half in 1960 (American Demographics: www. demographics.com).

6   A. Friedman, *The Grow Home* (Montreal: McGill-Queen's University Press, 2001) .

7   A. Friedman and D. Krawitz, *Peeking Through the Keyhole* (Montreal: McGill-Queen's University Press, 2002).

These socio-economic and demographic phenomena were the catalysts for the author's quest for a new housing paradigm, one that will foster a better fit between homebuyers and their chosen accommodation. The thrust of the approach was to regard the buying procedure as a process of selection from a menu. The author recognized that this choice and flexibility must be reflected in all aspects of housing design and marketing. It has to be factored into the composition of varied households within a single structure, the component choices available, and the minimal inconvenience with respect to future modifications to facilitate changes in the occupant's space needs.

This approach stands in stark contrast to current marketing practices of homes whereby only a small number of options, primarily in interior layouts and finishes, are offered to buyers. Having a variety of prototypes – either single- or multi-family dwellings – within the same development, enabling buyers to purchase the amount of space that they need and can afford, and permitting them to actively take part in the interior design of their home (e.g. choose kitchen types, locate partitions) is not common in today's housing market. The Next Home intended to demonstrate that a flexible approach to the design, construction, and marketing of dwellings can contribute to lowering the financial burden that buyers assume at the outset, thus making housing more affordable.

The Next Home – Flexibility and Cost Reduction

One of the fundamental distinguishing features of the Next Home was the option extended to prospective buyers of purchasing the type and 'quantity' of house they presently need and can afford. The feasibility of this option was attained by designing a three-story structure which can be built, sold, and inhabited as a single-family house, as a duplex, or as a triplex, and at a construction cost of $26 per square foot ($380 CAN per square meter). The interior of the units can also be configured according to the wishes of the occupants. Some, as noted in figure 2, may choose to have a home office as part of their unit.

The dimensions of the Next Home have been chosen by adhering to modular sizes and by balancing the advantages and critical limitations of various unit widths. In order to reduce waste of materials, the framing dimensions were subsequently adjusted to a 2 foot (610mm) module to enable sub-floor material which has been cut to be used elsewhere in the frame. A 20 foot (6.1 meter) width produces spaces of comfortable dimensions and compatibility with municipal regulations while liberating the interior of loadbearing partitions. With diligent planning and material selection the same principle was implemented to accommodate interior finishes such as drywall and floor tiles. Furthermore, cost savings were achieved not only through efficient use of materials but also through reduced labour requirements as a result of less on-site cutting and fitting[8]. The flexible choice of interior components combined with the efficient design reduce

---

8   Canada Mortgage and Housing Corporation (CMHC), *Canada's Exportable Housing* (Ottawa: CMHC, 1995).

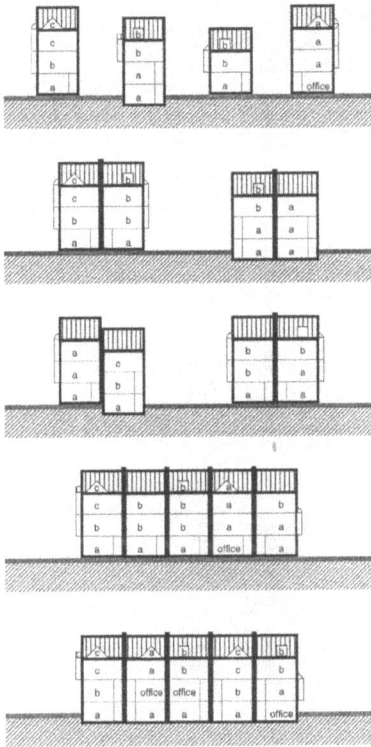

Figure 2. Subdivision and volume options (letters indicate households).

the cost of each 750 square feet (75 square meters) floor to an average of $37,000 ($50,000 CAN) (including serviced land at a cost of $7.50 per square foot ($108 CAN per square meter)) in Montreal.

The Next Home was designed to be subdivided and rearranged in both the pre- and post-occupancy stages in order to accommodate change from one housing type to another with minimal inconvenience and cost. In order to facilitate future transformation of the dwelling units and to maximize the impression of open space, the stairs were placed along the side longitudinal wall in the middle of the unit and adjacent to the front entrance. By positioning the stairs lengthwise against the side wall the available floor space was more efficiently increased (Figure 3).

Another characteristic of the dynamic and flexible design was the confining of the mechanical systems to a vertical shaft and horizontal chaser. The vertical shaft enclosed the water supply, drainage, venting (including heat recovery ventilator – HRV), as well as electrical, telephone, and cable. The horizontal chaser was installed to run the length of each floor and facilitated future relocation of rooms. Such an arrangement of chasers permits access to the building systems through the floor – not the ceiling

The owner of the ground-floor unit is a widower, age 57, who has worked as a civil servant for many years and has been offered an early retirement package due to budget cuts.

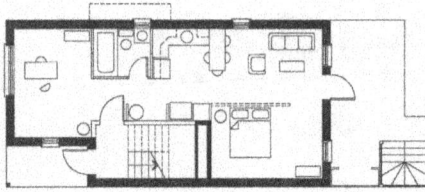

Figure 7. Ground-floor layout plan

The owners of the second-floor unit are a young couple without children who have been married for three years and who, until the purchase of their Next Home unit, rented a one-bedroom apartment in a suburb not far from the city centre.

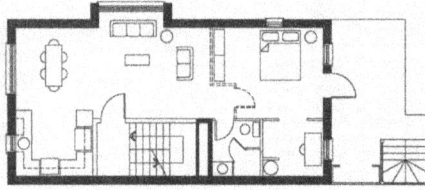

Figure 8. Second-floor layout plan

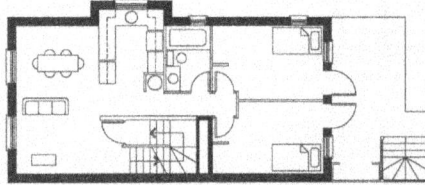

Figure 9. Third-floor layout plan

The owner of the unit on the third floor and the mezzanine at the top of the house is a single mother, age 41, with two school-age children.

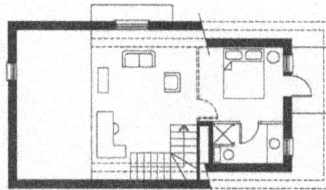

Figure 10. Fourth-floor (mezzanine) layout plan

or the walls – thus facilitating all changes without disrupting the neighbouring units. Consequently, regardless of the initial configuration of a Next Home design, the household and its evolving nature are accommodated with minimal renovation work and expense.

Components à La Carte

In the interest of responding to today's diverse demographic, lifestyles and the economic capabilities of buyers, the Next Home included a menu of pre-occupancy choices. Prospective occupants choose from a catalogue of interior components

Interior Partitions	($)	Kitchen Layouts	($)	Bathroom Layouts	($)

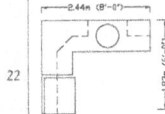

305mm (2') in length: 22

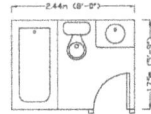

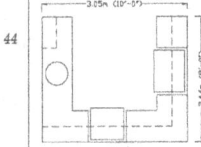

610mm (4') in length: 44

Cabinets in
Oak: 1736
Melamine: 1162

1410

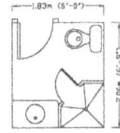

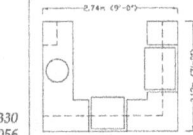

610mm (4') in length with door: 100

Cabinets in
Oak: 2976
Melamine: 1992

985

Floor Finishes

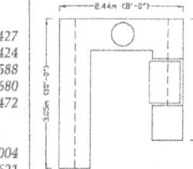

Cabinets in
Oak: 2852
Melamine: 1909

1084

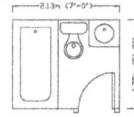

Ground Floor

Carpet:	1330
Hardwood:	5056
Laminated wood:	3344
Linoleum:	3430
Tile (in bathroom):	472

Second Floor

Carpet:	1427
Hardwood:	5424
Laminated wood:	3588
Linoleum:	3680
Tile (in bathroom):	472

Cabinets in
Oak: 3224
Melamine: 2158

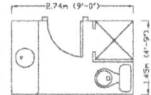

Third Floor and mezzanine

Carpet:	2004
Hardwood:	7621
Laminated wood:	5041
Linoleum:	5170
Tile (in bathrooms):	854

1785

Figure 4. Menu of interior elements and their costs in 1996 Cdn.$.

designed by an architect, determined and made available by the builder (Figure 4). User choice enables occupants to 'consume' only the type and quantity of features they currently require or can afford. These options also include a range of components to assist physically-challenged occupants to live independently.

Despite the large number of potential lifestyles that the Next Home aims to accommodate, current trends indicate that the average time spent by an adult on productive activities is 7.8 hours per day, compared with 5.7 hours spent on free time[9]. Such reduced leisure time is acknowledged and applied directly to the variety of configurations of Next Home units. For example, the pre-occupancy flexibility and the capacity for post-occupancy modification of the Next Home have inspired the design of a variety of kitchen layouts to suit a wide range of household configurations. These kitchen arrangements cater to desires for increased work surfaces, space economy, and the inclusion of washer, dryer, and recycling facilities within this area[10]. Moreover, due to the prefabricated nature of kitchen cabinetry, builders can offer a wide selection of layouts without significantly increasing the administrative costs that are incurred by allowing these choices.

Similarly, bathroom choices also vary according to the occupants and their individual needs. Living in a small home does not mean being restricted to a single bathroom: if the number of occupants and their schedules justify a second bathroom, one can be included. Consequently, the bathroom options offered by the Next Home builders will range in size from powder rooms to complete bathrooms with shower, bath, toilet and sink.

An analysis of the layouts of the three units of the Next Home demonstration house, which was displayed on the McGill University campus, illustrates the manner in which various pre-occupancy selections of interior components formed three highly personalized, versatile living spaces. Household scenarios have been created for the three units in order to account for choices made at the pre-occupancy design stage of each unit, and to illustrate the potential inherent to such flexibility.

Flexibility of Building Exterior

Façades of housing developments where identical units are built are often repeated for reasons of economy. Using the same size of window openings and the same style of windows gets a builder a volume discount from his framing team and manufacturer. The effect of such a streetscape, primarily one with rowhousing, is frequently unpleasant and sterile. In conversation with builders, the author has found that when a carpenter is alerted in advance (i.e. prior to the construction of the frame), he generally does not mind alterations in façade openings, as long as the variations are not radically different from one another. With regard to the opening sizes and to the windows themselves, small numbers can be selected and alternated within the composition.

The principles underlying the design of the Next Home façades are the same as those governing the design of the structure and plan: flexibility, individual identity, and affordability. The three basic formal strategies for the location and treatment of windows (the essential component in the articulation of residential façades) are:

---

9   C. Lindsay, M.S. Devereaux, and M. Bergob, *Youth in Canada, Second Edition: Target Groups Project.* Ottawa: Statistics Canada. Catalogue no. 89-511E, 1994.

10 A. Friedman, V. Cammalleri, J. Nicell, F. Dufaux, and J. Green, *Sustainable Residential Developments: Planning, Design and Construction Principles ('Greening' the Grow Home)* (Montreal: McGill School of Architecture Affordable Homes Program, 1993)

systematic repetition, random order, and composition. The strategy of systematic repetition accommodates the concept of flexibility by allowing the application of a universal standard of window placement which could accommodate any function, but such a strategy eliminates the potential for personal expression and must therefore be considered unsuitable. The second option, of random placement of windows based on user preferences and plan consideration, accommodates a high degree of individual identity, but runs the risk of undermining the reading of a single module as a unified whole. The result of absolute random placement of windows would be visual chaos. Some vertical emphasis is required to carry the eye upward and indicate the importance of a single unit over the row. The second strategy has therefore been applied to the Next Home façade in combination with the third strategy – that of composition – to obtain a balance between flexibility and unit identity. While compositional concerns impose some measure of constraint on the sizing and placement of windows, they impart a sense of stability and recognizability to the façade. The element of personalization in the placement and the specific sizing of windows reduces flexibility in the long term, in the sense that interior modifications could also lead to changes in the façade. While this aspect may be considered as an obstacle to flexibility, the appropriate choice of façade materials (such as stucco) makes such façade changes relatively easy.

Application of the Next Home Concept

The Next Home concept was implemented in the design and construction of several communities in the greater Montreal area. The builders' main objective, although different in each site, was to take advantage of the flexibility that the design offers both in the unit and the urban levels. Attracting a variety of households with a range of socio-economic backgrounds was meant to expand the builders' profit opportunities. In collaboration with the author the builders adopted the principles of the demonstration unit to their site as per their specific marketing needs. Affordability through flexibility remained a key factor in all the built projects. The units were sold at an average cost of $48,000 ($65,000 CAN) per 800 sq. ft. of floor area, a price equivalent to 50 percent of the median price in the Montreal area. The sites were all infill and the projects benefited from existing infrastructure and access to civic amenities. Descriptions of three of the projects' main features follow.

Le Faubourg du Cerf

Le Faubourg du Cerf is a 130-unit project in Longueuil, a suburban town near Montreal. In 1998, the builder, Cleary Construction, sold each floor for $44,000 ($59,900 CAN) in a relatively affluent area of town. The structures faced a communal green space and were built without a basement. The outdoor parking was designed for a ratio of one parking space per unit.

Units of two dimensions were designed in the three-story structure and mezzanine: 20 feet by 37 feet (6.15 meters by 11.6 meters) and 25 feet by 43 feet (7.7 meters by 13.2 meters) (figure 5). It led to the creation of a floor plate with an average footprint

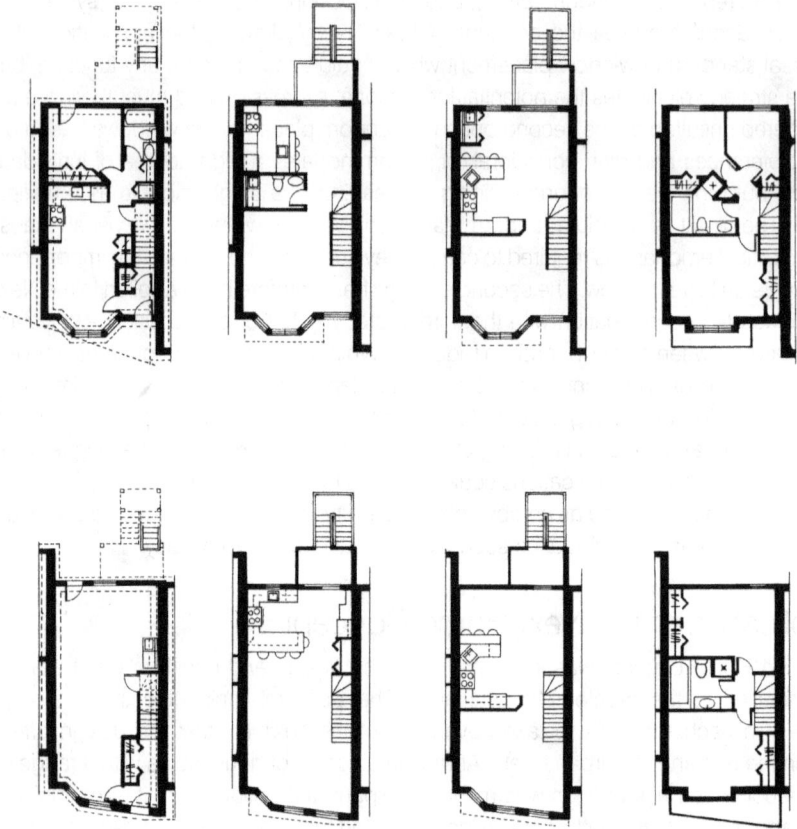

Figure 5. Plan options in the Le Faubourg Saint-Michel project

of 800 square feet (80 square meters). The developer offered the option to purchase one, two, or all three floors as was proposed in the original concept. He subsequently commented in a conversation with the author that buyers like the flexibility offered to them, which became a significant draw for clients with smaller means. This was demonstrated by the large number of single-storey units sold compared to two- or three-storey units, which enabled many young households to become homeowners.

As part of the marketing process, the developer constructed a temporary sales office near the site. In it there was a display of drawn floor plans and scale models of possible interior layout options. In addition to pre-conceived designs, the developer permitted buyers who were interested to participate in the design of their chosen floor. His firm's technicians assisted these clients for a modest administrative fee. The offered unit and those designed by the occupants demonstrate a wide variation of interior arrangements. Some of the units have one bedroom and others two. There is also a variety in the interior components (e.g. kitchens, bathrooms) chosen by the occupants and the placement of these components on the floor. The choices made and their location was an outcome of the household's demographic composition, lifestyle, and affordability level.

Conclusion

The evolutionary nature of the Next Home – the notion that housing be designed to evolve in layout and use – requires a thoughtfully developed urban design code which balances individual expression with the overall continuity of the street or neighbourhood. Another essential design element is the realization that lifestyle – as one of the defining characteristics of peoples' lives as citizens, consumers, and householders – is a feature that shifts in accordance with a dynamic lifecycle process. A home that can be altered, with a minimum of effort and expense at a time of change in the lives of its owners, is a home that evolves with the lifecycles of its household, rather than becoming an impediment.

The assessment of the application of the Next Home principles in building sites demonstrated that they responded to the two underlying objectives: affordability and flexibility. Although the builders had to invest more time in the marketing process, buyers were willing to pay the small administrative cost in return for having their choices built. It is no doubt a change to current approaches to home building and marketing. The flexible, affordable, and sustainable design principles of the Next Home respond sensitively to the urgent need to accommodate a wide diversity of contemporary users and household types and to extend affordable housing to a wider portion of the population.

Bibliography

Canada Mortgage and Housing Corporation (CMHC). *Canada's Exportable Housing*. Ottawa: CMHC, 1995.

Filion, P., T.E Bunting. *Affordability of Housing in Canada*. Ottawa: Supply and Services Canada, 1990.

Friedman, A. *The Grow Home*, Montreal: McGill-Queen's University Press, 2001.

Friedman, A., V. Cammalleri, J. Nicell, F. Dufaux, and J. Green. *Sustainable Residential Developments: Planning, Design and Construction Principles ('Greening' the Grow Home)*. Montreal: McGill School of Architecture Affordable Homes Program, 1993.

Friedman, A. and D. Krawitz. *Peeking Through the Keyhole*. Montreal: McGill-Queen's University Press, 2002.

Lindsay, C., M.S. Devereaux and M. Bergob. *Youth in Canada, Second Edition: Target Groups Project*. Ottawa: Statistics Canada, 1994. Catalogue no. 89-511E.

Rybczynski, W., et al. *The Grow Home*. Montreal: McGill School of Architecture Affordable Homes Program, 1990.

Statistics Canada. *Annual Demographic Statistics, 2001*. Ottawa: Statistics Canada, 2001. Catalogue no. 91-213.

KATHRIN GOLDA-PONGRATZ

FROM HOUSING AS A VERB TO HOUSING AS A PRODUCT. CONTEMPORARY TENDENCIES IN HISPANO-AMERICAN METROPOLITAN REGIONS – A FOCUS ON LIMA AND MADRID

Introduction: Paradigm Changes in a Postcolonial Constellation

Discussions on cultural identities, migrations, segregation, and the concepts of place and belonging mark our contemporary thinking and the experience of living together in urban settings. Voices like the German philosopher and sociologist Jürgen Habermas suggest we might be gradually led by cosmopolitan solidarity to a new form of integration beyond the concept of nation-states[1]. However, in the Hispanic and Latin American context – and not only there – the experience of colonization has produced a seemingly persistent dependency and interrelation with the 'colonisers' at a social and cultural level. This, it is arguable, persists today in the contemporary context of globalization that increasingly bypasses the nation state. What this chapter considers, is how this reconfigures the urban along similarly 'global' lines in the shaping of living environments in the capital city regions of Lima and Madrid respectively.[2]

---

1   Jürgen Habermas, *Die postnationale Konstellation. Politische Essays* (Frankfurt am Main: Suhrkamp, 1998), 90.

2   See: Neil Smith, 'Revanchist City, Revanchist Planet', in *Urban Politics Now. Re-Imagining Democracy in the Neoliberal City*, ed. BAVO (Rotterdam: Nai Publishers, 2007), 39.

Colonization – from Latin *colere*; to 'inhabit, cultivate, frequent, practice, attend, save, respect' –describes the process through which one or more groups inhabit a new territory; in the urban vocabulary it also stands for territorial expansion. By imposing a catalogue of norms on the newly discovered territories where cities had to be founded for example, the Spanish King Philip II envisioned the colonies as an ideal physical world. These would be models for social living in which the relationship between the ideal city and the 'ideal' behaviour of its inhabitants would be perfect.[3] The impact of this vision was such that the Spanish colonial grid has become *the model* for the urban in Latin America not only in those cities built by the Spanish, but also in the self-built peripheries – a phenomenon that suggests that even the very *notion* of space was colonized.

In a reflexive way the Latin American experience, which served Spain as a kind of a laboratory[4], was reimported back to Spain during the 19th century: the Catalan engineer Ildefons Cerdà developed his influential expansion plan for Barcelona – and his economic and social ideas – from a careful observation of Latin American examples. He had not only studied the expansive structures of the colonial cities – especially the city of Buenos Aires, which served as a model to define the size of the street blocks – but also their post-colonial dynamics, and the consolidation of democracy that Ibero-American cities experienced after their independence from Spain. The creation of a new city with housing options for all social strata and maximum flexibility in use and architectural design are consequently two basic principles of the Barcelona grid system.

Despite this, it is less the ideals followed by Cerdà, but rather the definition of colonization as a tool for territorial expansion, that has had most impact – contributing to suburban expansion all over the planet. Suburbanisation fulfils the colonizing dream and has become the most prevalent matrix today for urban development. In this sense, the production of housing – beyond its role as a primary response to the human right of dwelling and provision of human shelter and welfare – has gradually shifted towards being a synonym for the capitalization of land, profitability and speculation in metropolitan regions worldwide. At the turn of the 21st century, major Spanish urban agglomerations have shifted from 'necessity-driven housing' production and towards speculation-driven developments disconnected from real needs and human-oriented urban planning. As a consequence of the global financial crisis many of these recently built housing complexes, in which the home is seen as a consumable product, have become both under-utilized and even financially inaccessible, and have, as such, completely transformed the perception of housing production. This is very different to the context only half a century ago in the years after the Spanish Civil War, when

---

3   Lars Lerup, *Das Unfertige Bauen. Architektur und menschliches Handeln.* (Braunschweig: Vieweg, 1986), 48.

4   A most insightful publication that explores this notion of Latin America as a laboratory is: Roberto Fernández, *El laboratorio americano. Arquitectura, Geocultura y Regionalismo* (Madrid: Biblioteca Nueva, 1998).

informal production of housing on the one hand, and the state-driven provision of mass housing in growing metropolises like Barcelona or Madrid, on the other, responded to a massive real demand.

At the time cities like Madrid and Barcelona were developing their social housing programmes, the British architect John F. C. Turner described informal housing production and strategies of self-organization in Peru, in a similarly demand-respond context. His article 'Housing as a verb'[5] would become a major reference point in the field and saw housing as a constructive process, as an alternative to mass housing and as an activity that corresponds to the real needs of its inhabitants at every step of their personal stories. Today however, Latin American cities reinvent new mechanisms and policies of mass housing production which, whilst responding to an existing demand, neglect any of the participatory achievements of the past half-century as celebrated by Turner. As a result, they are gradually moving along the path towards adopting the speculative tendencies of the West in a post-colonial context.

Challenge of the Informal: the Emergence of the Barriadas of Lima as *Housing by People*

We are currently confronted with a crucial contradiction. As a product of the modern principles of rationalization, formalization, industrialization, specialization, and professionalization, the world's large urban agglomerations have incubated their opposite – the rise of spontaneous and informal structures. This has in fact, always been the case and as a result, we find constant conflicts in which the ephemeral, spontaneous and transitory have been turned into permanent settlements. Clearly, in these contexts, planning is failing and non-existent in standard forms. On this scenario we might ask: *'How do we explain the paradox that urbanism, as a profession, has disappeared at the moment when urbanization is everywhere and is on its way to establishing a definitive, global 'triumph' of the urban scale?'*[6]

Continuing on from this, it is possible to suggest that the urban scale has actually become the global scale – a phenomenon that started with colonial expansion and came to a climax in 2007 when, for the first time, more than half of the world's population lived in cities or urban agglomerations.

The urban agglomerations of Lima, Peru, are just one example of such territories. Here, as elsewhere, the migration of rural populations has been the primary factor – and has been since the mid-20th century. Between 1940 and 2000 the population of Lima increased from 645,000 to 7.5 million and its urbanized territory enlarged by nearly 16 times. Today, 8.2 million – out of Peru's population of 29 million – live in greater Lima,

---

5   Chapter 7 in: John F. C. Turner and Robert Fichter, *Freedom to build. Dweller control of the housing process* (New York: Macmillan, 1972).

6   Rem Koolhaas, 'Whatever happened to urbanism?', in *SMLXL*, ed. Rem Koolhaas and Bruce Mau (New York: Monacelli Press, 1995), 961.

Figure 1. Extensive horizontal urban growth north of Lima/ Peru. Photo: Kathrin Golda-Pongratz, 2010.

with 40 percent of them living in the more or less consolidated informal settlements.[7] These figures reveal a development that has surpassed the logics of modernity – they help visualize unforeseen consequences that are, and will continue to challenge our previous systemisation and enactment of urbanism.

Since 1961 the so-called 'Barriada Law' in Peru has acknowledged the unplanned occupation of public and private land in urban fringe areas.[8] It has provided legality, infrastructure, and technical assistance to the self-construction process, which different governments have recognized as a cheap and easy solution to the housing problem.[9] When in August 1963, John F. C. Turner guest-edited an *Architectural Design* issue on 'Dwelling Resources in South America' he focused on the *barriadas* of Lima and on the *Pampa de Comas* settlement, which is the origin of the so-called *Cono Norte*. At that time *Pampa de Comas* was entirely self-built by spontaneously formed associations of low-income blue- and white-collar workers and their families. It had 30,000 inhabitants.

---

7   Numbers according to the INEI (National Institute of Statistics and Informatics), 'Distribución de la población total por regiones naturales', accessed June 15, 2012, http://www.inei.gob.pe.

8   Julio Calderón Cockburn, Julio, 'Official registration (formalization) of property in Peru (1996-2000)', (paper presented at the ESF/N-AERUS International workshop, Leuven and Brussels/Belgium, May 2001).

9   Detailed information in: Eberhard Kroß, *Die Barriadas von Lima. Stadtentwicklungsprozesse in einer lateinamerikanischen Metropole* (Paderborn: Schöningh Verlag, 1992).

The initial occupation of the land was carried out by a group of families evicted from an inner-city slum, demolished for the construction of an office block.[10] Turner observed how this act of simple survival was followed by the emergence of 'values' such as progress, hard work, savings, and communal living. In his book 'Freedom to Build' he concludes that '...if housing is treated as a verbal entity, as a means to human ends, as an activity rather than as a manufactured and packaged product, decision-making power must, of necessity, remain in the hands of the users themselves.'[11]

In 1971, the Peruvian government engaged in its first massive formal construction processes. In the south of Lima, *Villa El Salvador* which housed 50,000 inhabitants, was officially planned by the military government. It was seen at the time as an exemplar project for poverty eradication, modernization, and social reform. Functionaries of the *SINAMOS*[12] provided water, healthcare, and transport connections to Lima. Since then, the continuation of this urban prototype has been, more or less, directed and instigated by the state. In 1979, the *Barriadas* were classed as *Urbanizaciones Populares*, and areas with irregular plots were recognized as ordinary districts with municipal rights and responsibilities. The neoliberal dictatorial government of Alberto Fujimori (1990–2000) promoted further suburban growth and classed the self-built settlements as *Pueblos Jóvenes* (young towns). Propaganda boards promoting self-construction all over the city evoked the dream of 'having one's own house' in these new suburbs. As a populist instrument of power centralization, the Commission for the Official Registration of Informal Property (*COFOPRI*) took over the municipalities' task of distributing land titles to facilitate the resettlement of residents in these settlements and more distant desertlands. It was presented as a demonstration of social engagement and was intended to gain the votes of the poor.[13]

In today's young towns second and third generations of immigrants have formed their own families but as their own *barrios* and parents' houses become too small for their growing familes and aspirations, they are gradually occupying and urbanising vacant plots within the existing settlements. This challenges the quality of public space they offer and vertical densification has become a trend – a solution that may alleviate the negative effects of occupying communal spaces.

---

10   John F.C Turner, 'Lima barriadas today.' in: *Architectural Design*, vol. 33, n° 8, ed. Monica Pidgeon (London: The Standard Catalogue, 1963), 375.

11   John F. C. Turner and Robert Fichter, *Freedom to build. Dweller control of the housing process* (New York: Macmillan, 1972), 154.

12   SINAMOS: *Sistema Nacional de Apoyo a la Movilización Social*, state organ to mobilize the population during the military government of General Juan Velasco Alvarado (1968-75).

13   Kathrin Golda-Pongratz, 'From self-built periphery to metropolitan business district. Spatial transformations, emerging urban identities and the concept of citizenship in the Cono Norte, Lima/ Peru' in *Local Identities – Global Challenges*, ed. Jorge Vanegas and Sabouni Ikhlas. (ACSA Press: Washington DC, 2012), 418-419.

Image 2. Gradual vertical densification of the consolidated self-built neighbourhoods in Lima. Photo: Kathrin Golda-Pongratz, 2013.

When the Ephemeral Becomes Permanent

The sensation one gets looking at contemporary Lima is the one of a never-ending city along the coastline, a band of low-scale settlements that densifies into nodes, stretches out into the dry hills and dunes along the Pacific and eventually fades out into the desert. If one follows the predictions of local planners and carefully observes the ongoing metropolitan expansion along the Pan-American Highway towards the North and the South, it is to be expected that *Lima Metropolitana* will constitute a continuous urban agglomeration of nearly 400 kilometres in length within the next few decades.[14]

The unplanned expansion of the city through ephemeral architecture on the periphery – thought initially to be a problem to be dealt with – has turned out to be the solution to the housing problem itself. Planners have been incapable of reacting to these developments which have become ever more consolidated.

The process of consolidating these settlements depends on political interests intersecting with the capacity of self-organization and solidarity amongst the dwellers. A close relation exists between the official registration of property and the standards of living evident in it and thus, property titles seem to encourage residents to improve their homes – probably because it symbolizes personal fulfilment and the feeling of social acceptance. The process of consolidation often goes through several phases: from cane or cheap wood shelters, to houses of *noble* material like brick or concrete. A whole industry of basic building materials, like wooden piles and rush-mats, has developed on the edges of the Pan-American Highway. Building materials and architectural styles are a clear manifestation of social status, and the upgrading dweller

---

14   Kathrin Golda-Pongratz, 'From self-built periphery', 417.

Image 3. The emergence of *Mega Plaza Norte* and other commercial centres has completely changed the face and the spatial logics of the area. Photo: Kathrin Golda-Pongratz, 2010.

imitates the wealthy neighbourhood's buildings, as well as some kinds of international architecture seen on television. This architecture is ambivalent, modern and traditional. It is ephemeral, as the houses are never finished; forms and materials change, and the use of rooms is often unspecified; the garage can turn into a shop, and the hall into a workshop.[15]

The *Cono Norte* of Lima, as a conglomerate of informally developed districts and self-built neighbourhoods, has become the most successful and surprising territory of the *Gran Area Metropolitana*. There, self-built settlements have been getting transformed into a fast-growing commercial district since the end of the 1990s and its previous peripheral status has become a form of centrality. This seems to prove the thesis formulated by Turner and William Mangin in the 1970s, according to which the hard-working and progress-oriented immigrant decisively determines the urban economy of future generations. The squatter settlement proves to be 'architecture that works,'[16] and as such, a real solution to the demand for housing.

What we are observing is the spatial consolidation of the ephemeral as it surrounds, overtakes and conquers the traditional city, creating a new model for a pluricentric metropolitan area. It can be argued that group and self-identification, and the definition of these new self-generated living environments, are based the Andean tradition of a shared economy that enables the creation of urban self-employment. In fact, a mixture of rural customs and global influences have created this new urban culture.

---

15   Kathrin Golda-Pongratz, 'From self-built periphery', 420.
16   John F.C. Turner, 'The squatter settlement: Architecture that works' in *Architecture of Democracy*. AD 8 1968, ed. Monica Pigeon (London: The Standard Catalogue 1968), 355-360.

In this context the marginal city has generated an industrial and artisanal economy of small and medium-sized businesses which have emerged out of improvisation and the needs of the population. Indeed, such is the success of the area that it one of the most economically active parts of the country. After the first economic phase of consolidation in which nightlife establishments, discotheques, gambling places, and amusement arcades emerged – such the *Boulevard El Retablo* in the late 1990s – big shopping malls such as the commercial mall *Mega Plaza Norte* have followed. After eight years of existence, *Mega Plaza Norte* claims to be the most successful shopping centre in Lima Metropolitana and another major commercial mall, *Plaza Lima Norte*, has just been opened and occupies a plot of 138,000 m². As such, it is the largest mall in the country.[17]

Another Extreme: Housing as a (Useless) Product

In contrast to the example of Lima, the case of Spain, and particular Madrid here, should be looked at as a case to learn from, rather than a model to export. The expansionist urban policies and planning practices of the last two decades, together with the creation of a real estate bubble and its recent collapse have both engendered a dramatic change in Spain's built landscape. A report by the Spanish Ministry of Housing reveals that never in the history of Spain has more land been urbanized and housing built on it than in the decade between 1997 and 2007.[18] A massive overproduction of multi-family housing for the middle classes evoked and incited the mass dream of ownership. Juan Herrera has summed up the phenomenon and its enormous consequences thus: '*Unfortunately we have, among other things, missed out on the potentials and possibilities of housing production. On the peripheries, we have built hundreds of new housing units in one go, to the extent that urbanized and built land in Spain has doubled within the last thirty years*'[19]

As a consequence of the global financial crisis territories in which the global flow of money during the period 1997–2007 enhanced the local urban development and real estate speculation are now at a standstill. In response to this economic bottleneck *ephemeral* architectures of a very different kind appeared in a very paradoxical sense: vast planned city layouts and housing structures that have not even been inhabited for a single day.[20] Areas that urbanized at an astonishing pace in the first decade of the 21st century have been left unfinished and now constitute urban fringes. This not only

17 Kathrin Golda-Pongratz, 'From self-built periphery', 421-422.
18 Ministerio de Vivienda, ed., *Informe sobre la situación del sector de la vivienda en España* (Madrid: 2010), 8.
19 Juan Herreros, 'De la periferia al centro. La ciudad en tiempos de crisis.' in: *La ciudad, de nuevo global*, ed. Luciano Alfaya y Patricia Muñiz (Santiago de Compostela: Colegio Oficial de Arquitectos de Galicia, 2009), 253.
20 Kathrin Golda-Pongratz, 'You can imagine the opposite. Terminological reflections on ephemeral architecture' in: *Moinopolis. Ephemerality and Architecture*, ed. Moinopolis Laboratory of Thoughts on Spatial Matters (Mannheim, 2013), 37.

Figures 4 and 5. Unfinished housing structures and urbanized open spaces in Valdecarros, a speculative urban development south of Madrid/ Spain. Photos: Kathrin Golda-Pongratz, 2012.

applies in and on the outskirts of established cities but also in holiday resort locations along the Spanish coast. These unfinished projects are sparsely populated ghost towns of orphaned housing structures and half-finished infrastructures.

Until a few years ago the logic of dispersion, spatial segregation and the need for new construction that they generated were seen as key to economic growth and job creation in Spain. This, together with increasing migration pressures and ever more real estate speculation on the part of local and international investors, constructors, and banks, together with corruption in certain city councils, converted the country into a sprawling, suburbanized territory. Under social pressure to buy, large sectors of the population incurred debt to finance their first, and in some cases second, home. Throughout the boom period real estate developers promised modern, comfortable, and harmonious lives in new housing developments, in close contact with nature, conveniently connected to the metropolis. Everyone wanted what was (and still is) considered a status symbol – owning one's own home was seen as a sign of integration and success for immigrants and a guaranteed investment for small speculators or people who wanted some financial security for the future. The large colourful billboards and adverts that promoted this all over the country however, did not mention water supply problems, the massive loss of rural territory involved on city peripheries and the coastline, the severe ecological disequilibrium or other long-term side effects.[21]

The Spanish capital Madrid has a series of these uninhabited new towns, colloquially known as *barrios fantasma*. They are tangible 'urban monuments' to the rampant

---

21 Kathrin Golda-Pongratz, 'Formen der Mixicidad und Segregation in Spanien' in: *Soziale Mischung in der Stadt*, ed. Tilman Harlander and Gerd Kuhn (Stuttgart: Krämer, 2012), 221-222.

economic speculation of the recent times. These satellite towns of immense extensions (the largest one intended to provide new homes to 75,000 people) had been planned since the mid-1990s under the name of *Programas de Actuación Urbanística* – or Programs of Urbanistic Action (PAU's). The development of *Vallecas* foresaw the construction of 28,000 new flats; that of *Valdecarros*, a kind of mega-PAU to the southeast, projected 48,000 new flats, a new business district, and several amusement attractions. These, and even more peripheral new towns that were rather 'hostile' and not very 'urban' in their design, spread out into the landscape and have become a physical symbol of blind urban expansionism and its failure.

El boom del ladrillo (the construction boom), which seemed to guarantee welfare and realize the dreams of citizens and politicians alike for over a decade, has brought about a dramatic change in the social and physical landscape. With the outbreak of the financial crisis, the construction sector has ground to a halt, unemployment has risen dramatically, and people who can no longer pay their mortgages are losing their properties to the banks and still remain in debt.[22] Consequently, a whole sector of Spanish society – its middle class – is in danger of sinking into poverty, while no political solutions are given, and citizen unrest is on the rise.[23]

Conclusions

Towards new territorial imaginaries and identities

Contemporary politics of land management respond primarily to the logic of the global economy, and consequently convert any territory within a metropolitan agglomeration into an object of speculation. Urban peripheries, in the sense of fallow waste land surrounding the consolidated city, offer a perfect portrait of these contemporary social and globalized economic pressures. The appearance of gated communities is a similar manifestation of related issues. These develop as an economy grows and have been, since the turn of the century, an increasing phenomenon in emerging cities which, as discussed previously, shift from being the self-built periphery to a profitable terrain of speculation.

Our case study Lima is perfect proof of this – its newly created infrastructures and mega-projects such as an airport, its harbour enlargement and the massive construction of highways and by-passes are all related to urban and economic growth. They all, simultaneously, put at risk the fragile coastal landscape, its ecological equilibrium and

---

22   Kathrin Golda-Pongratz, *Landscapes of Pressure* (Barcelona, 2014), 6.

23   The PAH (*Plataforma de Afectados por la Hipoteca*, http://afectadosporlahipoteca.com) is a voluntary civic association which helps affected citizens facing eviction to find legal support and a new place to live. In several larger Spanish cities it has started occupying empty buildings to resettle evicted families. In June 2013, the PAH brought the Spanish case to the European Parliament and was distinguished with the European Citizen Prize 2013 for its anti-eviction commitment. In May 2015, its former speaker was elected as the new mayor of Barcelona.

its pre-hispanic heritage. The earmarking of a semi-rural district in the *Cono Sur* for the installation of leisure facilities and service industries to serve the luxurious spas and second residency urbanizations (that have developed more than 50 kilometres away Lima) is a clear sign that these remaining rural territories will be sites of dispute between the last *campesinos* and the real estate speculators of the next decade.[24]

Clearly, the traditional central city, classic spatial denominations and the various forms of suburbanization that have developed in the second half of the 20th century are failing to respond to social changes today. *Barriadas* or *pueblos jóvenes* are becoming consolidated and economically active sub-centres; old seaside resorts are densifying and grow vertically; and the remaining rural territories we do have are already earmarked as spatial capital and, as such, will be completely absorbed by the economic development of their macro-regions sooner or later. To imagine an urban future beyond the old concept of the metropolis opens up new perspectives on its diverse realities, its contemporary tendencies of land colonization, its promising hybridity, and its actual fragmentation. It makes us understand that an attitude of centralism is obsolete and will have to be replaced by a regional and pluricentric mode of operation. It makes us see the importance of instigating an interaction between different local actors, finding of mechanisms for a well-balanced connectivity, and developing infrastructural networks that strengthen and protect the diversity of cultural, spatial, economic, and social potential of all the regions in which we live.

The multiple paradoxes laid out here remind us of Marshall Berman. There are the self-contained paradoxes of self-built and ephemeral architectures consolidating into liveable and highly productive urban agglomerations. We also have the paradoxes of well-planned, formally structured, and preliminarily equipped settlements ending up as contemporary ruins and short-lived failures. There is of course also the paradox between both these phenomena as well. In the terms of Berman, this is the insecurity inherent in the contradictions with we we live daily.[25] In light of this, we could argue that it is necessary to rethink housing as a space-making activity, relate it more to social needs than to the logic of economics and reimagine ephemerality as a transitional quality.

Bibliography

Berman, Marshall. *All That Is Solid Melts Into Air.* New York: Penguin, 1982.
Calderón Cockburn, Julio. 'Official registration (formalization) of property in Peru (1996-2000).' Paper presented at the ESF/N-AERUS International workshop, Leuven and Brussels/Belgium, May 2001.
Fernández, Roberto. *El laboratorio americano. Arquitectura, Geocultura y Regionalismo.* Madrid: Biblioteca Nueva, 1998.
Golda-Pongratz, Kathrin. 'From self-built periphery to metropolitan business district. Spatial

---

24   Wiley Ludeña Urquizo, *Lima. Reestructuración económica y transformaciones urbanas. Periodo 1990 – 2005* (Lima: PUCP, 2010), 47.

25   See: Marshall Berman, *All That Is Solid Melts Into Air* (New York: Penguin, 1982).

transformations, emerging urban identities and the concept of citizenship in the Cono Norte, Lima/ Peru'. In *Local Identities – Global Challenges*, edited by Jorge Vanegas and Sabouni Ikhlas, 417-424. ACSA Press: Washington DC, 2012.

Golda-Pongratz, Kathrin. 'Formen der Mixicidad und Segregation in Spanien' in *Soziale Mischung in der Stadt*, edited by Tilman Harlander and Gerd Kuhn, 220-225. Stuttgart: Krämer, 2012.

Golda-Pongratz, Kathrin. 'You can imagine the opposite. Terminological reflections on ephemeral architecture' in: *Moinopolis. Ephemerality and Architecture*, edited by Moinopolis Laboratory of Thoughts on Spatial Matters, 30-39. Mannheim, 2013.

Golda-Pongratz, Kathrin. *Landscapes of Pressure*. Barcelona, 2014.

Habermas, Jürgen. *Die postnationale Konstellation. Politische Essays*. Frankfurt am Main: Suhrkamp, 1998.

Herreros, Juan. 'De la periferia al centro. La ciudad en tiempos de crisis.' In *La ciudad, de nuevo global*, edited by Luciano Alfaya y Patricia Muñiz, 251-265. Santiago de Compostela: Colegio Oficial de Arquitectos de Galicia, 2009.

INEI (National Institute of Statistics and Informatics). 'Distribución de la población total por regiones naturales.' Accessed June 15, 2012, http://www.inei.gob.pe.

Koolhaas, Rem. 'Whatever happened to urbanism?' In *SMLXL*, edited by Rem Koolhaas and Bruce Mau. New York: Monacelli Press, 1995.

Kroß, Eberhard. *Die Barriadas von Lima. Stadtentwicklungsprozesse in einer lateinamerikanischen Metropole*. Paderborn: Schöningh Verlag, 1992.

Lerup, Lars. *Das Unfertige Bauen. Architektur und menschliches Handeln*. Braunschweig: Vieweg, 1986.

Ludeña Urquizo, Wiley. *Lima. Reestructuración económica y transformaciones urbanas. Periodo 1990 – 2005*. Lima: PUCP, 2010.

Ministerio de Vivienda, ed. *Informe sobre la situación del sector de la vivienda en España*. Madrid, 2010.

Smith, Neil. 'Revanchist City, Revanchist Planet' in *Urban Politics Now. Re-Imagining Democracy in the Neoliberal City*, edited by BAVO, 30-42. Rotterdam: Nai Publishers, 2007.

Turner, John F.C. 'Dwelling resources in South America: Government-aided rural housing. Mass urban re-housing problems. Lima barriadas today. Barriada integration and development. Minimal government-aided settlements. Cooperative housing project. Evolution of a government housing agency. Aided housing in a new industrial city.' in: *Architectural Design*, vol. 33, n° 8, edited by Monica Pidgeon, 371-388. London: The Standard Catalogue, 1963.

Turner, John F.C. 'The squatter settlement: Architecture that works.' In *Architecture of Democracy*. AD 8 1968, edited by Monica Pigeon, 355-360. London: The Standard Catalogue, 1968.

Turner, John F. C. Turner, and Robert Fichter. *Freedom to build. Dweller control of the housing process*. New York: Macmillan, 1972.

SECTION THREE:
STUDENT DESIGN PROJECTS

The more theoretical engagements with housing, its social conditions, practical implications, inherent contradictions, seemingly intractable problems and economic models just described, all come from researchers engaged in academia. It is, as suggested earlier, from there that their particular strengths come. Free from the time and money strictures of practice the authors of these essays offer a broader contextual understanding of the problems faced by those seeking to improve the provision of affordable quality housing in diverse contexts. Despite their academic backgrounds however, many of these authors are also practitioners and, as a result, clearly address very real problems – even when their scholarly approach brings theory and social criticism into sharp focus. Perhaps more pertinently for what follows in this book however, many of these authors are also teachers.

In a number of the chapters in Section Two this teaching focus was actually the basis of the text. Some documented the work already done by students and the academics leading them in workshops, others discussed ongoing programmes of research that feed into design projects carried out by students, and some specifically laid the theoretical groundwork for the projects that follow in this section. From a pedagogical perspective some of the previous chapters and the subsequent projects are purely hypothetical – in that they seek to understand core issues and propose semi-utopic solutions that (knowingly) require a major restructuring of the economic systems at play in the design and constructions industries for them to come to fruition.

In some cases, this means questioning the profit motive, for others, it involves a level of financial support from the State, or similar sources, for the projects to be realised in the detail – or on the scale – imagined. For others, it is the pre-empting of social and cultural changes that seem to be on the horizon that make the projects in question utopic – or at least speculative. However, in all cases the projects developed and presented here are framed in a clear understanding of the socio-cultural context that shapes, for good and for bad, the built environment. It is to the credit of their teachers that such issues are at the fore of the thinking of these students.

Within this schemata the projects presented in this section address issues such as the reuse and renovation of existing properties to meet the needs of a changing society. They also address the possibilities of rethinking the arrangements, living patterns and urban fabrics of historic residential areas in need of rehabilitation for modern habitation. In some instances, they look at the need to ensure active and interconnected communities in areas currently suffering from sustained loss of families and inhabitants, or the continued decline of their housing stock. These, and numerous other issues of social, theoretical and cultural import, are threaded through these projects that come from various countries and are set in several others.

The importance of foregrounding the work of these students in a book like this should not be overlooked. Facilitating and encouraging the next generation of architects and urban designers to have a clear focus on, and developed knowledge of housing is essential. After at least two decades of 'starchitecture' (in reality a lot longer than that, depending on how one defines the term), it is important that the next wave of designers of the built environment direct their criticism and skills to the issue of housing. It is as a reaction to the lack of opportunities for these new designers that do wish to address this subject, that this book has, in the final analysis, been put together.

The works presented inevitably have their weaknesses – they are the products of young minds searching for alternative approaches to housing design in an overwhelmingly conventional set of social contexts. Breaking out of these contexts whilst still proposing solutions that can, without excessive exaggeration or hope be realised, seems to underpin each and every project represented in the following pages. Some are ingenious and radical, others offer a lighter touch and a more Fabien approach to how one could move the debate forward around housing and the conventions of its design.

As indicated previously, we do not pretend that these projects represent anything like a *comprehensive* sample of the work student architects and planners are doing on the issue of housing globally. They do however, represent a sample and, more importantly, represent an attempt to promote housing as an issue of central importance to this generation who will, in the very near future, be responsible for developing and implementing the house designs, residential planning solutions and urban design proposals that our societies will have to live with, and in, for the coming decades and more.

EUSEBIO ALONSO GARCÍA

Universidad de Valladolid

ESCUELA TÉCNICA SUPERIOR DE ARQUITECTURA DE VALLADOLID

The Technical Superior School of Architecture of Valladolid (ETSAV) is the section of the University of Valladolid (Spain) dedicated to architecture. It has undergraduate, graduate, doctorate and postgraduate courses and is split into the following departments: Department of Architectural Construction; Earth Engineering and the Mechanics of Continuous Media; Theory of Structures; The Department of Theory of the Architecture and Architectural Projects and the Department of Urban Planning and Architecture Representation. It was established in 1968 as the only public school of architecture of Castilla y León and was expanded in 1980 and 2010. It has approximately 1,300 students and 100 teachers engaged in practice and theory. The School offers complementary training of students in countries outside Spain with fifty-two agreements with European and American institutions. Concomitantly, the School opens its doors to foreign students.

Pedagogy is based on a complete humanist education with a proper balance between the technical and the artistic aspects. Special emphasis is placed on propaedeutic knowledge, project management skills, design and technical ability, and an understanding of construction and urban developments. The training offered provides additional opportunities for professional development in heritage and archaeology, interior design, scenography, museology, graphic design, landscaping, bioclimatic and energy studies, sustainability and construction management. The aim is the development of graduates competent in design and in directing projects – whether they be rehabilitation, new build, urban planning projects or any of the other types of projects associated with the overarching disciplines of the School.

Research in the School is conducted through the following centres and initiatives: The Wood Chair, Earth Group, University Institute of Planning, the Photogrammetry Laboratory, the Laboratory of Architectural Landscape, the Heritage and Cultural

Centre, and the Laboratory of Ventilation HS3. It also has several recognized groups of investigation (GIR) including: The Analysis and Representation of the Architectural Heritage; Architecture, Art and Science; Architecture and Cinema; Architecture and Energy; Development of Contemporary Architecture; The Laboratory for Research and Intervention on the Architectural Landscape, amongst others.

Within this broad research framework, the School approaches the issue of housing from the perspectives of different specialisms – each determined by the particular department addressing the issue. At least one semester per year is assigned to residential questions in each department. This means housing is dealt with in terms of analysis, representation, case studies, history, the relationship between housing and the city, theory and legislation. Projects deal with the issue in different contexts resulting in design proposals operating at different scales of intervention, that engage with historic fabrics, and which seek to understand the new contemporary ways of living. It also involves the study of the structural, construction, energetic and bioclimatic systems. The projects included here reflect this scenario and come from the workshop of international students and academics outlined in Chapter Seven for the renovation of peripheral areas in Valladolid, Spain.

Project A: STREET EVERYONE

Vicent Agustí Visedo, Sofía Cuadrillero Rueda, Ana Garrido García, Nicolás González Arboleya, Alba Zarza Arribas

This proposal is aimed at clarifying the relationship of the neighbourhood of La Rondilla with the city centre of Valladolid and at clarifying the spatial structure of both. Despite its proximity to the centre, La Rondilla has no relevant relationship with the city and is, in itself, a labyrinth for those who do not know the area well. In addition, road traffic hinders the enjoyment of the few public spaces it currently has. This proposal attempts to improve the district in relation to its connection to the centre, improve its public spaces, and provide a reference point to the district.

The project is premised on the creation of a pedestrian axis at the ends of which are located two car parks that will largely eliminate the presence of cars on the streets. It also incorporates the creation of a new centrality in the area with the design of a new square. The proposed new axis, Cardenal Torquemada Street, connects the city from the Church of San Pablo with the Plaza Ribera de Castilla, it connects downtown with nearby public and green spaces, and will strengthen the businesses that currently gather around this area.

The new street will become the principal focal point of the project and the neighbourhood. It is understood as a route, a place to enjoy and occupy, and a place of coexistence and social interaction between neighbours. Structurally, it is a folded concrete slab that creates a new topography for the street and generates places to stay or areas for services. These spaces can be banks, playgrounds, toilets, kiosks, urban beaches, or gardens, and can be complemented by the introduction of vegetation or the addition

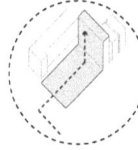

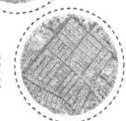

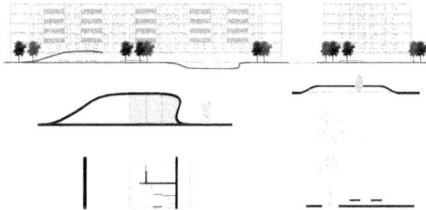

Figure 1. Site model. Strategies of intervention. The new square of the neighbourhood. A versatile shaping system.

of flooring with different textures. The new district square is located at the crossing of this new axis with Cardenal Cisneros Street. Here, some old buildings are to be demolished and replaced by a high-rises that are intended to free up space at ground level for the new square.

Project B: BREAK / LIBERATE /RECOVER

Raquel Álvarez Arce, Laura Barrientos Turrión, Iago Pérez Fernández, Álvaro Pérez Uzuriaga

This project proposes three actions on three scales: the house, the block, and the district. The proposal is to release the lower blocks of the housing units so as to break the rigidity of the neighbourhood and retrieve a public space of quality for La Rondilla.

The strategy employed produces spaces and habitats seen as more adapted to 21st-century living. It involves the fragmentation of the block so as to reconfigure the public space of the neighbourhood, the private neighbourhood spaces, and the home. It allows for the penetration of adequate lighting into different parts of the houses and creates spaces that have a common relationship to the block – away from the current narrow approach streets. It creates a natural sequence from the privacy of the house to the public realm of the street and the neighbourhood.

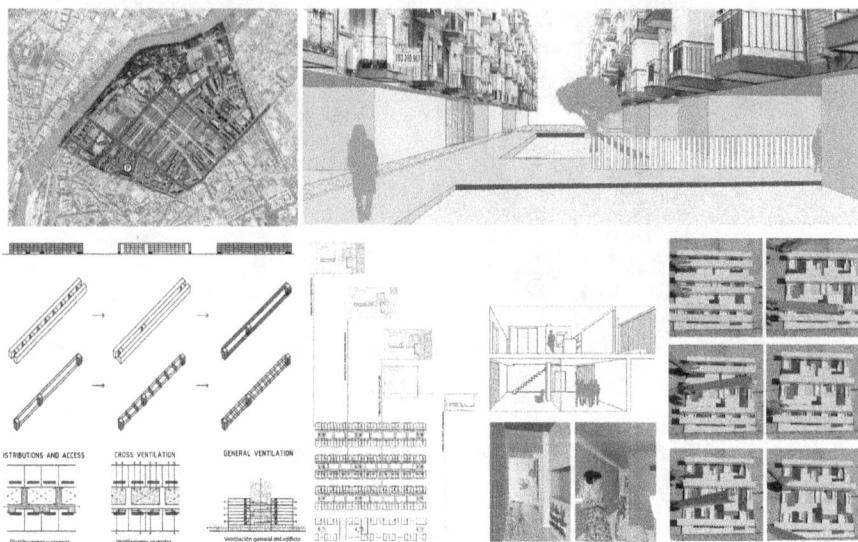

Figure 2. Site plan. View of the encounter space. Plans, sections, interior views. Ground floor tapestry.

The ground floor relationship between the current blocks and the street is very rigid and solid. This proposal frees up parts of the ground floor to make a more flexible arrangement and breaks the current visual homogeneity. The new ground floor plan permits movement in more directions connecting areas that were previously isolated. This interconnectedness applies to the interior of the housing blocks as well, and is achieved through emptying of the central strip of the block. The emptying of the inner part of the blocks allows the rearrangement of access points and the nuclei of interaction, which can be reduced in number because of the use of bridges and galleries. These provide spatial interest to these new areas of interaction and communication.

The location of functions on the ground floor is determined by the parameter of sunlight: dwellings are located under direct sunlight, and work spaces (workshops, retail outlets etc.) are placed in areas that get north or reflected light. The new entrances are positioned to both reduce the number of gateways required and to provide privacy to the most exposed homes. In turn, these are redesigned so as to be capable of accommodating new types of family living in the 21st century. They do this by having large flexible areas divided by furniture, rather than solid elements. The positioning of the kitchen and bathroom serves as a filter between the living area and the central space of the block, thus creating a transition that resolves problems of lighting, ventilation, and privacy that would otherwise exist between the living areas and the public gateways. This is reinforced by the housing access which is configured and is accessed directly or through the bridge, allowing a balance between functionality and privacy.

Project C: LANDMARKS

Sergio Abril, Miguel Ángel Cerro, Javier Mínguez, Soledad Moreno, Carlos Paredes

The neighbourhood being addressed in this project, La Rondilla, is characterized by homogeneity and density. There is no sense of orientation. It is impossible to determine reference points. This proposal is to form open spaces in the dense network of the city by creating squares and public spaces that are currently absent. In key points of the district some parts of its buildings are to be removed, namely, at points of entry, and at its main axis crossings. It is a strategy aimed at creating the possibility of having some urban landmarks in the existing homogeneous residential neighbourhood.

Figure. 3. The new skyline and the site plan. The new tower: shaping strategies. Views and axonometric. Proposed site model.

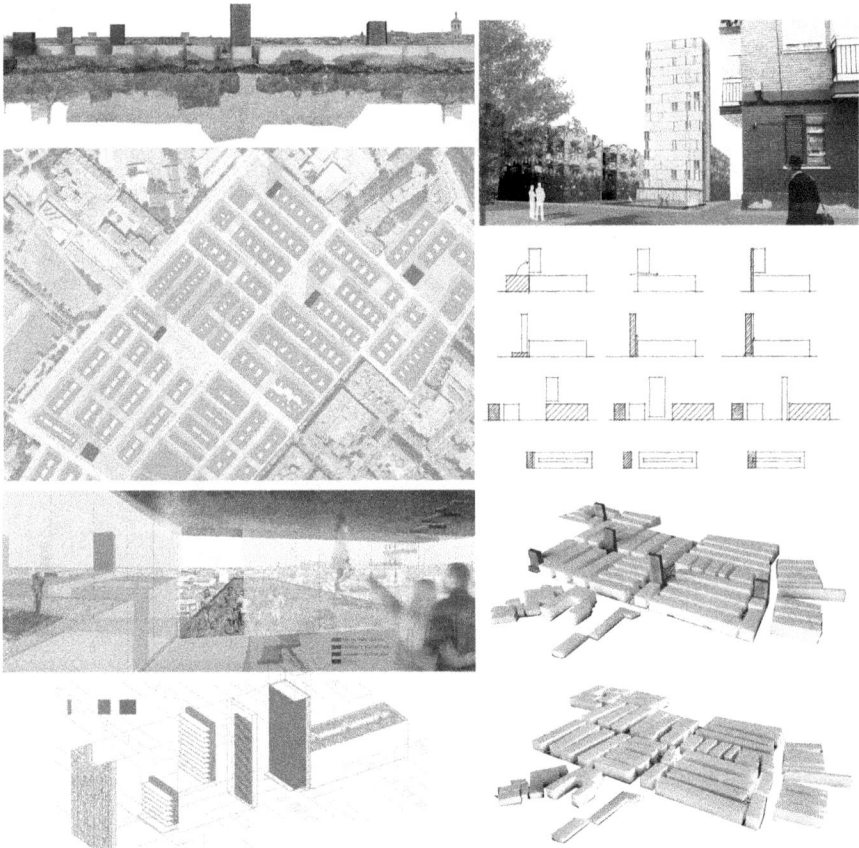

These landmarks are to be structures that will a have different character from the existing fabric, and will be linked to the gaps, or public spaces, carved out of the city. These gaps are almost hidden to the pedestrian because of the labyrinthine structure of streets, so it has been decided to 'perforate the city' and form access routes through the ground floors of buildings at key points. This new pedestrian structure overlaps with the existing traffic ways of the city, which are limited to specific areas by making some routes exclusively pedestrian. Parking is located in car parks and buildings on the periphery.

New towers are proposed to create a new skyline, reflecting a new urban image and celebrating new public and collective spaces. These buildings will permit the collective use of their roofs as spaces of public encounter and as urban orchards. Other buildings can also have community spaces on the roof. Incorporating vegetation, urban gardens are created for the inhabitants of each block. The strategy is to 'append' the landmark to the existing block; to facilitate links between the ground and the roof; to successfully join old and new constructions; to create new roof gardens; and to open the ground floor space to more common usage rather than limiting it to residential functions.

At ground floor level the plan is to be composed of three distinct bands, communication systems and terraces, services systems, and housing. The housing unit itself is to be a flexible system that allows for the restructuring of old housing typologies based on two- and three-bedroom models.

Project D: INHABITED ROOFS

Jacobo Abril, Gema Hernández, María Laspra, Ana Prada

Our critique of the neighbourhood of La Rondilla in Valladolid focuses on the social housing blocks of the area. The projects address the lack of public spaces and services for the community, dark interiors to many of these buildings, poor spatial dispositions inside and out, and weak links from the interiors to the exterior. Doorways and pathways in the blocks are poorly lit, dwellings overlook small courtyards, and streets are narrow and long. They also lack the multiple access points that would give greater opportunities for neighbours to interact.

These inherited difficulties inspired us to create the public spaces that these houses never had, and to prepare them for current urban conditions. We propose to create this public space of encounter between neighbours wherever it may be possible: on lower floors, roofs, intermediate levels, and interior courtyards. We want to generate a structure of collective spaces, articulated with appropriate connections, and adapted to facilitate greater civility.

We propose different initiatives to solve these problems.

Existing roofs are to be transformed into places of encounter, spaces for relationships, and spaces for community activities such as small promenades, gardens, and sports facilities. Also, the connections and access points of the partially submerged lower

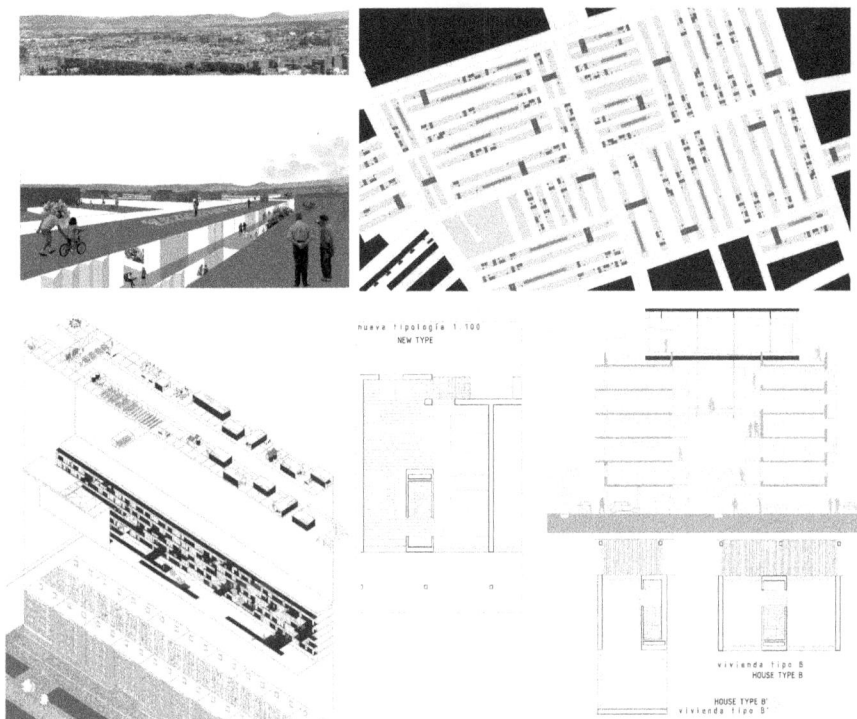

Figure 4. Inhabited roofs. The old and the new roofs. Sections and plans.

level houses are to be opened and increased in number to improve their connection with the rest of the block houses and streets.

The small courtyards are grouped into large central open spaces in each block of flats. The old stairs that divided those courtyards are to be abolished and replaced by more open stairs located in new strategic positions. These will resolve the connection between street, houses, and roofs, in a smoother way.

Along with these new stairs, new voids on the ground floor of the blocks are proposed to provide alternative connections between streets. At intermediate levels, and alongside these stairs, are small areas for meetings and encounters between neighbours. Overall, accessibility is to be improved with more access from new stairs, through gateways, and across galleries that all facilitate communication between each of these spaces and the roofs. In short, we propose the re-articulation of standard spaces into new public and collective spaces that allow multiple meeting spaces and the generation of community activities.

IAN WROOT

Liverpool John Moores University

SCHOOL OF ART AND DESIGN

The MArch programme in Architecture at Liverpool John Moores University focuses on sustained scholarly activity underpinned by the research interests of staff engaged in the strategic theme of urbanism, and concerned with identifying the value of design thinking and practice in new urban contexts. It addresses questions around dwelling, health and well-being, and public space in a range of contexts, driven by an ambition to produce visionary strategies for sustainable urban futures.

The principal building design project of the first year of the MArch is based around issues in contemporary housing. The current political context of this critical aspect of the built environment forms the backdrop for consideration of how architects should respond to the pressures and demands in meeting the residential needs of future generations. Groups explore differing typologies: urban blocks, urban terraces, and suburban semi-detached. The various types and their urban/suburban locations are selected to cover the principal design issues faced by the profession in meeting the challenges posed by Britain's chronic housing shortage. Issues addressed by the students include the diminishing size of the average British house, the potential of residents to adapt and change the physical fabric of the house, construction technologies and pre-fabrication, provision of public social space, and changing patterns in family models

Urban Block

Liverpool's historic core used to exhibit some of the highest residential densities in the United Kingdom. Emptied of its population during the 1960s, 1970s, and 1980s, it is only now being rediscovered as the heart of urban living. One part of the city which is coming under increased development pressure is the Baltic Triangle, a former industrial and warehousing zone on the edge of the city centre. The standard speculative developers' two-bed apartment solution currently preferred in this area offers little to the city by way of either social space, or variants upon the typological norms. Students were tasked with questioning these norms and examining alternative possibilities for city centre living, questioning the apartment layout and the form of the urban block, whilst maintaining high densities. A constant theme was consideration of larger units suitable for family living, and in meeting the demands of family life innovation in provision of private and communal gardens.

Terraced House

The much loved Georgian terraced house, considered one of the most robust housing typologies, is often regarded as an urban ideal in a country that struggles to shake off its suburban passions. Liverpool is lucky enough to have maintained, in the Canning Street Quarter, a significant inner city Georgian residential district of considerable architectural and urban quality. Within this largely intact and popular district there exist a number of gaps created by lower density redevelopment from the 1970s – one such space is the Falkner Street primary school site. Students were required to propose reinterpretations of the local terraced house typologies which reflected the differing patterns of the contemporary family, whilst accommodating new external social space and the displaced functions of the primary school. A number of interesting solutions were designed, playing with the subtle relationships of the section to create courtyards and integrated semi-independent mews, each of which maintained the urban terraced character of the area whilst addressing modern social structures.

Semi-detached House

The British semi-detached house has been a little-changing model since the 1900s. Developed to service the needs of the nuclear family it has proved very resistant to the challenges of the 20th and 21st centuries. How fit for purpose is this typology for this century? Can one bathroom deal with the needs of a step-family? Can the technology of bricks and blocks meet the energy use limitations of affordable homes? Does the type permit sufficient site densities to prevent reliance upon cars? The questions facing the semi-detached house as a typology are numerous and students have been encouraged to challenge the perceived norms of this staple for the mass housing developers. Projects have been located on typical suburban 'greenfield' sites with limited urban context to define the parameters. Each site offers up subtle but important relationships with the natural context of woodland and open landscape views. Solutions include: communal living clusters set in allotment gardens, self-build student pre-fabricated dwellings constructed for the same cost as three years rent, and houses with the capacity to accommodate mature children returning home.

Project A: The Interblock

Amir Izzat Adnan

The site of this project is located between Liverpool's China Town, Anglican Cathedral, and docks. It presents valuable opportunities for pedestrian accessibility with a distinctive presence in an area classified primarily as residential, but which includes some commercial and service industries. Since the site is already active with pedestrian movement the project seeks to further enhance social interaction amongst the residents through a variety of programmes and public spaces. The Interblock's planning is conducive to sustainable living, and it provides infrastructure and facilities that are lacking in the area at present. The existing park will also be enhanced for the established community to use to its full potential. At the core of the block is an elevated soft landscaped courtyard, which has car parking provided beneath.

The overarching concept is to provide high-quality healthy living in an affordable community of new housing. The Interblock will be suitable for a variety of different occupants – including both tenants and buyers – through a diverse range of dwelling types. The target market for the Interblock includes single person households, couples, families, and extended families. Multiple and flexible dwelling types will allow occupants to dictate the form of a particular unit, thus providing alternative possibilities for them to design and redesign what they want in a practical way.

The Interblock's structure and fabric are designed in response to the context of the dock area and China Town. This surrounding context was highly influential in informing the design, which creates a new block terrace orientated for optimum solar penetration.

Figure 1. Site perspective. Unit typology. Sectional perspective. Interior perspective.

The material rationale is evident from the front façade, with its composition of brick and precast concrete structures. Another aim is to express the massiveness of the overall proposal through a complex façade treatment on flat surfaces. Full height and recessed windows offer a sense of exposure to the surrounding context for the occupants.

The Interblock creates the possibility of having a luxurious-looking home for its occupants that is designed by the occupants in accordance with their individual needs and wants. This is achieved through the use of design and construction systems that enable the occupants to customize the dwellings to their preferences. Therefore, the focus on sustainability is thought of in terms of maximising the longevity of materials and reducing embodied energy, as well as other green strategies such as sunlight penetration, natural ventilation, recycled rainwater usage, and occupation energy savings. The building orientation also means that every dwelling will receive sun penetration, and will have a garden for the occupant's individual use.

Project B: The Return of the Courts: The Revival of an Archi-Type

Christopher Wells

Over the centuries Liverpool has witnessed a variety of housing types which have fragmented and reconfigured the urban fabric that is seen today: from back-to-backs, to Georgian and Victorian, to the municipal housing projects. Each new idea introduced a distinct way of living, while losing a piece of Liverpool's collective memory along with it. How can housing be reconnected back to its original context whilst providing the society of today with their needs?

Forming a Cooperative

An objective of the project is to embrace an experimental idea generated from the works of Bill Halsall (Senior Partner, Halsall Lloyd Partnership) and Robert McDonald (Reader in Architecture, LJMU) called 'Alternative Third Wave Housing Futures.' They proposed to revisit the housing cooperative model in a way that befits today's residents.

The project focuses on starter families and couples who will be able to opt in and out of the housing scheme, to enable people to get onto the housing ladder. These families will form a cooperative that uses shared communal areas and facilities to their benefit, whilst creating a sustainable community that care for the housing types provided.

Chosen Archi-Type: Liverpool's Courts

'The Return of the Courts' is a revival of the back-to-backs (courtyard housing), which will be used to stich new residential schemes back to the city by creating street patterns of public and semi-private spaces that Liverpool was once renowned for. With this building type being highly dense, other precedents are used to develop these back-to-back terraces into a semi-detached housing type that sits contextually within the site of Aigburth.

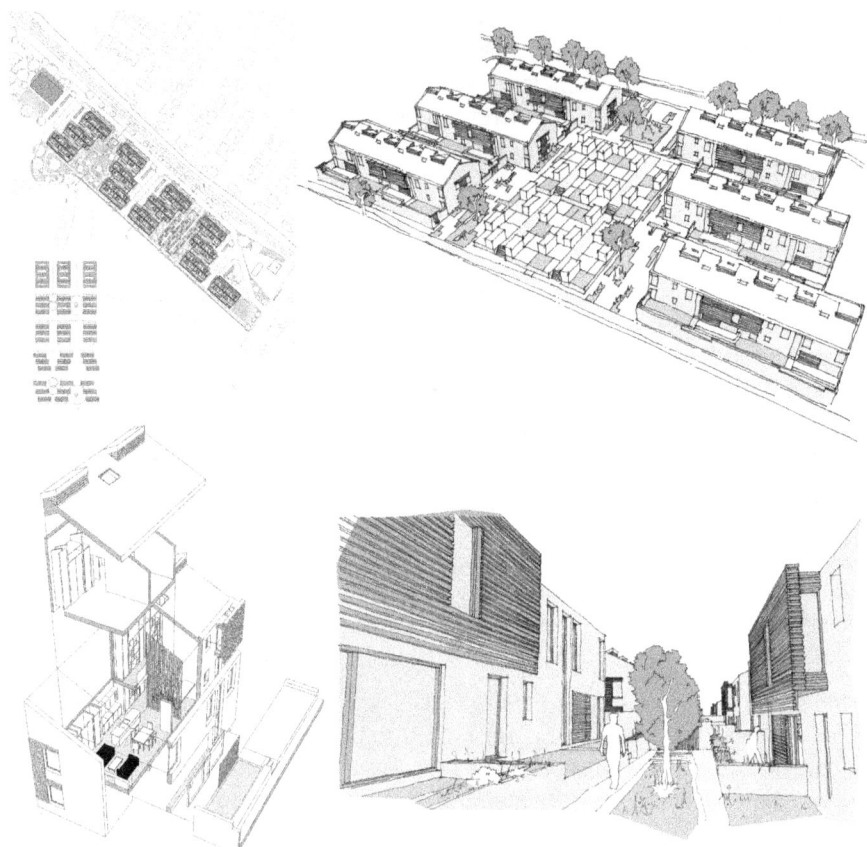

Figure 2. Master plan and concept. Communal clusters formed around shared allotments.
Exploded diagram. Courtyard perspective.

The typology will be revived not for its aesthetics, but for the courtyard located off a street, which once housed the communities that thrived within. Throughout the scheme there will be a relationship between the courtyard house and its surroundings, creating transitions through space. In places there will be a relationship with the community space and street, but in the majority it is a study on the individual courtyard and its relationship with the key space within the dwelling.

Individual Dwelling

A key aim is to improve the condition of the chosen housing type by focusing on light, ventilation, comfort, and space. By incorporating different sustainable elements throughout the design the project ensures that health and well-being is of a high standard. The party-wall is utilised for storage and ventilation, and acts as a buffer between the dwellings.

The north and south façades play an important role due to the dwellings' orientation. Both share the same language, but differ to reduce the carbon footprint. The south is composed of sizeable windows for solar gain during the winter, while louvres restrict excessive gains in summer. The north façade will be made of smaller openings to minimise heat loss. The roofline allows clerestory windows to penetrate the first and ground floors through the ventilation voids and to admit sunlight to the northern houses.

Project C: Grow Home

Gethin Hughes

Floor plans and housing typology now need to offer a platform for living to people who are constantly undergoing change and are involved in a great variety of living situations.

Christian Schittich

The topic of housing in the UK is a controversial one, to say the least. As housing demand is on the rise once again following the recession, there is a need for more dwellings to be built across the country; the Government has set a target to provide 3,000,000 homes by 2020. What should these dwellings be like? Should they be designed to suit a particular lifestyle, or certain types of society? Is space within the dwellings an issue that needs to be considered?

After investigating and exploring the dilemmas faced, it became apparent that future dwellings should be easily adaptable, in order to provide sufficient space for families to develop and grow. It has been said that the average UK homeowner moves at least seven times in their lifetime. Why should this be the case? A homeowner should have the option of owning a dwelling that not only fulfils their present needs, but also their future needs. By providing such a house, a young family could live comfortably within it, and if the time comes when they need more space, they should have this option in their existing dwelling.

The proposed project would address these issues in eighty dwellings across a vacant site on Jericho Lane, Liverpool. Both detached and semi-detached dwellings have been carefully arranged across the site, incorporating pockets of public green space to provide families with spaces to socialise. Each dwelling has been designed to be both flexible, and easily adaptable, in order to accommodate the evolving needs of a family unit. This removes the need for occupants to relocate when they want to upscale, by providing a dwelling that can 'adapt its lifestyle.'

The main living space can be found at the front of the property on the ground floor – a multifunctional space that would give a family enough room to develop and grow – which, being a double-height space, gains ample daylight. Large windows are provided, with careful consideration given to their proportion and composition in order to maximise the space's potential. Alongside the living space is a bespoke staircase and kitchen-diner, which overlooks the private garden to the rear of the property, and

Figure 3. Master plan. Detached dwelling floor plans. Isometric view. Street elevation.

connects the internal spaces to the outdoors. The number of bedrooms on the upper floor can vary from two to four, to enable a variety of family configurations across the development.

It was considered vital that the proposed scheme blend with its surrounding context, so that it would appear as if it had been a part of the setting for numerous years. In terms of materiality and construction, a traditional brick and block structure is proposed. It can be constructed entirely onsite, and provides higher thermal mass than a timber frame structure.

Project D: RE I CON [vive]

Kevin Hiew

Liverpool's creative quarter has been known as the city's workshop and creative playground. It is roamed by musicians, photographers, artists, fashion designers, architects, film makers, young entrepreneurs, and recording artists. Around the so-called Baltic Triangle there are drinking holes, eateries, nightlife venues, galleries, and internationally acclaimed arts festivals are held.

Ever since the waterfront began regenerating pedestrians have been attracted to use a waterfront route instead of heading towards the Baltic Triangle; current development plans propose a route for pedestrians to navigate from the ACC Arena towards the city centre. Regeneration on the waterfront may therefore be to the detriment of the

Figure 4. Floor plans. Axonometric of components. Concept diagram. Street view.

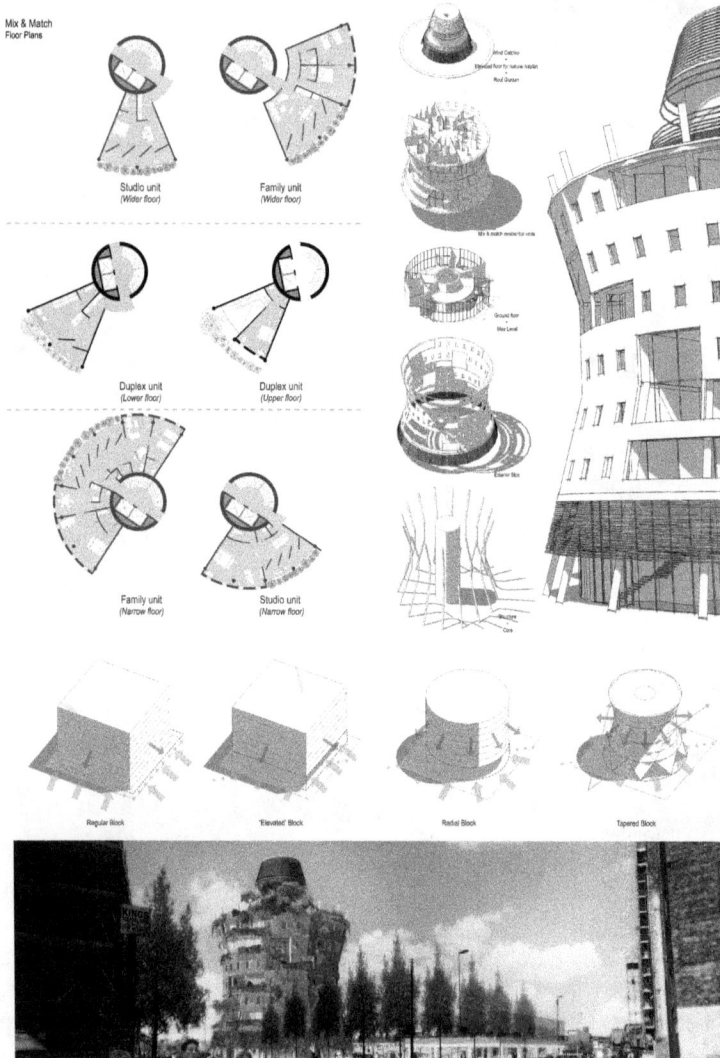

creative quarter. Consequently, a key objective of this project is to identify a prominent site and create a community that both sustains itself in the central city area, while simultaneously attracting the public to the heart of the Baltic Triangle.

The design approach proposes to create homes suitable for families, and to encourage them to remain in the city centre through balancing density, nature, public open space, and the inherent creative character of the area. There are various industries located within the Baltic Triangle. The project aims to utilise these resources available locally for prefabrication systems, instead of global products; a bazaar instead of globalised shopping centres. The site also benefits from close proximity to the city centre, and the development of education institutes and numerous block developments that house a growing population density.

Design Concept

Regular Block. Regular blocks tends to be unfriendly to pedestrians by creating a boundary that distinctively demarcates private spaces from public spaces. As a result, there is no interaction between the building and pedestrians other than for the people who live within it.

Elevated Block. By elevating the residential units and opening up the Ground Floor a direct route is created toward the waterfront from China Town. Adding public access services – such as cafés, bars, or convenience stores – nurtures interaction between the public and private spaces. A disadvantage of a square surface for a building block is that there is only one view outwards toward the street.

Radial Block. Creating a radial block instead not only opens up more views outward, but it also allows more fluid pedestrian movement.

Tapered Block (Diagrid or Slanted Structure). The tapered block carves out more views toward the Cathedral. A much neater entry point is formed by the radial grid, as consistent openings provide a homogenous form. Once through the perimeter there will be a landscaped area within the boundary inviting people to linger. It will also provide a hangout space for students living around the site.

Since the building is planned in a radial form there are 'mix and match' dwelling units that range from studio to duplex to family dwellings. This variation – as well as wider to narrow floor plates – determines the fenestration arrangement of the exterior façade.

Project E: Habitus: Homes not Houses

Matthew Kerrod

The house is the most intimate of all architectural spaces. The design of these spaces directly influences the rituals of people's daily lives, and in turn the inhabitants' own preferences and idiosyncrasies are reflected in the ordering of the house. Yet we live in a society dependent on the mass housing developer. In contrast, before the rise of

Figure 5. Site plan. Existing perspective. Cross section. Perspective to park space.

Modernism and World War II, self-building homes was the norm. As a consequence of the need for mass housing from the post-World War II period to the present day, housing estates with repetitive house-types have been built all across the country. The main objective of this project is to allow the inhabitants to reclaim their space and appropriate it to suit their particular needs and desires.

There are two main precedents for this approach to housing, but they use differing strategies. Diagoon Houses in Delft, by Herman Hertzberger, were designed in such a way that allows the occupants to alter the internal layout to suit their needs. Whereas Monterrey Housing in Chile, designed by Elemental, adopts a strategy of building only half a house – with only a bathroom and a kitchen unit as defined spaces. The rest of the dwelling is then constructed by the occupants, which allows them to appropriate their home in any way that they see fit. It was these two strategies which informed the configuration of the project's two core structures. Unit A is designed with the intention that the internal fit out is the primary area of adaptation, whereas the aim with Unit B is that the occupants not only adapt the internal layout, but also extend their house to develop additional meaningful, personal spaces.

Habitus seeks to provide a housing type that can be appropriated by various users to create a house that is more personal and tailored to the individual needs of its inhabitants: a home. The project proposes two different shells that contain a stair core, a kitchen, and a ground floor bathroom. Beyond these, it is up to the end-user as to how the house is subdivided into its various spaces. This concept of appropriation and adaptability was explored by applying three different scenarios to each of the house shells and examining how different 'family types' could develop the space in different ways, including the utilisation of double-height spaces, and extending the given shell.

In terms of a strategy for the overall site, a few of the houses are not given gardens to allow the occupants to make a conscious decision as to whether they want a garden space or not. This lack of private open space was then mitigated in two ways: firstly, through the provision of roof terraces, and secondly, by incorporating a community park space which is enclosed by the terraced rows. The park is there to promote community spirit through shared use of the space, encouraging the home-owners to interact with each other in this area.

GEORGIOS ARTOPOULOS AND IOANNIS A. PISSOURIOS

Cyprus Institute and Neapolis University

SCHOOL OF ARCHITECTURE, LAND AND ENVIRONMENTAL SCIENCES

The School of Architecture, Land and Environmental Sciences of Neapolis University, comprises the Programmes of Architecture, Real Estate, Construction Management, and Landscape Architecture. Although these Programmes run simultaneously and in parallel as distinct disciplines, they support one another on both the organizational as well as the educational level. The Programme in Architecture acknowledges the significant social responsibility of architectural practice for the study and development of everyday space, public or private.

In this respect, each individual student on the architecture programme is regarded as a distinct personality, open to freely shape a system of values and skills concerning aesthetic development, imagination, ethos, and consistency. At the same time, the programme utilises the heterogeneity of its highly qualified teaching faculty as an educational tool, in order to establish an architectural field of study that takes into account the multiple approaches on offer, thereby provoking an essential transformation of students' thinking. Within the context of university education, the programme combines the provision of broader humanistic values for students while granting them the necessary skills for their professional life and research.

In its home, the city of Paphos, the School operates as an intellectual and cultural hub, building on its own activities, as well as on synergies with the city, its institutions, and its citizens. At the same time, it establishes connections with the wider context of Cyprus, the Mediterranean and beyond, facilitated by contemporary modes of communication and transportation, such as student exchanges, EU-funded research projects, international workshops, conferences, and exhibitions. In line with its social agenda, local, regional and international focus the projects on housing included here are local in site but draw upon ideas and theories that come from around the world and have potential applications on every continent. They are, in this regard, representative of the work of the School and the University.

As indicated previously in this book, the projects documented come from the Module ARCH S05: Urban Design and Housing. They are second-year projects from the Bachelor in Architecture Degree programme and are focused on two sites: one located in the historic core of the city, in Mouttalos, and the other in the Universal area, which exhibits all the typical characteristics of newly (after 1990s) built-up areas in most Cypriot cities. The research the students engaged with in developing these projects focused on spatial irregularities and social associations emerging in everyday activities on these two culturally contested sites between Cypriot Greeks and Turks. The aim was to approach the challenged identity of the quarter of Mouttalos, and the ubiquitous urban fabric of the Universal, as unique parts of the city that negotiate interaction opportunities, rather than as areas that define boundaries in the daily experience of the city, performing as borders of 'otherness'.

Thus the educational outcome of the Studio is to enable students to communicate how this negotiation can replace distinctions of identity among users, in order to embrace shifting identities and create a space that allows irregularities and idioms to emerge and promote co-existence. In this context what is documented here is an attempt to study the architectural terms of convergent urban scenarios. These spatialised scenarios look at what emerges between quotidian, mundane, repetitive strings of actions – that individuals follow in their everyday interaction with the built environment – and the uncertain encounters they have in the city. In doing so the overarching goal of the Studio, reflecting what we need to do in practice, is no longer about (over)designing housing typologies, but rather to devise inclusive design strategies that associate narratives, memories, and experiences with the communal spaces of housing projects and the public space of the neighbourhood. To achieve this aim, the Studio brief pursues the following micro-objectives:

- to study the impact of cultural heritage on the form and level of interaction/ exploitation of resources by distinct populations; and,

- to map particular complexities (i.e., social, operational, organizational) that the site exhibits and associate patterns of movement, use, and performance in the neighbourhood of the site.

The Design Studio acknowledges that the participation of socially active, culturally motivated and eager to learn citizens is necessary in order to achieve the holistic development of the city. The student projects were designed to accommodate spatially organized activities and offer an alternative to typical urban experience in Cyprus with a view to promoting opportunities of collective learning and engagement with the local natural and cultural resources. Offering multiple narratives and experiences to their visitors, by means of alternative and complementary circulation paths and use of space, the proposed housing projects, and primarily their associated communal spaces, were designed to become an inclusive environment, where individuals become active users of the space and are invited to explore it. The design of these spaces resorted to a performative understanding of common spaces, which respects diverging identities and localities, while promoting shared activities. In doing so the Design Studio offers a potentially fruitful contribution to the architectural discourse about contemporary transregional challenges in the cities of the Eastern Mediterranean.

Project A: Housing and Culture as Means for Social Integration

Kostas Economou and Pieris Ioannou

The main idea of the project was the creation of a neighbourhood of culture built around a social housing complex. Housing and commerce already exist in the area and this project aims at improving and upgrading the conditions of the site through the rehabilitation of existing structures and new interventions. In Moutallos, the co-existence of two ethnicities with different intangible cultural heritages can potentially be used for the emergence of new, shared activities that could take place in the in-between space, the common spaces of the neighbourhood. Music is a common language that anyone can understand and enjoy, irrespective of his or her nationality, ethnicity, religion, or educational background. Hence, in this project we propose the creation of the necessary built spaces to host and support music events during specific periods of the year and visiting artists from various countries. Thus, a row of guest rooms is proposed to complement the social housing project and accommodate the participating artists for the duration of the organized music events.

Music is the vehicle of facilitating cultural integration in the area. For this purpose, a music stage was created to host cultural events. The music stage lies on a recess to the rest of our intervention level so that anyone standing around the stage, or passers-by, can watch the events unobstructed. There are several communal spaces between the dwellings and the rest of the proposed intervention. We envision these shared spaces to become places of social activation and meetings, bringing visitors from various countries in contact with the locals. Our aim was the creation of 'deep' enjoyable pathways; our objective was to explore how public space, movement, and the built environment can interweave without the disintegration of the existing urban fabric. An effort for the preservation and conservation of the existing buildings on site was made, and thus we propose the demolition of structures without historical value, which are considered in very bad condition.

The concept of the proposed design stems from a network of pathways that is created in order to integrate the new spatial interventions with the existing urban fabric. The design of covered passageways was inspired by the typical characteristic of Cyprus' vernacular architecture. In traditional Eastern Mediterranean architecture the passageways were created in urban spaces to protect inhabitants from the weather, and mainly from the hot sun, while they, for example, hosted social and commercial activities. The housing block was formed out of the integration of residential, commercial spaces, guest units and communal spaces, into a continuous whole. The continuous curvy outlines of the building's shape organize the various spaces in groups of uses, like residential and commercial, while creating canopies and cantilevered slabs that offer shading in the communal spaces. Combined with the covered passageways, these canopies enable the natural ventilation and accelerate airflow through the buildings, contributing to the bioclimatic performance of the design, an architectural solution that is deemed necessary due to the tropic climate of the area (see Figure 1).

Figure 1. Plans and design proposals.

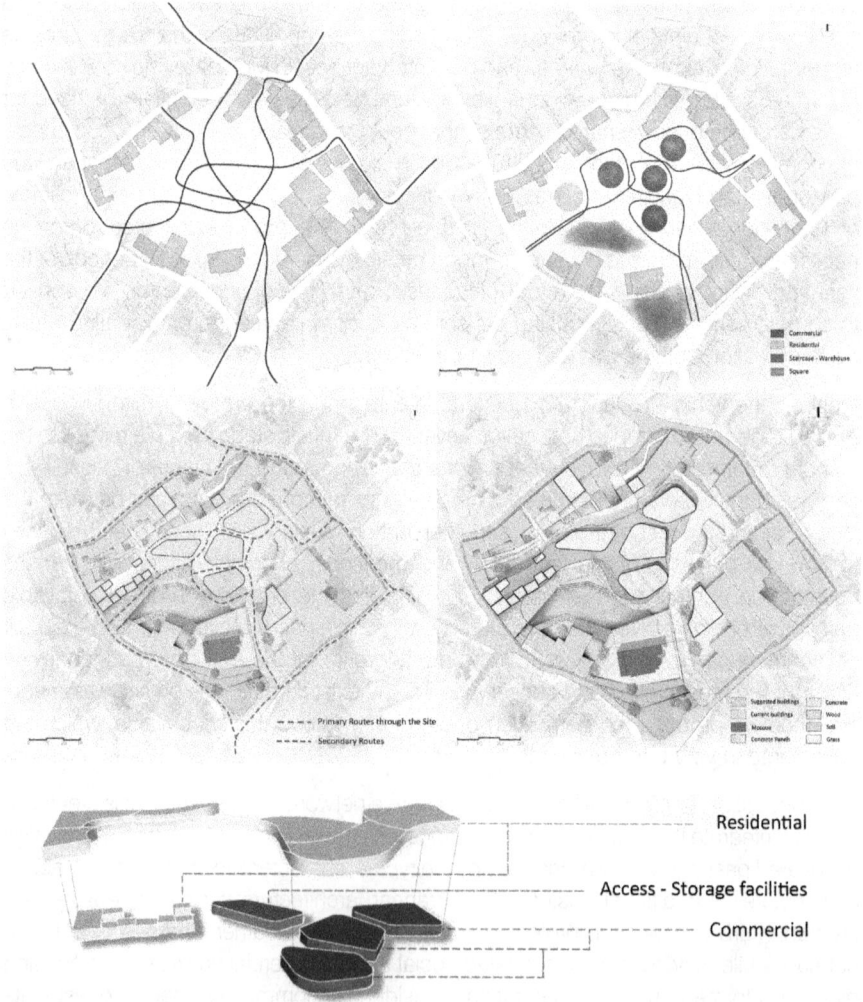

From left to right:

- Pathways, access points and movement on site

- Generation of social condensers / Activation field: the resulting pathways from the three defined access points. The access points are defined in conjunction with the proposed land uses, creating a network of movement. This circulation network was used as a diagram for the spatial organization and geometric configuration of the proposed building.

- Main and secondary routes through the site that connect the cluster proposed with the wider area and its landmarks: the mosque, the historical city center and public buildings, like the town hall and the schools.

- Master plan design proposal.

- Shows the urban uses in the area. The commerce, guest rooms and hostel, the entrance to the housing project, as well as the storage rooms that support the units of the housing block, are all located on the ground floor, whereas the housing units are laid on the first floor.

Project B: Spiral Housing for Social Resilience

Petros Kaloterakis and Andreas Savva

The quarter of Moutallos is part of the historic core of Paphos and therefore it was necessary that any interventions should be made with sensitivity and respect to its cultural significance for the community. Our preliminary site analysis pointed to the many abandoned buildings, the poor building conditions and construction quality of prefabricated structures, and the numerous under-operating retail shops in the area that challenge the coherence of the local urban-scape.

Our proposal attempts to respond to these challenges and link the quarter's history with future aspirations for a vibrant and inclusive urban environment. Aiming at achieving higher densities, our design project proposes an alternative solution to housing that integrates services (e.g., residential, corporate offices, and shops) and amenities, both existing and new. We propose three distinct types of blocks, each adapted to the formal specificities and operational needs of these three conditions of occupation (i.e., housing, retail trade, and entertainment). Distinct from both typical high-rise and low-rise typologies of housing our spirally organised blocks allow open space to penetrate the complex and offer opportunities for social interaction and associations, while permitting for future vertical expansion and higher densities.

The establishment of points of interest and the re-formation of the built environment and the natural resources that surround the housing complex were our criteria for the implementation of this spiral diagram on site. Our design motives were achieved by positioning the spiral housing complex in the centre of a concave 'circulation belt' that runs through four sub-centres: the main square of the Mosque Hagia Sophia, the public market, a skate park, and a terraced, small-scale and more private square which is designed to function as a stage for free movie projections and theatrical plays.

We envision that these places will attract new users and possibly permanent residents in the area, as they offer opportunities for social interaction and activation. By integrating a wide range of cultural and entertainment activities with sales booths for local products and culinary arts, this network of secondary centres is expected to contribute to the popularity of the neighbourhood among locals and tourists of all ages, and by doing so, to enhance the life of the quarter. Essentially, the bodily movement through this network of proposed social activation points encircles the housing complex and consists in a journey through the flavours and odours of past times, linking the present life of the housing complex with the history of the site and its neighbourhood (see Figure 2).

Figure 2. Plans, concepts and design proposals.

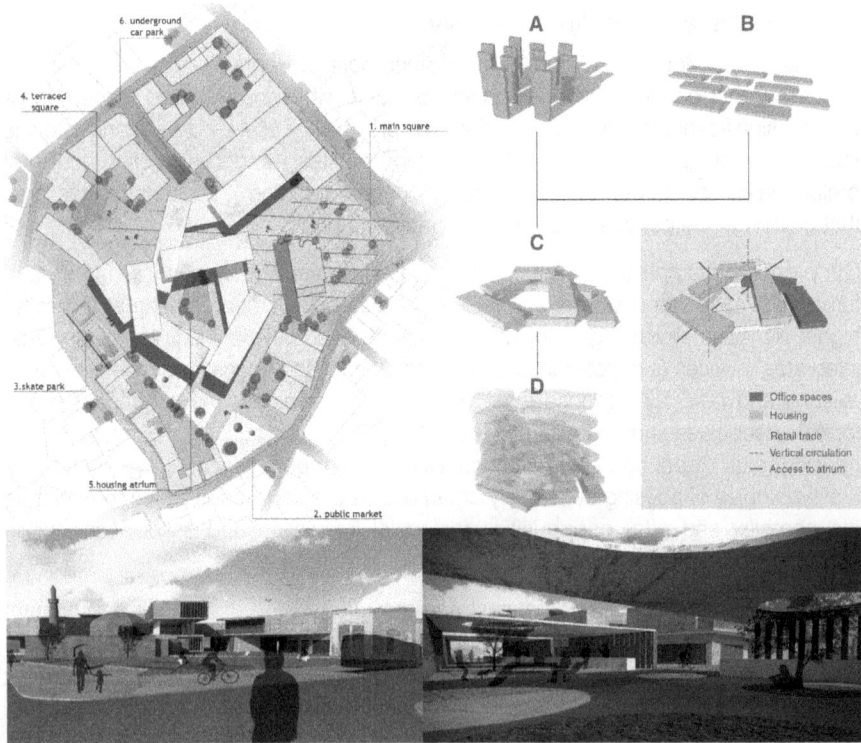

From left to right:

- Plan of the design proposal

- A. Typical high-rise housing blocks isolate users from open green spaces. B. Typical low-rise blocks reduce available green space. C. Spirally organised blocks allow open space to penetrate the complex and offer opportunities for social interaction and associations. D. The spiral organisation of the blocks allows for future vertical expansion and higher densities.

- Main square and entrance to the cluster; the monument of Mosque Hagia Sophia punctuates movement around the square.

- The area of the public market is organised around a network of benches to be used for bazaars and crafts display.

- A terraced square will host free movie projection events and theatrical plays.

Project C: Re-thinking the Universal

Christina Dimitriadou and Maria Gerogiannaki

The city of Paphos is one of the most popular tourist destinations on the island. In particular, Kato Paphos is renowned for its abundance of tourist resorts, shops, and archaeological sites, like the UNESCO World Heritage site. However, the mono-dimensional focus of the area in providing tourist services is challenging not only the development and integration of the numerous residential complexes and housing projects with the city, but also, and more significantly, its public space. One of the most populated residential areas of the city is Universal, where our site of intervention is located.

During the design process, our main concern was the lack of public space, where its inhabitants could meet, interact, and engage in cultural and social activities. Trying to find a point of interest that would be common among all age groups, we decided to build on culture. To do so we propose a central square that includes a cultural center, a movie theater, a stage for music events and art performances, art exhibition galleries, a library, and a coffee shop. We believe that the Universal quarter could accommodate all these facilities successfully as it is located near the main entrance of the city from the highway, and it is easily accessible from the existing road network.

Regarding the design of the housing complex, our motive was to incorporate key elements of bioclimatic architecture, like dense plantation of indigenous vegetation, arcades (as shaded transitional spaces in-between the units), and the use of water for cooling, all in order to adapt to the local climate. We further pursued this ecological approach beyond the architectural scale and explored possibilities for its application in urban design. In doing so, we integrated the proposed set of housing units in the existing linear park and green open spaces, located on the east side of our intervention site. True to our ecological approach, these housing units are designed as a three-

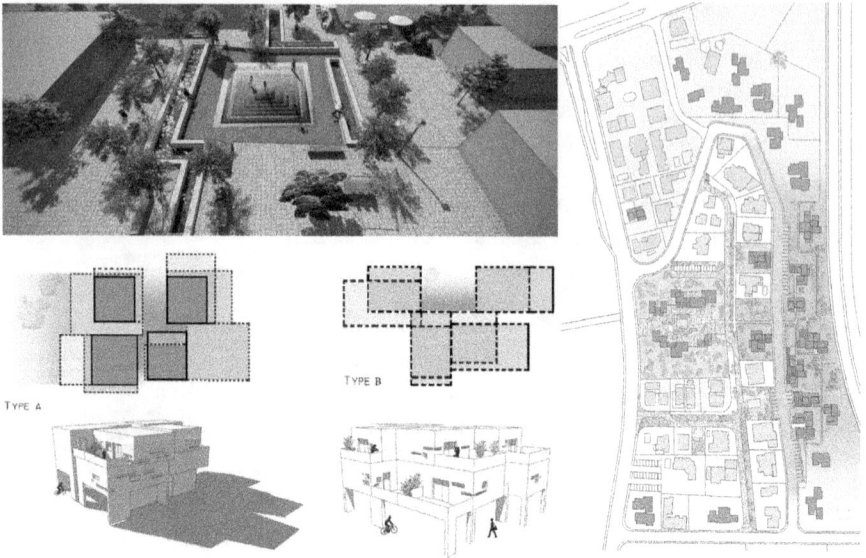

Figure 3. Exterior view, master plan, unit typologies.

dimensional composition of cubes (of a room size each) that expand vertically in order to achieve the smallest possible footprint and allow for transitional open air spaces in-between the cubic rooms. At the urban scale, the houses do not form a continuous front, but are scattered within the park, in-between the existing trees. This way existing plantation is used to protect the housing units from the noise of the main city road that runs parallel to the site. The proposed housing complex in the park is complemented with a network of walking paths and canopies-pavilions for recreation (see Figure 3).

From left to right:

- Photorealistic representation of the multi-functional central square. The combination of water, green, and hard surfaces renders the area capable to accommodate multiple uses.

- Housing Unit typology. Type A: The two-storey building is deconstructed in smaller parts-cubic rooms, in order to allow the formation of semi-public spaces and green corridors to penetrate the building

- Housing Unit typology. Type B: The use of *pilotis* allows the continuity of green spaces and the formation of protected private spaces.

- Master plan

Project D: Living on the Edge: a Parametric Housing Model

Nikolaos Varlagkas

One of Paphos' major problems is the way in which the city grows. The low-rise building scheme used in planning resulted in a scattered urban form with no density and lack of coherence. My proposal provides a mix of land uses that the area needs desperately if it wants to become a lively urban environment. In particular, the list of proposed uses includes commerce, leisure, sports, cultural activities, and housing units. All the buildings are connected with meandering footbridges and paths enabling users to walk and explore the area. The form of the proposed buildings is influenced by the follicles

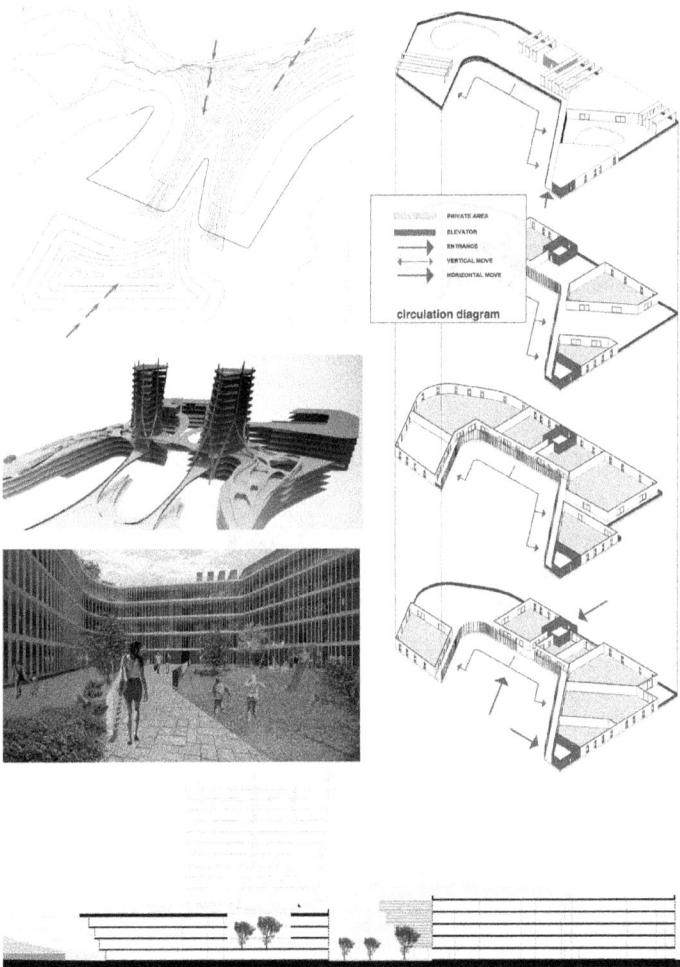

Figure 4. Concept images, spatial diagrams and exterior views.

of the urban web, with linear housing blocks twisting around the plot and defining enclaves of green open spaces while enabling public space to penetrate the housing complex at different heights (both at the ground level and on roof tops).

The project's main idea was to create a housing complex with a strong identity that will provide a new habitation model/scheme for Paphos. Each level of the housing block consists of residences with their own courtyard and a network of circulation routes, like streets in the air, that are reminiscent of the famous Peter and Alison Smithson's 'Golden Lane' model. The communal areas and access to the housing units are located on the inner side of the block overlooking the green open spaces. An integrated design approach with the use of parametric tools enabled the generation of structural elements that operate on multiple levels (responding to circulation, and formal and construction criteria).

The housing units are designed so that all residents have access not only to the communal spaces, but also to their private courtyard, a design rule that when repeated for each unit generates a formal interplay of solid and void spaces across the whole block. In addition, the largest part of the roof of the block is used as a public space for recreation and social activation that is accessible by both the residents of surrounding blocks, and passers-by through the network of footbridges. Integrating all these communal spaces in the housing complex will hopefully offer new opportunities for interaction to the users of the area and promote an alternative approach to diversity, accessibility, and social engagement that is deemed necessary for the sustainable development of Paphos (see Figure 4).

From left to right:

- Concept of the design proposal inspired by the stratification of the geological formations of the landscape.

- Detailed circulation diagram of a typical housing block.

- Three-dimensional impression of the housing complex. A network of bridges/'street in the air' allows circulation between housing blocks. As integrated design approach with the use of parametric tools enabled the generation of structural elements that operate on multiple levels (responding to circulation, and formal and construction criteria).

- Longitudinal section of the housing complex.

AMADEO RAMOS, MIGUEL ÁNGEL DE LA COVA
AND ALFONSO GUAJARDO

Universidad de Sevilla

ESCUELA TECNICA SUPERIOR DE ARQUITECTURA

The Technical School of Architecture at Seville University (Escuela Tecnica Superior de Arquitectura), Spain, opened almost 50 years ago. Its current site was inaugurated in 1967 and was designed to accommodate about one thousand students. At that time, there were only two Schools of Architecture in the country – one in Madrid, and the other in Barcelona. Today, after significant transformation, it has grown to approximately four thousand students. At present, there are twenty-two architecture schools, the School of Architecture being amongst the biggest and most prestigious.

The projects discussed in the chapter from students of the University aim to address the need for the regeneration of the housing stock in the neighbourhoods of 'Virgen del Carmen' (1955–60), and 'Los Diez Mandamientos' (1958–63), both publicly funded projects in Seville during the dictatorship. These areas are noteworthy for many reasons, but are in need of upgrading in various ways. Improvements are required in access to public spaces, housing provision, accessibility, construction quality, and energy efficiency, amongst other things.

The residential programmes that are presented here are based on an expected three year rental period. The new dwellings are all intended to increase flexibility in use so as to facilitate adaptation to the changing uses and demands of the contemporary inhabitants of these neighbourhoods. Each project includes ideas for the renewal of the main entrances to buildings, promoting an overall regeneration for the current housing conditions that could be repeated in similar housing projects in the future. More specifically, the projects seek to reactivate the use of the roof-terraces, and look at the presumed need for installing air conditioning systems and clothes-drying facilities. Additionally, attention is paid to elevators to serve the whole of the buildings, and the new level, which is indispensable given that the vast majority of people inhabiting the existing houses are elderly. The proposals are all based on a mixed tenure system of purchased and rented units, and the proposals are designed to be economically sustainable.

Project A: 'Anywhere'. Neighbourhood – Los Diez Mandamientos

Ana Sollero and Rafael Sollero

The absence of a clear formal configuration of the neighbourhoods of Virgen del Carmen and Los Diez Mandamientos is caused by a lack of parallel arrangements between buildings facing each other and orientation in acute angles creates uncertain and poor quality spaces. In this difficult situation this proposal is to engage in the north-eastern area of the district and reconfigure the area by the overlapping of the existing layout with a new circular geometry. This manoeuvre turns one of the existing urban problems into the core idea of the new proposal.

Figure 1. Site axonometric. Exterior view. Floor plans. Exploded axonometric.

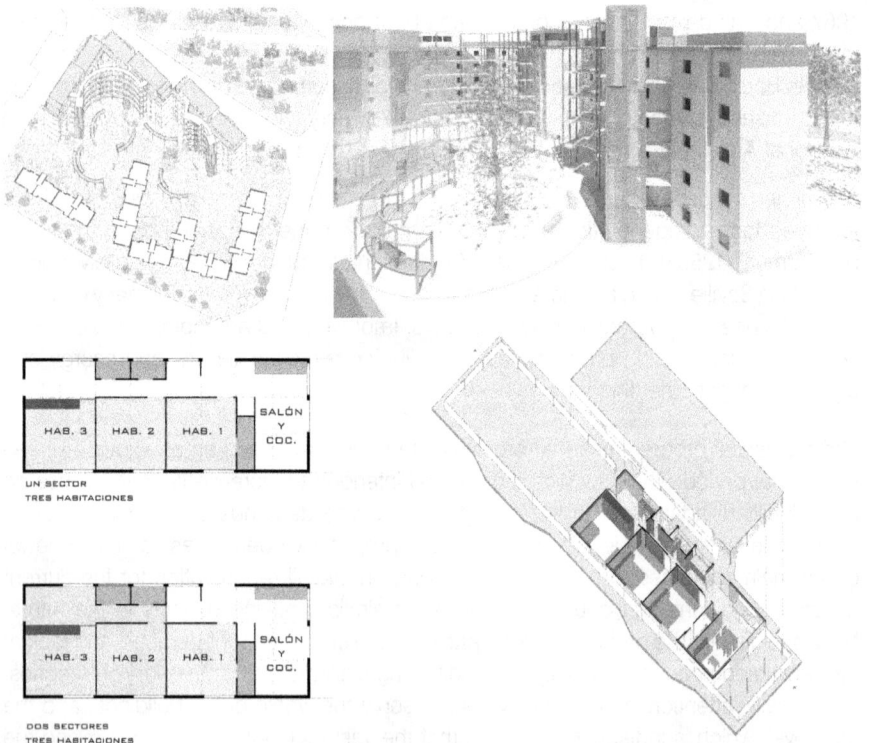

The public space of this new geometry is expressed by the creation of two connected squares enclosed by pergolas, whilst two prism-shaped volumes of the lifts that enclose the project from both sides – and which are built as lamps with colourful polycarbonate – also help to control and define the exterior space. Also fundamental to this project are footbridges constructed with curved forms and access routes to the housing that are also curvilinear in form. The rationale behind this composition is the prevention of the tunnel effect and the creation of a gradual, continual change in view when walking. Central to all this external work, is the respecting of the existing vegetation which is retained and protected.

Focusing on the buildings themselves: each of the roofs of the buildings in the neighbourhood is reworked with a living unit designed in such a way as to allow for greater use of the roof by other occupants of the building. Internally, flexibility in the living space arrangement is key and a lengthwise gallery articulates all the spaces, connecting the access routes and rooms. It can be divided using sliding doors to create sections for different uses and the flexibility this created is supported by a movable partition as a cabinet that gives better versatility to the module. Consequently, even inside the buildings, a sense of community if fostered.

Project B: 'Better Together'. Neighbourhood – Virgen del Carmen

Javier Lopez and José Antonio Castro

Virgen del Carmen is a neighbourhood located between the streets of Rubén Darío and San José de Calasanz. It was built between 1955 and 1960 and it has a total of 636 homes distributed in 10-storey towers and 4-storey linear buildings in a 31,586 m2 area. Although the original architect, Luis Recaséns, proposed many public urban voids as public spaces, today we find a monofunctional neighbourhood with empty community spaces where interaction between residents is not common. Moreover the linearly arranged buildings show a state of decay that is worrying and accessibility routes and other facilities are obsolete. This project proposes the urban revitalization of the neighbourhood with an intervention on the pedestrian streets sited between the linear buildings. Rather than fight against these monofunctional spaces we think that it is possible to exploit their potential so as to improve social interaction across the whole neighbourhood.

The intervention is inspired by a Sevillian form of architecture whose origins go back to the fourteenth century, 'el corral de vecinos' – houses with a courtyard space as the principal site for relationships between the people who live there. Staircases are removed and replaced by walkways which bridge the gap of 8.25 meters between two blocks. These are supported by hidden pillars on the wall, preserving and improving the image of the street at pedestrian level. Moreover, the walkways provide a secondary access routes to houses which helps the accessibility of the complex that will be improved primarily through replacing interior stairways with lifts and adding an exterior

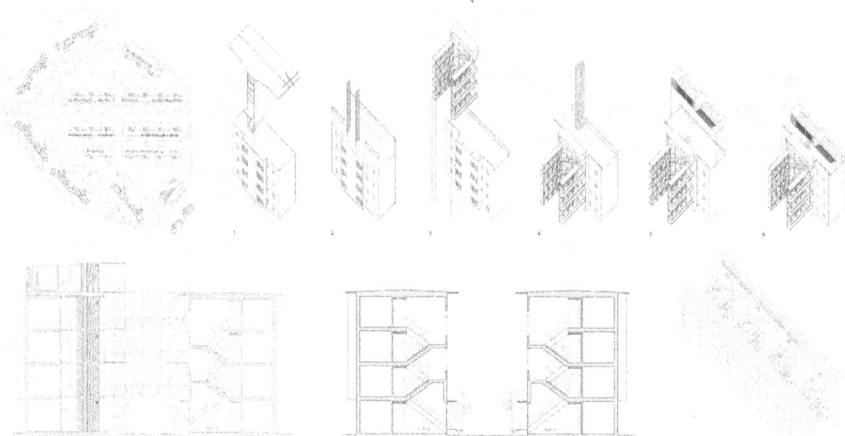

Figure 2. Neighbourhood plan. Development diagrams. Proposed cross sections. Axonometric.

stair which links the ground floor to the walkways – all of which helps cover of the building. By repeating this intervention across the blocks in question we can generate a sequence of courtyards within which neighbourhood interactions can occur.

On the top of the rehabilitated buildings prefabricated houses (8.3 x 2.8 meters) are incorporated on a new floor which facilitates carrying out domestic chores such as hanging out clothes –.8 meter potential community and meeting place. These prefab houses are built with modular metal panels with internal insulation and a swing jalousie in order to improve comfort and will be fitted with all necessary climatic technologies. The main challenge for this project however, is not individual buildings, but rather the provision of urban and individual building renewal with a minimum of apparent intervention.

Project C: 'Rehab'. Neighbourhood – Virgen del Carmen

José Carlos Menasalvas and Helena Cumbreras

The main aim of this project is fourfold: to adapt the blocks to the living requirements of the modern age; to control the pedestrian and vehicular traffic in the building immediate areas around the renovation to make it more usable public space; to ensure the renovated blocks meet today's sustainable requirements; and to respect the original buildings through minimizing, or even eliminating, any 'aggressive' contact by the new renovations.

The concept of family today has changed. It is a concept which has become blurred - due, in part, to the state of impermanence of the family. Today, it is typical that a family may move several times as it grows and changes it needs. To avoid this cost and

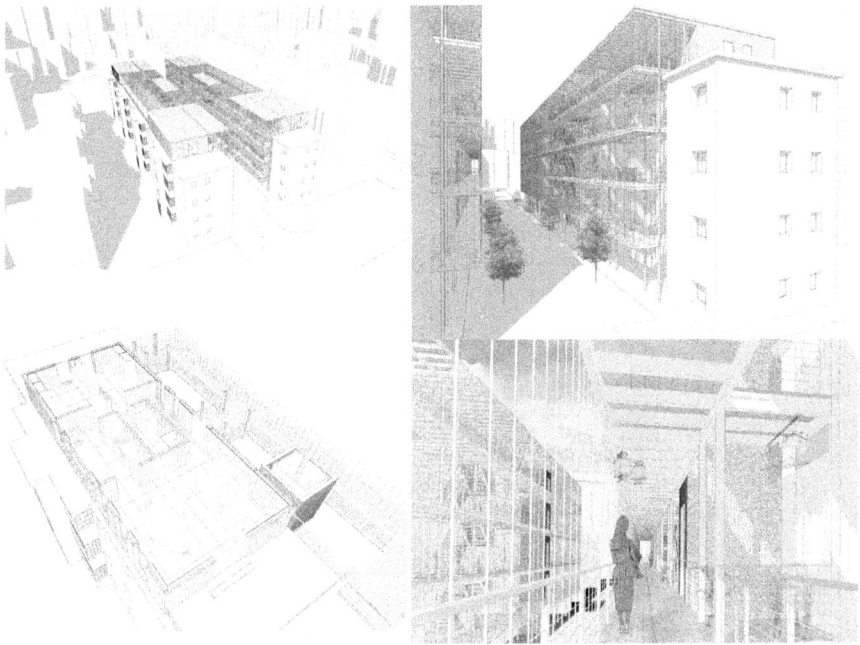

Figure 3. General view. Street view. House 3D plan. Perspective view.

inconvenience, this project seeks flexibility in the planning of the units to accommodate different people at different stages of life. As a result, fragmentation of spaces is avoided and rooms are designed for dual purposes.

In terms of sustainability emphasis is placed on energy efficiency in use. Equally as important however, is the notion of 'recycling' the buildings themselves and using minimum resources to do so. For that reason a lightweight construction system is employed for the new constructions that can also easily be altered – a metal structure with wood panels on the walls and floors, and a modular raised floor and false ceiling.

To accomplish its objective of making more public or shared space, the project involves 'taking back' part of the street and dedicating it exclusively to pedestrian use; it establishes new housing on the roofs of the blocks in question for people with special needs, or for temporary stays; and it adds communal clothes-drying areas that meet a very specific need of the current inhabitants which potentially also functions as a shared social space.

The use of light and porous new elements for rooms and facades facilitates a light touch to the existing structures and creates a type of veil which reduces the harsh aesthetic aspect of the original building. These contain the access elements such as stairs, lifts, and gangplanks and also emphasise visually a concept of gradation between public and private space.

Project D: 'On the Top'. Neighbourhood – Virgen del Carmen

Marta Moreno and Paula Cano

Like many of the residential developments of the 1960s and 1970s in Spain, Seville's Virgen del Carmen district is a neighbourhood in which we see a series of deficiencies that are leading the district to obsolescence, but also some virtues which need to be encouraged and further facilitated. This project is consequently intended to renovate, change and adapt where necessary and retain and reuse where possible. Overall, the project deals with issues identified at both an urban and individual unit scale. The buildings were seen as in need of a 'new aesthetic image'; the desirability of unifying elements that had been modified over the years by residents themselves (such as the jalousies and balconies) was identified; and the reorganization of green areas and other public spaces was seen as essential – including car parks which understandably featured less prominently in the original designs. More specifically, this project deals with the issues of accessibility and the potential of the roof spaces for new developments and public spaces as key features.

The issue of accessibility is particularly problematic for the elderly who now represent a large proportion of the population, in complete contrast to the original make-up of the neighbourhood when first built. For this reason the connection points between access routes and pedestrian walkways, as well as the squares, are altered and rationalized. Additionally, new 'vertical communication hubs' are proposed to improve access to the existing units and, in turn, to the roof spaces which are at present inaccessible but feature heavily in this proposal.

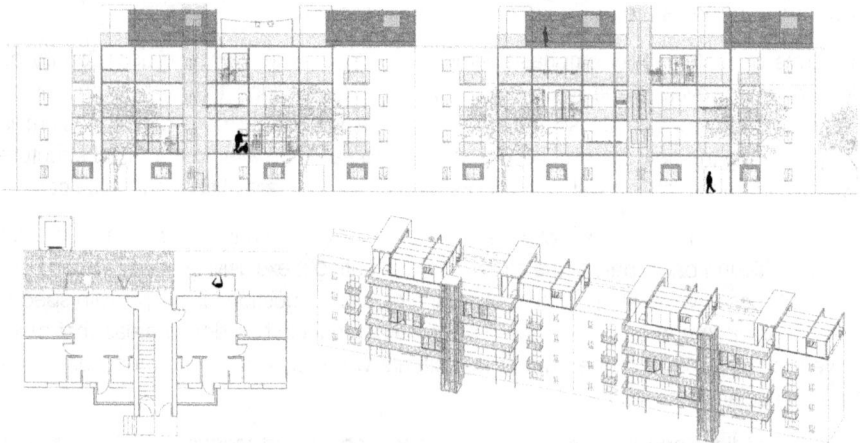

Figure 4. New façade. Typical plan (renovated house). Overall view.

The roofs of the blocks are to be 'colonised' and used as private and communal areas through the incorporation of temporary housing and resident facilities such as clothes-line areas. A series of houses made of lightweight and recycled materials are to be implanted directly onto the roof. It is a system that reduces the costs of labour and materials and meets certain basic sustainability requirements. These modules are 46 m^2 and consist of a living room, kitchen, terrace, bedroom, and bathroom. They are also flexible with, for example, the possibility of moving the bathroom and adding one more room near the terrace. It is envisaged that the apartments will be rented to young people and care workers who help the area's elderly population.

GUYA BERTELLI

Politecnico di Milano

SCHOOL OF ARCHITECTURE AND SOCIETY

The Politecnico di Milano is a public university with a science and technology focus. It was founded 1863 and in 1987 opened additional campuses in Como, Lecco, Cremona, Mantova and Piacenza. It incorporates engineering, architecture, urban planning and design into its portfolio. The Piacenza Campus was founded in 1997, and hosts the three-year course, Bachelor in Environmental Architecture, as well as the Master's in Sustainable Architecture and Landscape Design, established in 2007. Issues dealt with on the programme include environmental sciences and technologies, and sustainable regeneration and urbanism. It offers a combined theoretical, methodological and technical-constructional approach.

The work on housing as expressed in the projects collated in this chapter are drawn from the design studio 'Multi-Scale Architecture and Urban Design' and concludes work from Italy and work carried out in conjunction with the Universidad de Sevilla in the neighbourhood of La Virgen del Carmen. It is premised on the need to provide affordable, healthy and sustainable dwellings as an integral part of broader regeneration of residential neighbourhoods. The projects are located in several countries in which the question of housing is seen as 'critical' for different reasons. They are based on the *process* of transforming existing neighbourhoods and buildings, and consequently emphasis is placed on practices of reuse, recycling and the regeneration of existing urban landscapes and the retrofit of existing buildings.

Students have been encouraged to rethink the 'product' of the house, but also the 'act of inhabiting' it. They have done this at the scale of the room, individual buildings and the urban intervention. As a result, projects engage landscape architecture, planning, architecture, public space design and the study of contemporary aesthetic scenarios. The common denominator in this multi-faceted approach is 'multidisciplinary practice'. Dealing with the question of housing in this way means some of the projects deal with issues of planning prevision, others address community empowerment, and some proposals develop alternative forms of space planning – such as an *urban foyer*. In other cases, technological fixes, new forms of construction and alternative models are used and sought. Examples include the employment of resilient materials, easily transportable 'kit-of parts buildings' and hybrid typologies that combine the small office and the home etc. The projects collated here were coordinated by Martina Sogni with Giuliana Bonifati.

Project A: Creative Housing. Diaphragm as a Tool Generating New Spaces

Anna Chiari, Ana Laisa Chiroli, Irene Manzini Ceinar, Aigesha Ospanova

Today, the neighbourhood of Virgen del Carmen feels like an isolated enclave in the city of Seville. It falls into the category of projects known in Spain as *polìgonos* and has a mono-functional residential character. The goal of this project is to integrate the neighbourhood with its surrounding context through two paths. The first of these paths relates to agriculture and establishes a direct relationship between Virgen del Carmen and Charco de la Pava – it is a path that interacts with towers, both supporting native flora and fauna (*Barriadas Verdes*). The second is a 'cultural path' – a succession of creative spaces connected with the Conservatorio Público Elemental de Música and the Colegio Publico de San Jose de Calasanz. It is intended to completely change the meaning of the areas public space (*Barriadas Creativas*).

The idea of memory is represented in the project through maintaining the existing buildings and redefining a new border that spreads out towards the river and, at the same time, offers protection from the street (*Barriadas Seguras*). The project thus aims at maintaining the existing structure to preserve the identity of the place, whilst also giving a new meaning to its spaces. In particular, it tries to preserve the idea of the neighbourhood: a community with a defined border and spaces of internal relations operative at the human scale.

Key to the project is the design of a filter space between the totally private residential areas and the public road – seen as *a diaphragm* that generates a sequence of spaces that interact with the 'housing'. This diaphragm, made of corten steel, spreads along the cultural path in different forms – sometimes being a sign on the ground, at others rising up to be benches. When appearing between buildings generating public spaces on the ground and first floors it creates public space. These become creative spaces: theatres, exhibition spaces, sharing spaces, co-working spaces, and interactive spaces. It changes the surroundings of the houses in the area radically.

Next to these are apartments (*Vivienda Hìbridas*). Designed to be flexible, they can accommodate artists and other residents. They are integrated with creative spaces

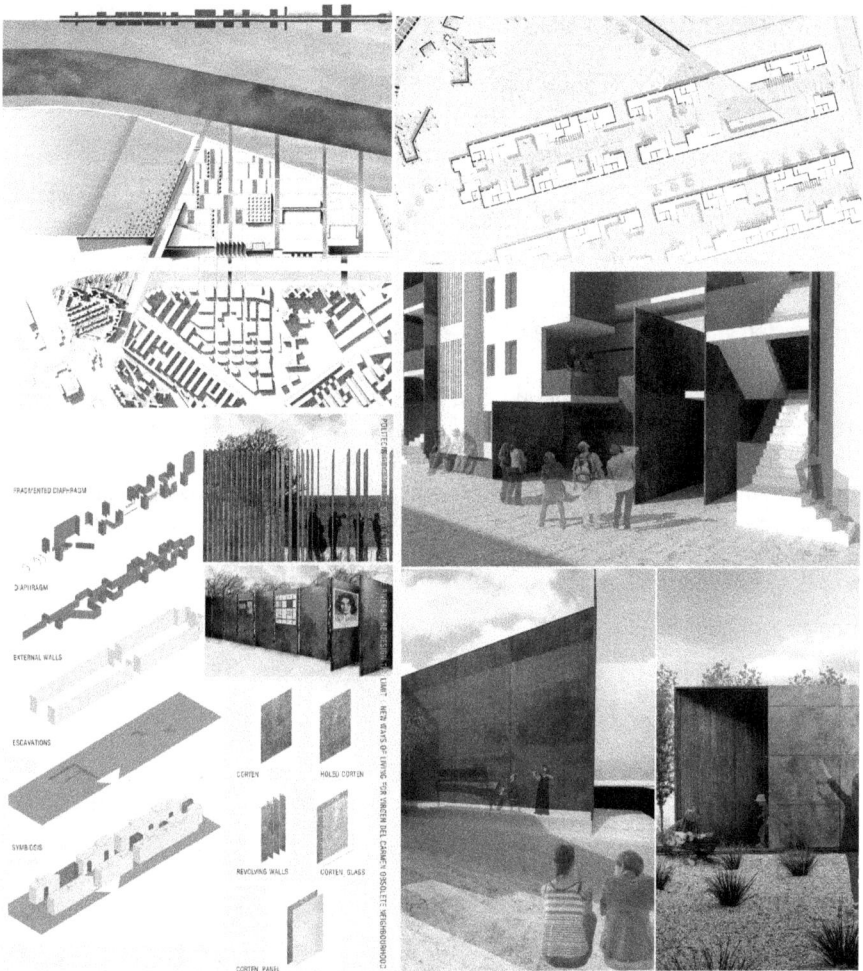

Figure 1. Site concept. Floor plans. Exploded concept axonometric. Visual perspectives

that, in most cases, result in houses connected directly to an exhibition gallery or private workspaces (*Viviendas en Comunidad*). They are spaces that can be private most of the time, but opened out to be public exhibition spaces at others (*Viviendas Flexibles*). Other apartments are seen as duplexes or triplexes, with private roof spaces that can be ateliers and/or secret gardens (*Viviendas Diversas*).

Project B: Re-Naturalization of Milan

Marina Di Pumpo, Federica Farè, Martina Gasparoli, Sara Grassi, Giorgia Zocchi

The reading of the city in this project provides macro and micro fragments of vacant courts and gardens along the historical axis *Corso Sempione* in the contemporary city of Milan. The strategy employed in the design is a *fil rouge* that brings a discontinuous sequence of built-up and open spaces which includes residential blocks that will improve the living conditions and suitability of the housing in the area.

The masterplan of *Piazza Firenze* is the key element in this initiative to improve housing / living conditions. It was born from the concept of folding that allows different levels to become detached from the ground. It is divided into four functional areas connected through public open spaces. The first area is occupied by a series of greenhouses, the second by a covered market, the third by a co-working space, and the fourth is an exhibition place. The public space is accessible through a walkway that runs through the area to the social housing at one end. The objective is to ensure a vibrant and sustainable urban context for modern living.

Figure 2. Area plan. Site plan. Urban concepts. Floor plan. Elevations and sections

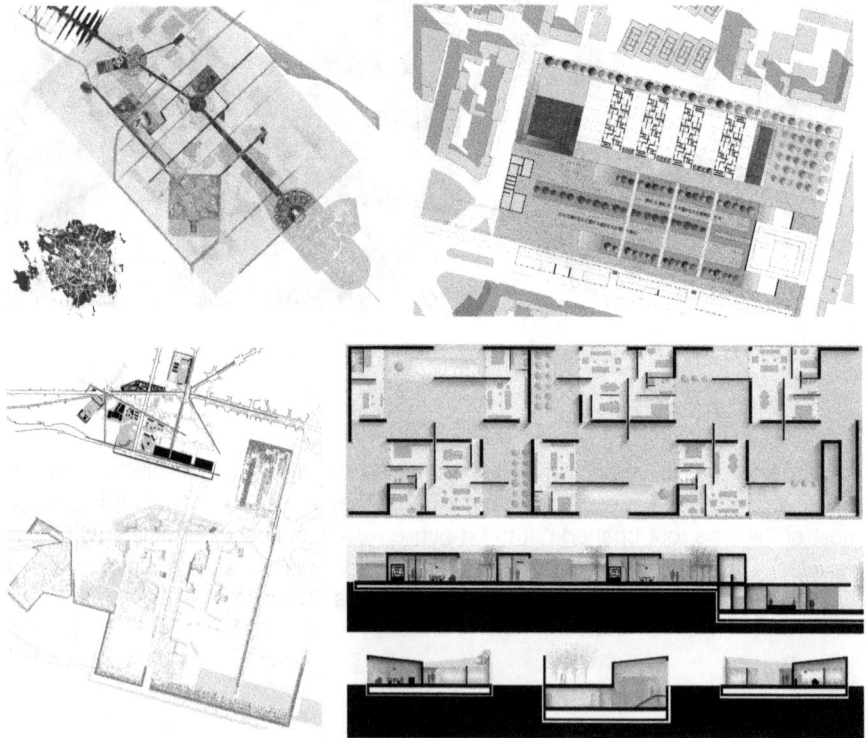

Four separate residential buildings are connected underground by a series of collective services and spaces, such as a gym, children's play areas, and common laundries. The interiors of the housing units themselves are integrated with the external space, producing a hybrid space. In the design of these homes, particular attention has been paid to the architectural details with, for example, the interpenetration and the nodes between surfaces using different materials that allow an interesting façade composition to be formed. The central point behind the proposal, is that for quality housing, one has to consider the urban context, the facilities required and desired by modern residents and the need for common spaces to facilitate community life.

Project C: Through the River. The Spaces In-Between, Gate of Seville

Iman Gerveh, Nguyen Anh Tuan, Nazila Salehia, Vulov Mihail, Vuong Thuy Duong

There has always been an attraction to Seville since its Roman origin years ago, one that grows stronger today, with the layers of architecture showing the combined influences of two thousand years of artisan work. The city itself is an *urban palimpsest*. From here comes the suffocating confrontation between old and new, the need to change, the need of unchanged perception, the urge to grow, and the reality of *shrinking cities*. This project is situated on the edge the city near the flow of Guadalquivir River and is composed of residual spaces on the river bank and the social housing area named Virgen del Carmen.

Naturally, the perception of *rhythm* and *time* became an inspiration and led our design thinking to the well-known theories of Henri Lefebvre; *'The city is constructed by overlapping and interacting rhythms, to become one single flow that is city life'*. It was not only a very powerful metaphor, but also had a strong visual impact on the design. Using landform and green stripes as the background, the city and nature can both be said to reach out to each other. Where these contradicting elements meet the concept of *in-between* is introduced through subtle, sensible interventions that make a series of transversal, open spaces.

The centre point of the urban plan is the diagonal axis that connects both sides of the river and re-discovers the human traces on one bank, and the landscape on the other. This axis is continued as a creative garden that leads straight to the re-generated social housing area, which the project includes in its art-and-action process.

The concept for the social housing site is to keep the familiar residential towers surrounding the site, but then to confront them with emotionally charged dramatic 'events'. A water mirror is created on the ground floor of specific low-rise inner buildings; walls are dismantled and replaced by partitions, surfaces, and walkable routes that lead through several spaces; and activities are placed on top of the 'water mirror'.

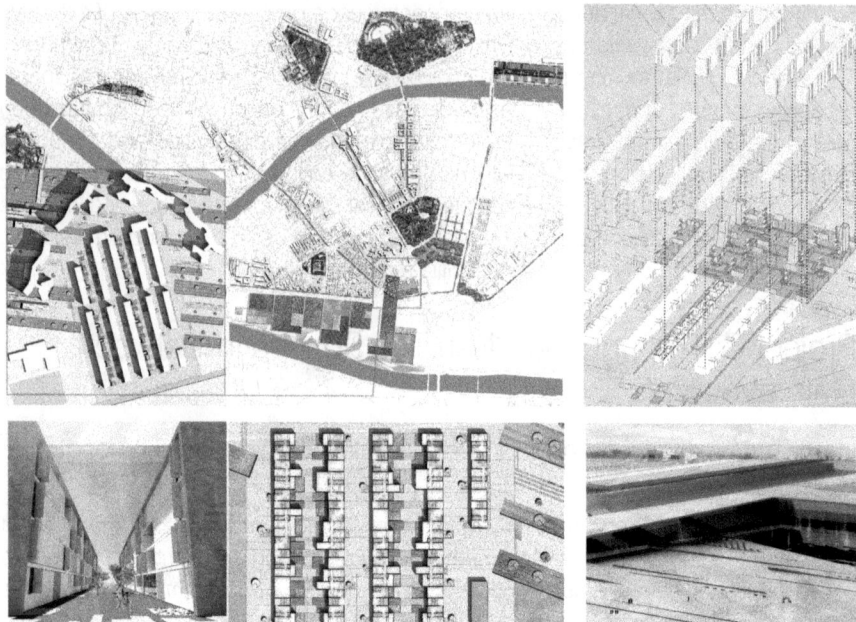

Figure 3. Site plan. Axonometric. Perspective and plan. Aerial perspective.

The mirror is the heart of this neighbourhood. From this heart grows the *aortas* and lesser *blood veins* – metaphors that flow from a hierarchy of water streams that circulate to the other side of the neighbourhood, enhancing the tranquil feeling of peace and quietness of the place. Where these small streams connect with the residential blocks small communal spaces are inserted and treated with a surface pattern inspired by the famous Alcazar water garden.

The new intervention is distinguished from the existing façade by a small gap between them. Spaces inside the apartment are shaped by their own use through partitions that also function as furniture. There is a minimum use of doors and diffused light and ventilation. The spaces define themselves. Less is more.

Project D: Special Symbiosis and Seasonal Dwelling. Exploring the Opportunities of Transformable Living Space.

Lida Ansari, Behdad Bolouhar, Ana Maria Estrada, Khaled Kaddouh, Krasimir Krumov, Yosif Histrov, Ivanka Ivanova, Ralitsa Yordanova, Cesar Mauricio Sanchez, Mihails Zuravlovs

Seville is famous for its architectural richness but the recent economic crisis has had a very negative impact on the city, with particular implications being felt in its housing.

The area examined in this project, Virgen Del Carmen, is in a state of obsolescence and not able to offer residents what they need for contemporary life. This project attempts to deal with these deficiencies from an urban and sociological point of view. Virgen Del Carmen is an urban enclave detached from the city. People complain they do not feel secure. Houses do not accommodate the diversity of the ways people live, and the common external spaces are empty and abandoned. The project aims to provide a new architectural and social environment by upgrading these existing dwellings and open spaces.

At the urban scale, the project develops active relationships with the consolidated city, whilst at the architectural scale, it creates an interactive space in which the public and private work in symbiosis. The project sees dwellings as places in which people can work and live at the same time. It proposes a hybrid typology for the housing aimed at providing a flexible habitat. The units are thus designed to allow the easy rearrangement of architectural components through the use of moving walls and service elements. During the day, residents can reduce the sleeping area and increase the living space. This increased living space can also be used as working space. This space in turn is linked to an urban foyer and placed between the apartments in which a co-working space is located. The expected effect is the regeneration of the buildings, but also the giving of new meaning to the entire area and its public spaces.

Figure 4. Urban site plan. Plans and visual perspectives. Façade – day and night. Interior view.

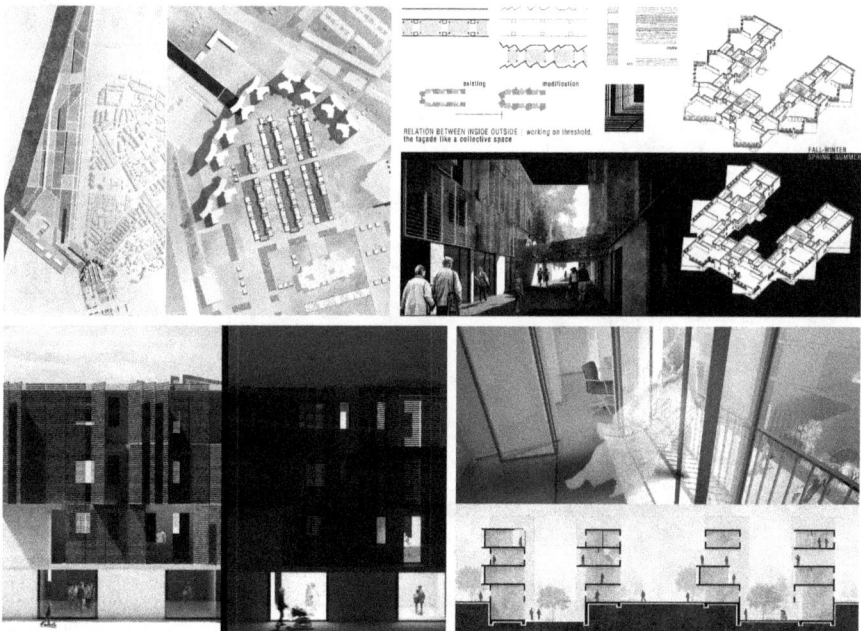

Project E: Housing the Future. Alternative Approaches for Tomorrow

Lida Ansari, Behdad Bolouhar, Ana Maria Estrada, Xavier Mendez,
Fernanda Ordoñes, Shenona Rodrigues, Cesar Mauricio Sanchez

The Virgen del Carmen site is located on the edge of Seville, next to the Guadalquivir River in the Triana neighbourhood. It is comprised of residential apartments for families, but it lacks collective spaces. It was only constructed during the 1960s, but today many of its buildings are unoccupied. Over the years they have increasingly failed to meet the needs of changing users and, as a result, many people have opted to move out. Today, the social housing programme of the city has an important role to play in the successful and sustainable regeneration of the area. However, given the financial crisis, there is very limited expenditure possible. In this context we as architects have a social responsibility to bear.

Figure 5. The existing site. Proposed site plan. Axonometric plans and proposed exterior.

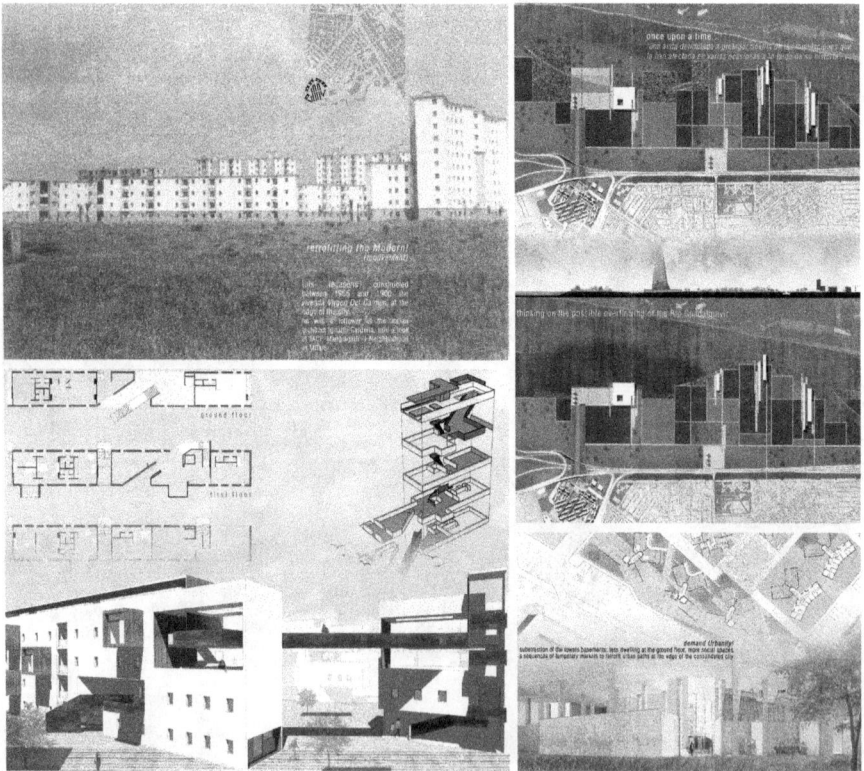

The design strategy employed here tries to revive the connection of the peripheral neighbourhood to the city of Seville and its forgotten landscape alongside the river. For this reason the neighbourhood and the landscaped areas nearby are bridged so as to turn the site into a hinge, and in the process, bring about urban regeneration. The central space of the neighbourhood is opened up to create a site for social interaction, around which are collective services that create flux and movement.

As for its approach to the housing units, this project focuses on the interiors, redefining the boundary between public and private spaces, and turning them into semi-public or semi-private spaces. For example, selected staircase cores were linked to the rejuvenated landscape and elevated public spaces were created on the buildings' roofs, thus livening up the space and creating a further positive flux of movement through the neighbourhood. These elevated public spaces were in keeping with the social culture of Seville, where terraces are often used to enjoy its Mediterranean climate.

The inhabitants of the apartments are given the flexibility to create or modify their own space. This is achieved by providing a service core inside that frees up the rest of the space for different uses by employing a module of moveable panels. As a result, a 2-bedroom apartment can be adapted to a 3-bedroom one, and possibly even a 1-bedroom apartment. This DIY approach allows growing families to adapt the house as per their needs and requirements over the years, thus making it a sustainable housing solution for their future.

GARY SANDS

Wayne State University

DEPARTMENT OF URBAN STUDIES AND PLANNING IN THE COLLEGE OF LIBERAL ARTS AND SCIENCES WAYNE STATE UNIVERSITY

Founded in 1868, Wayne State University is a nationally recognized metropolitan research institution offering more than 370 academic programmes through 13 schools and colleges to nearly 28,000 students. Wayne State's main campus in Midtown Detroit comprises 100 buildings situated over 200 acres; its six extension centres offer higher education to students throughout Southeast Michigan. It is a nationally recognized urban centre of excellence in research. It is dedicated to preparing students to excel by combining the academic excellence of a major research university with the practical experience of an institution that by its history, location, and diversity represents a microcosm of the world we live in. The University's vision is to become the model public research university engaged in the urban community.

The Master of Urban Planning (MUP) programme is located in the Department of Urban Studies and Planning in the College of Liberal Arts and Sciences. It offers a professionally oriented degree that focuses on preparation of planners who will be employed primarily by local governments, planning consultants, and community-based organizations. Students have the opportunity to specialize in Housing and Community Development, Urban Economic Development, or Managing Metropolitan Growth. The specialization in Housing and Community Development provides students with an understanding of theory and practice in urban development, particularly physical development in neighbourhoods. It requires students to address both housing and its community context (as opposed to focusing more narrowly on either housing or neighbourhoods alone). While the principles and skills included have broad applicability, course content emphasizes metropolitan areas and pays particular attention to conditions, policies, and strategies central to the challenge of strengthening disadvantaged urban core communities.

The Detroit metropolitan area provides an outstanding laboratory for the study of these issues and processes. The economic and demographic restructuring of Detroit has led to conditions that are prototypical of older central cities and mature suburbs. At the same time, portions of the region continue to experience growth and development with the attendant problems of planning and management. This broad range of existing conditions provides students with the opportunity to gain experience in all facets of the housing and community development process.

The WSU Urban Planning faculty is actively engaged in policy-focused research that seeks to improve public policy related to housing, neighbourhoods, and communities. This engagement ranges from basic research on how urban systems and markets function, to more narrowly focused programme evaluations. WSU Urban Planning students are engaged with the community through both individual and group projects. As part of their capstone course, student teams provide analyses and projects to meet the needs of their community based organization clients. Capstone reports have received national and statewide recognition. The projects collected here are all examples of this approach.

Project A: City of Change – Documenting the Condition of Detroit's Housing Stock from 2009 to 2014

Noah Urban

Over the past fifteen years the City of Detroit has been swept up in international conversations for reasons both positive and negative. Whether being panned for an oft-cited population decline of 25 percent between 2000 and 2010, or being hailed as America's great comeback city, the years since 2000 have seen a surge in discussions about this extremely complex metropolis. This diversity of residential communities means that, even in a city facing as many challenges as Detroit, there are fascinating trends that can be teased out, and neighbourhoods across the street from each other may have seen very different fates. Here we will examine one particular indicator – Average Residential Structure Condition – to illuminate how the physical condition and character of Detroit's neighbourhoods has changed over the past five years.

This analysis is based on information from two large-scale data collection efforts – the 2009 Detroit Residential Parcel Survey (DRPS), and the 2013–14 Motor City Mapping Survey (MCM). Both surveys focused on collecting condition information on properties in the city (for structures, DRPS focused only on 1–4 unit residential buildings, while MCM surveyed all structures in Detroit). It is possible to compare the structural condition data for about 840 Census block groups in the City of Detroit (out of roughly 880) at two points in time – 2009 and 2014.

Every structure surveyed was assigned a value from 1 to 4, with 1 indicating the best possible condition. For each block group, a weighted average was created by summing condition values for all residential structures in the block group and then dividing the total by the total number of residential structures in the block group. Values closer to 1 indicate stronger average condition, while a value closer to 2 (or more) indicates an area with much poorer structural condition. The data were separated into quartiles and mapped.

Average Residential Structure Condition in 2009

In general, the condition of residential structures appears to be related to their age. Many of the block groups with the strongest average condition ratings were found at the outer edges of the city, while those with the poorest quality housing stock were located in older neighbourhoods near the core of the city. The Brightmoor neighbourhood in northwest Detroit stands out as a pocket of blight among areas that are generally in better condition. The poor initial construction quality of the housing in this area makes it similar to the older areas near the city centre. With limited exceptions, the area south of Interstate 94 included very few block groups in the highest two quartiles.

There was typically a gradual transition between the average condition ratings in adjacent neighbourhoods. That is, neighbourhoods in the top quartile were typically bordered by neighbourhoods in the first or second categories. There were, however, a few instances where simply crossing the street can result in a significant change in average housing condition.

Average Residential Structure Condition in 2014, Compared to 2009

The average condition rating for each of the block groups in 2014 is shown in the central image of Figure 1. While the overall geographic distributions of good and poor quality housing are similar to 2009, there are some important differences. Southwest Detroit has seen a decline in housing condition, and the concentrations of blight that were evident in northwest and northeast Detroit seem to be spreading. The neighbourhoods near the intersection of M-39 and M-5 are no longer solidly in the top quartile; similar declines can be seen on the Far East Side.

When the 2014 condition ratings are mapped using the quartiles defined by the 2009 data, the decline in average housing quality is evident (Figure 2). The top two quartiles contained a net total of 79 fewer block groups, a decrease of nearly 19 percent. The growth in the quartile with the lowest average condition – an increase of 70 block groups – is particularly concerning, and indicates that an increasing number of neighbourhoods across the city may be entering steeper spirals of structural decline.

Absolute Changes in Residential Condition from 2009 to 2014

The two surveys recorded a small overall decline in the average residential condition rating for the city of Detroit from an average rating of 1.23 in 2009 to 1.27 in 2014. As shown in far right image of Figure 1, more than 500 block groups had declines

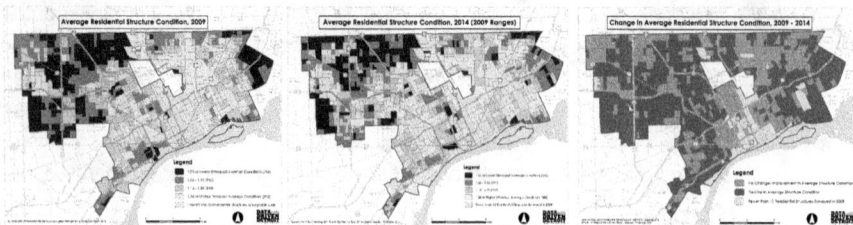

Figure 1. Left: Average residential structure condition, 2009. Middle: Average residential structure condition, 2014. Right: Change in average residential structure conditions.

Average Condition Rating	Number of Block Groups		
	2009	2014	Change
1.05 or lower (strongest)	210	150	-60
1.06-1.15	210	191	-19
1.16-1.35	210	219	+9
1.36 or higher (weakest)	210	280	+70

Figure 2: Change in residential structure condition

in average condition, while 315 saw an improvement or no change. Much of the improvement occurred on the East Side, including some neighbourhoods with the poorest structural condition ratings in 2009. Considering the relatively low starting point for many of these neighbourhoods, it is likely that much of the observed increase is due to demolition of blighted structures, rather than as a result of new construction or rehabilitation.

In summary then, although five years is a relatively short time in the life of a city, Detroit has seen a noticeable decline in the average condition of its housing stock since 2009. The areas of the better quality housing are shrinking, while the pockets of blight are growing. Where average structural condition ratings have shown improvement, this appears to have most often been the result of the demolition of the poorest-condition homes. Detroit's housing recovery is still far from a certainty.

Project B: Crime and Vacant, Open, and Dangerous Housing

Erica L. Raleigh

Detroit has experienced a decline of population, households, and jobs by half or more over the last five decades. As fewer residents pay lower taxes on properties that have declined in value, city government has struggled to maintain service levels with decreasing revenue; thousands of vacant structures became the visible manifestation of this ongoing process. Anecdotal evidence points to abandoned properties as magnets for criminal activity, but the assumption has not been rigorously tested. This analysis asks, are crimes more prevalent in proximity to vacant, open, and dangerous structures (VODs), all else being equal? Is there a significant positive relationship between the number of VODs on a block in a given quarter and the number of crimes occurring on that block in the following quarter? Is there a particular category of crime that is more highly related to the prevalence of VODs than others?

This relationship is explored using point data from the Detroit Police Department on the incidence of reported crimes, and parcel level data on housing from the Detroit Residential Parcel Survey (DRPS). The number and rate of violent and property crimes are considered below. The left and middle images of Figure 3 show the geographic distribution of violent and property crimes, respectively, for the first quarter of 2010. The majority of blocks recorded no violent crimes in this period; only a small number had a rate of more than 1,000 crimes per 10,000 residents.

Data on housing vacancy and condition were obtained from the 2009 DRPS. Three different conditions were used here: vacant but habitable housing; vacant, open, and dangerous (including fire damaged) housing; and vacant residential lots. The right hand image of Figure 3 shows the distribution of VOD residential properties. Comparisons of these three figures indicate there is indeed a great deal of overlap between VOD residential structures and crime rates. A regression analysis was employed to provide a more precise measurement of the relationships between crime and VOD housing. In addition to crime and housing vacancy statistics, a number of other demographic and socioeconomic variables were tested. A spatial lag model is used to account for probable spillover effects of both crime and VODs. The model is represented by the following equation:

$$C_{yit} = \beta_0 VOD_{it-1} + \beta_1 X_i + vw_i VOD_{it-1} + \rho w_i C_{yit} + \epsilon_i$$

Where C is the number or rate of crime type y on a given block i at time t, $\beta_0 VOD_{it-1}$ is the term for the independent VOD predictor variable, $\beta_1 X_i$ is the term representing the independent neighborhood characteristics, $vw_i VOD_{it-1}$ is the spatially lagged term for the independent predictor variable, $\rho w_i C_{yit}$ is the spatially lagged term for the dependent variable, and ϵ_i is the independent error term. There is a positive and highly significant correlation between violent crimes and the presence of VOD housing. The relationships with the spatially lagged variables were not significant, however.

Figure 3 Left: Geographic distribution of violent crimes. First quarter of 2010; Middle: Geographic distribution of property crimes. First quarter of 2010. Right: Distribution of vacant, open, and dangerous structures, 2009.

Interestingly, the percent of residential parcels that are vacant lots shows significant *negative* correlation with nearly all crime types, although the expectation was that this correlation would be positive. There was no significant correlation between vacant housing units and crime or crime rates.

Three other variables emerged as the most consistently related to all types of crime: percent of housing units that are renter occupied, number of liquor licences in the block, and population density. The first two are significantly positively correlated with crime, while the latter is significantly negatively correlated. These findings suggest other potential crime reduction strategies. Zoning changes that restrict or reduce the number of liquor vendors would be a relatively simple approach to reducing crime rates. While reductions in rental housing occupancy might have similar beneficial effects, implementation of such strategies is more problematic. Increasing homeownership is likely to require substantial increases in both household incomes and the availability of mortgage credit. (See other project reports in this chapter.)

Increasing population density is not likely to have a noticeable positive impact on public safety, however. Higher density neighbourhoods may have an effect on other objectives, such as transit planning and economic development, but would not be an effective strategy for combating crime. The significant negative correlation demonstrated between percent of parcels that are vacant lots and most types of crime suggests that demolishing VODs is another potential strategy for reducing crime rates; statistically, for every one-percentage-point decrease in VOD structures, crime incidents could decrease by between 50 and 200 offences per 10,000 residents, depending on crime type. Overall, these findings highlight the importance of reexamining theory as new data, technology, and research findings become available. Results shown here suggest that several neighbourhood characteristics typically associated with high crime rates may not be the most relevant attributes contributing to the occurrence of crime. Eliminating vacant, open, and dangerous buildings, either by demolishing them, or simply securing them from trespass, could contribute to a reduction in criminal activity.

Project C: Mortgage Origination in Detroit

Sylvia Tatman-Burruss

The availability of mortgage finance is key to the functioning of the American housing market. In 2013, 65.4 percent of US homeowners (43.1 percent of all households) had a mortgage. The situation is considerably different in Detroit. The homeownership rate in Detroit is lower than the national average – 48.0 percent compared to 65.8 percent – and just 55.3 percent of Detroit homeowners have a mortgage. The number of mortgages originated in Detroit fell from 11,715 in 2004, to just 378 in 2010, a decline of more than 97 percent (Ding, 2012).

Detroit's mortgage market during the middle years of the last decade included a large proportion of subprime loans, which were often the result of predatory lending practices. Such loans were inherently high risk and led to the subsequent spate of defaults, foreclosures, and short sales. With the decline in subprime lending activity, total mortgage originations in Detroit have decreased. When considering origination of mortgage loans, institutional lenders evaluate characteristics of the borrower, the home, and the surrounding neighbourhood. *Credit history* and the resulting *credit score* is a determining factor for origination. In addition, if the *debt to income ratio* is too high, the perceived risk of loan default is seen as too great.

In considering whether to originate a mortgage and the amount of the mortgage, the lender considers the collateral, that is, the property to be mortgaged. The physical condition of the home is a major factor in mortgage originations. Detroit has an 'inspection on sale' ordinance, which requires a local code inspection when a home is sold. Code violations must be corrected by the seller or the purchaser before the sale can be completed. Institutional lenders are prohibited from offering a mortgage in an amount greater than the market value of the property, as determined by an independent appraisal. Large numbers of Detroit properties have been foreclosed and returned to the market by the lender. In Detroit, the number of Real Estate Owned (REO) property sales has regularly exceeded traditional market sales since 2008 (right hand image of Figure 4). These properties are often sold at well below market prices, putting downward pressure on property values throughout the neighbourhood. Because distressed sales cannot be used by appraisers to establish market value, mortgage financed home purchases in Detroit remain at low levels (Ding, 2014).

How have these factors played out in the Detroit housing market in recent years? All regulated financial institutions are required by the Home Mortgage Disclosure Act to report mortgage application information (aggregated by Census tract). Left hand image of Figure 5 illustrates the extent to which the City of Detroit is disadvantaged in terms of mortgage originations. In part, mortgages are not being originated because Detroit properties generate relatively few applications; the suburban application rate is almost ten times that of Detroit. Moreover, suburban applications were more than twice as likely to be approved as were Detroit applications. The most common reason for denials, applicant credit history, was roughly comparable in city and suburbs, 26

Precipitous Decline in Inflow of Mortgage Credit
Home Purchase Mortgage Originations (ff in 2004 set as 100%)

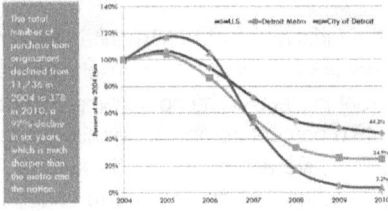

Dominance of Distressed Sales since 2008
Housing Sales in City of Detroit, 2005-Q22010

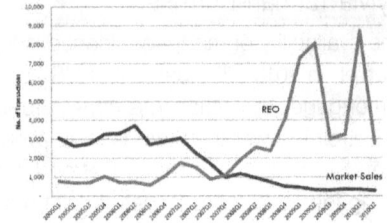

Figure 4. Left: Decline of mortgage credit, Detroit and surrounding region. Right: Distressed sales since 2008. Mortgage origination activity.

	Detroit	Suburbs
Applications	4,249	210,760
Rate/1,000	16.6	150.7
Originations	1,536	149,959
Percent	36%	71%
Denials	1,874	34,909
Percent	44%	17%

	Detroit		Suburbs	
	African-American	White	African-American	White
Applications	2,823	845	17,069	166,366
Denied	47%	30%	26%	15%
Originated	34%	51%	58%	72%

Figure 5. Left: Detroit area mortgage applications, Source: Home Mortgage Disclosure Act, 2009-2013. Right: Detroit mortgage applications and actions, by race, Source: Home Mortgage Disclosure Act, 2009–2013.

percent and 23 percent, respectively. But denials because of problems with collateral (typically as a result of low appraisals, lack of comparable sales, or condition of the property) were more prevalent in city than the suburbs, 26 percent compared to 19 percent. When controlling only for income and loan amount, an applicant is 73 percent less likely to obtain a mortgage in the City of Detroit than in the surrounding suburbs.

Although Fair Housing regulations prohibit the use of race in making mortgage origination decisions, African-American applicants are much more likely to be denied than are white applicants (right hand image, Figure 5). While these figures are suggestive, there is insufficient information available to conclude that there is bias in the mortgage origination process in the Detroit area.

As southeast Michigan and the country recover from the mortgage crisis of 2009, far fewer mortgages have been made in Detroit than in its suburbs. Origination rates in the suburbs have returned to pre-crisis levels, but remain low in the City of Detroit. The data reviewed here, as well as by experts in the field, suggest that Detroit's biggest issues are low appraisals due to a lack of comparable sales in Detroit, and the continuing dominance of distressed sales. This leaves the mortgage market in Detroit in need of some kind of incentive mechanism or gap-financing option to facilitate mortgage originations. Data also show that African-Americans are less likely than white applicants to get a mortgage in either city or suburbs. More sophisticated analysis and more variables are needed to gain a better understanding of this phenomenon.

Project D: Impacts of the Neighborhood Stabilization Program on Housing Values in Genesee County Michigan

Anna Pinter

Between 2008 and 2011, the United States government pumped almost $7 billion into the economy through the Neighborhood Stabilization Program (NSP). This was done in an attempt to arrest decline of neighbourhoods across the U.S. after the number of foreclosures increased by almost one million (81%) from 2006 to 2007. Grant awards were provided to all 50 states and to over 250 counties and cities throughout the nation. Yet, there has been little research done on whether NSP funding was successful at stabilizing property values in target areas where funding was expended, or if the funds provided a positive return on investment.

The foreclosure crisis contributed to accelerating neighbourhood decline in Genesee County, Michigan. Even outside of the hard hit city of Flint, the county saw a sharp decline in its residential tax base. Genesee County received $3.1 million NSP funding that it used to acquire and rehabilitate 31 foreclosed single-family homes and demolish 28 properties in NSP1 target areas.

How can the impact of housing and community development investments, such as the NSP, on neighbourhood change best be measured? The *adjusted interrupted time series* (AITS) model allows for the comparison of pre- and post-intervention observations between target and control areas, while controlling for coincident County-wide trends (Galster, Tatian and Accordino, 2006). Ideally, neighbourhood input and outcome indicators should be measured frequently, over an extended period before and after the intervention, and at a small geographic scale to assess impacts. 'Home sale prices are well known to capitalize many changes in the underlying desirability of neighbourhoods, and thus represent a powerful summary measure of neighbourhood trajectory' (Galster, Tatian and Accordino, 2006).

The AITS model was employed to find the difference between the value of NSP1 sales (a sale in a NSP1 target area, either pre- or post-intervention) and NSP1post sales (a sale in a NSP1 target area, post-intervention only). These results were then compared to the difference between the value of Control sales (a sale in one of the control areas, either pre- or post-intervention) and ControlNSP1post sales (a sale in one of the control areas, post-intervention only).

A semi-log linear regression was used to estimate that the average sales price in NSP1 target areas was 12.3 percentage points less than the County through the first quarter of 2010, the date of intervention. The average sales price in NSP1 target areas post-intervention (after the second quarter of 2010) was 16.9 percentage points less than the County overall. Thus, the average sales price of a home in NSP1 target areas decreased by an additional 4.6 percentage points after the intervention. However, in order to determine the impact of the intervention, these results must be compared to control areas. The pre-intervention control areas were equal to the County level, or zero difference. The average sales price in the control areas post-intervention dropped to 16.2 percentage points lower than the County average. Therefore, the average sales price of homes in control areas dropped by 16.2 percentage points pre-intervention to post-intervention.

When comparing NSP1 target areas to the control areas, the NSP1 areas fared better by 11.6 percentage points. This provides evidence that Genesee County's NSP did have a positive impact on sales prices in target areas; it moderated the decline in prices compared to what would have been expected. (See Figure 6 for a visual comparison between NSP1 target areas and the control areas).

Based on these results, the question becomes to what extent was there was a positive return on the $3.1 million NSP investment? Was this difference of 11.6 percentage points enough to justify the investment? For the County, the return on this investment can be measured by the impact on property taxes, which was calculated as follows:

- Actual average sales price with intervention: $57,204

- Estimated average sales price without intervention: $50,568

- Average increase in property values: $57,204 – $50,568 = $6,636

- Times number of homes: $6,636 * 8909 = $59,113,488

- Net property tax on increment: $59,113,488 – investment of $3,139,700 * tax rate = $1,436,029

- Divide the County's investment by the incremental tax revenue: $3,139,700/$1,436,029 = 2.19 year payback period.

These calculations indicate that the NSP1 investment was paid back through increased property taxes in NSP1 target areas (actually, a reduction in the decline of property

Figure 6. Left: Home mortgage foreclosures in the United States. Middle: Residential property value trends, suburban Genesee County. Source: Michigan Department of Treasury. Right: Percent difference from baseline value – NSP1 only and control. Source: Realty Trac.

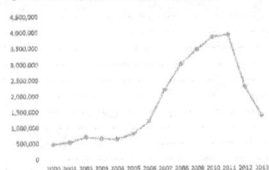

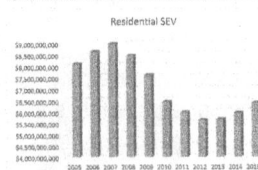

values) in just over two years. While NSP funding cannot claim to have arrested decline and turned a declining market around, the research indicates that the intervention slowed the decline of these neighbourhoods and provided a quick return on investment. Without NSP investment in the NSP1 target areas, sales prices would have fallen further, to levels equal to the control areas. That decline in value would have created an even larger reduction in property tax revenues and created a larger strain on local governments relying on property taxes to provide basic services to residents.

KATHRIN-GOLDA PONGRATZ AND MICHAEL PETEREK

Frankfurt University of Applied Sciences

URBAN AGGLOMERATIONS – MASTER PROGRAMME

Frankfurt University of Applied Sciences (FRA-UAS) is an institution of higher education for about 12,000 students that systematically combines scientific approaches with practical applications. Within its four faculties – Architecture, Civil Engineering, Geomatics; Computer Science and Engineering; Business and Law; Health and Social Work – it offers more than 70 study courses. The Master Programme 'Urban Agglomerations' (MSc) is based on an interdisciplinary approach and an international orientation, addressing graduates from the different fields of architecture, urban planning, landscape planning, civil engineering, real estate, urban geography, and other planning-related disciplines.

The issues addressed in the programme are related to the most pressing challenges of urban agglomerations today. They include urban development, land management, housing, environmental conditions, mobility and transportation, socio-economic differentiation, segregation and migration processes, as well as urban and regional governance. They are dealt with from a global and intercultural perspective, comparing and exchanging experiences and practices of European urban agglomerations with recent developments in highly dynamic city-regions and mega-cities worldwide. Underlying its approach is the connection of theory to practice.

The topic of housing is central to a series of theoretical and practical study units in the master's programme which deals with global urbanizations processes, current developments, manifestations, and typologies of both formal and informal settlements in different social, cultural, and economic contexts. Social developments as well as segregation, marginalization, and fragmentation processes in contemporary cities are examined with regards to their impact on housing conditions. Based on an analysis of the roles of the different actors and stakeholders involved in the housing developments, new options of community involvement and public participation are discussed. Finally, in conceptual study units, concepts and projects for more sustainable and equitable housing conditions in our future agglomerations are developed.

The contributions to the UN-Habitat mass housing competition presented here were developed within the module 'Urban Renewal and Redevelopment' in the winter semester 2013/2014 under the guidance of Professor Golda-Pongratz. They are the results of the typical interdisciplinary project work in the master's programme 'Urban Agglomerations' at Frankfurt University.

Project A: Haram City

Amr Halawi, Mittal Patel, Rola Sayaydeh, Shima Buzari

Haram City is a major public-private affordable housing development in Egypt, located in '6th of October' City, 20 km west of Cairo. The construction of the project began in May 2007, covers approximately 8.4 million m2 of land and represents the largest private investment in affordable housing in Egypt. Of the over 70,000 projected affordable housing units proposed by the end of 2010 a total of 6,959 units had been completed and delivered. Beyond the provision of a wide range of facilities, the project also anticipated activities to create jobs and other benefits to the community such as the creation of a waste recycle company, an embroidery factory and a rehabilitation centre for homeless children.

Despite these intentions however, half of the city is still vacant. Residents complained very early on about the isolated location that is not well connected by public transport and this severely hinders opportunities of work. As a result, a new transportation system is now proposed with better frequency and less capacity per trip, due to low density. Another complication escalated after the 2007 rockslide in Cairo's Duweiqa neighbourhood. Its residents were displaced from their dilapidated homes and relocated into parts of Haram city. These 'refugees' rank amongst the poorest and least educated in Cairo and currently, of the 30,000 inhabitants living in Haram City, 6,000 of them are the refugees from Duweiqa. The two communities have created a buffer zone between them highlighting the problems of integration that exist.

In response to this, the proposal outlined here intends to turn the buffer zone – the most negative aspect of Haram City – into a 'positive' space by filling it with activities and services such as workshops, recreational spaces, a library, and more. The proposal also suggests using art as a metaphor for bridging the social gap through two art pieces that display each social group's spiritual values and beliefs to the other.

In addition, to deal with problems surrounding the emergence of a refugee 'illegal market' that includes enclosures for livestock, the proposal envisages a fixed more formal and properly designed space for this type of commerce. A weekly schedule is proposed that will see the market operate in different places each weekday. It will have uniformed stalls, interactive places to sit and eat and additional other activities for the original inhabitants of the city. It is hoped that these moves will help improve social

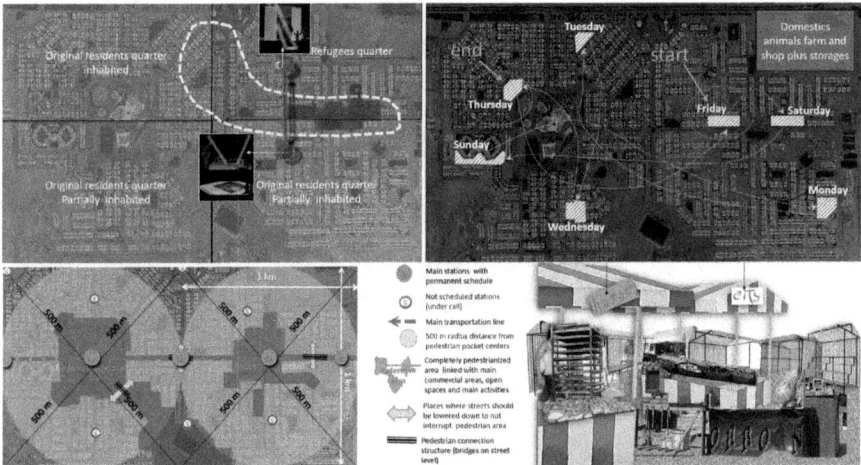

Figure 3. Relationships between original dweller and refugee quarters. Strategy for weekly market. Proposed plan for transport and pedestrian movement. Concept diagram. Perspective of formal market uniform stalls.

interaction by avoiding 'mono group dominance'; will avoid waste disposal and other problems associated with the informal and static current market and, in addition, help create jobs, enhance social interaction, and assist in getting back the city's original aesthetic.

Project B: Karoliniskes, Vilnius, Lithuania

Allyson Murillo; Eugenia Marinaki; Marvin Alvarado Brenes; Mina Mansourian; Öykü Ülgüner; Shikha Salla Mohanraj

Lithuania was one of three Soviet Baltic countries between 1944 and 1990. During this time housing management was highly centralized and focused on mass housing production – mainly prefabricated reinforced concrete. Karoliniskes was built as the second 'micro-district' of Vilnius in 1971 and in less than 20 years around 11,000 dwelling units in 5 to 9-storey residential buildings were constructed and provided homes for 31,000 citizens. After the collapse of the Soviet Union, the state-owned housing stock was privatized and today the homeownership ratio of Karoliniskes is 91%. For various reasons, including suburbanization trends and a lack of successful renovation initiatives, Karoliniskes' residential sites are in decline. Poor environmental conditions, vandalism and a feeling of insecurity have become major problems and open spaces are poorly managed.

Not only the starting point, but also the focal point of this project, is the community. It is suggested that it is possible to create and finance this project through creating

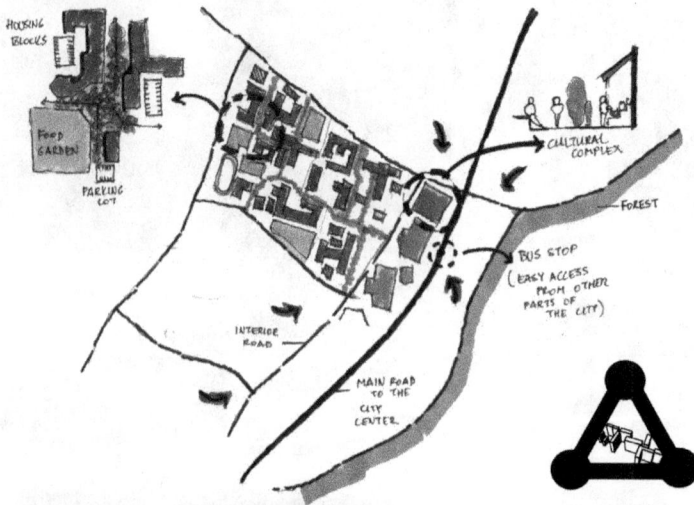

Figure 2. Site plan sketch. Strategy diagram and project logo. Before and after proposals.

engagement with, and communication between, residents. The project itself is centred on the urban revitalization of Karoliniskes through a triangulated startegy:

Meetings and workshops – These aim to create an environment of participation through introducing a cultural centre where meetings with professionals can take place, and which will enable the residents to discuss the future of Karoliniskes and gain expert advice from professional supporters.

Home-food gardens – The workshops will introduce knowledge about the basics of food local production to kick start an interest in food sustainability. Many unused areas in the city could easily be converted into gardens which the residents can use to produce food to consume or sell, helping both the environemnt and the small local economy.

Invest and develop – Renovations in the basement floors of existing buildings to turn them into shops and stores will be encouraged which, alongside food-led ecnomic initiatives will help generate additional income through retail activities.

When brought together these strategies, it is suggested, will create a 'knowledge atmosphere' and inititiate resident-led engagements in design to upgrade the physical environment, create a sense of community and help the local economy survive.

Project C: Al-Zarqa, Jordan

Gustavo Alberto Tánori Rivera; Carolina Zabas Roelandt; Khalil Albitar, Rajiv Irungbam; Talia Figueroa; Relder Legus

Founded in 1928, the city of Al-Zarqa grew as refugees from the neighbouring countries started to settle next to the military bases built in 1926. When the military bases were dismantled they left an urban void the size of Al-Zarqa. In 2008, the King of Jordan Abdullah II put the plan 'Decent Houses for Decent Living' into action. It was aimed at providing 70,000 housing units and benefiting 370,000 citizens. The project in Al-Zarqa was designed to be on the land where the old military base was located. The first phase of the project was developed in 2008, providing the first 20,500 housing units, streets, sidewalks, and urban infrastructure. However, the project stopped due to the financial crisis and the lack of citizens who could afford a new house. This turned the 'Decent Houses for Decent Living Plan' into another project in which market speculation, and an urbanization process focused on profit maximization, led to its abandonment.

This project for the *UN Habitat Mass Housing Competition* aimed at revitalizing the existing development, but also took into consideration the needs of the citizens of Al-Zarqa, in order to redesign the project and lead it in new directions. Based on the sustainability theory of the *Triple Bottom Line*, this project seeks to improve the wellbeing of citizens from economic, environmental, and social perspectives. As a result, the proposal is not based predominantly on a top-down urban planning process, but rather the need to develop bottom-up (grassroots) strategies to provide the citizens with the knowledge and skills needed to improve their living conditions for present and future generations.

The main aim of the project is to redesign so as to connect people, no matter what their social or economic situation – linking those who already live in the new development with those in the old parts of the city. In order to do that, the project emphasises the need to provide spaces and opportunities for the people of the old city to move into the new development by enhancing transportation. It also sought to a solid economic and social base through other forms of infrastructure and public spaces and take care of the environment by providing residents with training in issues of sustainability.

In short, the proposal is based on the following strategies:

- Redesign street networks as well as pedestrian and public transportation infrastructure.

- Develop a high-density neighbourhood in order to increase activities and reduce commuting time.

- Plan for mixed land-use in order to increase activities and activate a local economy around the residential areas.

- Train people with building knowledge so they can improve their living conditions in a responsible and skilled way.

- Create markets, squares, and places to enhance social cohesion, a sense of belonging, and local identity.

- Mix the sizes and types of housing units in order to avoid social segregation.

- Train people in local food production knowledge and skills.

- Create a waste and water management plan and facilities.

- Recycle grey water in order to irrigate green spaces.

Figure 3. Research analysis. Development phases. Design proposal summary sheet.

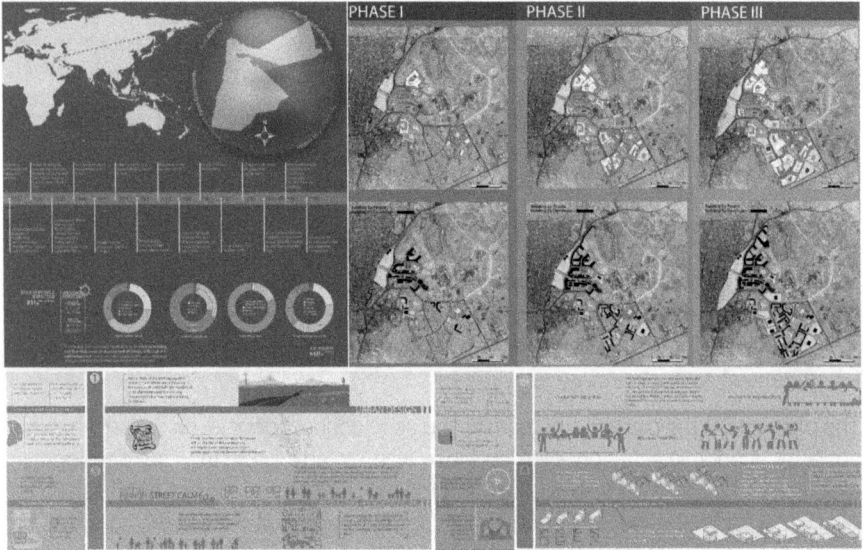

CONTRIBUTOR BIOGRAPHIES

SERIES EDITOR

Dr Graham Cairns has taught at universities in Spain, the UK, Mexico, South Africa and Gambia. He has worked in architectural studios in London and Hong Kong. The author and editor of five books, he has delivered keynote talks internationally and has published multiple articles on architecture, film and advertising in scholarly journals. Previously, he also ran a research-based performing arts company, Hybrid Artworks, with a specialism in video installation and performance. Currently, he is based at Columbia University, New York and is Honorary Senior research Associate at the Bartlett School of Architecture, UCL. He is principal editor of the scholarly journal *Architecture_MPS* and director of the research group AMPS (Architecture, Media, Politics, Society).

EDITORS

Dr Graham Potts works at the intersection of everyday and popular (digital) objects, focusing on what they say about how we understand the self and subjectivity. He is presently an Assistant Professor in the Department of Sociology at Trent University. He holds a PhD in Social and Political Thought from York University, an MA from the University of Toronto, and a BA from the University of Western Ontario. His previous publications can be found in *CTheory, M/C Journal, The International Journal of Baudrillard Studies*, and *Problématique*. He is presently working on the monograph *Posthumanism Punk'd* and writing about love, cars, and other drugs.

Rachel Isaac-Menard has a background in psychology, art history and information science (University of Toronto). She has worked at universities in the UK and some of North America's leading research institutions. She is Assistant Professor and Reference Librarian / Emerging Technologies Coordinator at Adelphi University, New York. She is also a Chartered Librarian who has participated in various publications and research projects in Canada, the US and the UK. She is the author of refereed articles, reviews and book chapters, and has presented at conferences in North America and the UK.

AUTHORS

Dr Avi Friedman received his degrees from Technion-Israel Institute of Technology, McGill University and Université de Montréal. In 1988, he co-founded the Affordable Homes Program at the McGill School of Architecture, where he is a Professor. He has authored eighteen books. He is is a practising architect and the principal of Avi Friedman Consultants, Inc. He has designed housing prototypes which were built as full-scale demonstration projects and were then constructed by homebuilders around the world. Avi has received several awards for his research, design, and teaching, including the Progressive Architecture Research Award, the J. Armand-Bombardier Prize for Technological Innovation, and the World Habitat Award.

Dr Eusebio Alonso García is an architect and educator. He is Professor Master of research in architecture at the Universidad de Valladolid. In 1984 he qualified as an architect from ETSA Valladolid; in 1992 he became professor of design and in 2006 professor of projects. He received the MEC Scholarship (1988–1992) and the Academy of Spain Prize in Rome (1990–91). His doctorate was obtained from the Universidad de Valladolid in 2001. In 2003 he was a finalist in the Arquithesis Award (2003). His publications include *Transparency and opacity in the houses of Marcel Breuer* (2002); *San Carlino: geometric machine of Borromini* (2003), *Mario Ridolfi, architecture, contingency and process* (2007, 2014); *Alvaro Siza* (BAU 1996), *Fisac* (2008), *Paulo Mendes da Rocha* (DPA UPC 2014). His awards include: First Prize, Benta-Berri, 1993; Finalist Europan III, 1993; First prize and second prize, Castilla y León Award, 98-99; Special Mention, Julio Galán Carvajal Prize, 2001; Selection, VI HISPALYT award, 2002; Third prize, Santander Award, 2002; Honorable mention, Sustainable construction in Castilla y León, 2007; First prize and finalist, Castilla y León Award, 2008-10; Third prize, Center entrepreneurs, Torrelavega, 2013.

Dr Gary Sands, AICP, is Professor Emeritus of Urban Planning at Wayne State University in Detroit, Michigan. During his 35-year teaching career at WSU, he taught graduate classes in Housing Policy, Housing Development, Local Economic Development Finance and courses on preparing and implementing neighbourhood plans. He also held a faculty appointment at the University of Windsor, Canada and has taught at El Colegio de Mexico in Mexico City. Professor Sands holds a Master's degree in Urban Planning from Wayne State University and a doctorate in Housing and Public Policy from Cornell University in Ithaca, New York. Prior to his academic career, Sands was a Senior Economist for the City of Detroit. Over the years, one of his research interests has been the structure of local housing markets and how the functioning of these markets is influenced by government development regulations and controls. Sands is the author or co-author of seven books and symposia and more than 50 book chapters and journal articles, in addition to numerous technical reports and working papers.

Dr Carlos Garcia Vazquez is an architect and Full Professor in the Escuela Tecnica Superior de Arquitectura (Universidad de Sevilla). He is also Visiting Professor in the Scuola Architettura e Società (Politecnico di Milano). His main field of research concerns contemporary urban phenomena. He is the author of the following books: *Antipolis. El desvanecimiento de lo urbano en el Cinturon del Sol* (Barcelona, 2008), *Ciudad Hojaldre; Visiones urbanas del siglo XXI* (Barcelona, 2008), and *Berlin-Potsdamer Platz: metropolis y arquitectura en transicion* (Barcelona, 2000). His other areas of scholarly activity are social housing in the contemporary age, and 20th century architecture as heritage. Garcia Vazquez has been the lead researcher of the following: 'Intervention in obsolete social housing neighborhoods. Best Practices Handbook' (financed by the European Union and the Regional Government of Andalusia), and 'The 20th century architecture in Spain, Gibraltar and Southwest France' (financed by the European Union).

Dr Charlie Smith is a Senior Lecturer in Architecture at Liverpool John Moores University's School of Art and Design. He teaches across both undergraduate and postgraduate programmes, specialising in sustainability and design. In the postgraduate studio he runs both design and research projects dealing specifically with contemporary housing design. His doctoral thesis studied ways in which to dramatically improve the sustainability of housing in UK cities. In this work the term 'sustainability' encompassed a broad church, including issues such as affordability and space standards. All of these factors were identified as interconnected, and the thesis proposed that they must be considered holistically, and never in isolation. The proposed integrated, holistic design tool was benchmarked against best practice in sustainable design, and used projects and competitions as a fundamental part of the research methodology. As a qualified architect Dr Smith has also worked as a consultant on a range of progressive carbon-neutral buildings, working collaboratively with architectural practices. This work has included winning and shortlisted projects in national and international housing design competitions.

Dr Giorgos Artopoulos holds a Master of Philosophy in Architecture and the Moving Image from the University of Cambridge, UK (2004), and a PhD from the Department of Architecture, University of Cambridge, UK (2010). The PhD received funding in the form of a Doctoral Award from the Arts and Humanities Research Council, UK, and he assisted as tutor and research assistant. Giorgos has participated in 12 European Research Programs and he received the Best International Short Film award in Mestre Film Festival, Venice. His work has been presented: at the International Biennale of Contemporary Art, Czech National Gallery, Prague; at the International Exhibition, Computational Turn in Architecture, MAV, Marseille; at the Hong Kong and Shenzhen Bi-City Biennale of Architecture and Urbanism; at the 11th and 12th Biennale of Young Creators of Europe; at the 63rd Venice Film Festival, La Biennale di Venezia, Venice; at the Royal Institute of British Architects, London; at the BALTIC Centre for Contemporary Art, Newcastle; at the London Design Festival, London; at the Ukrainian Institute of Modern Art, Chicago; at the ISEA 2006 and 2008; at the British Council; at the Byzantine Museum, Athens; at the Benakis Museum, Athens; and in many international film festivals and art exhibitions. His work has been published in more than 23 peer-reviewed journals and books of architecture, including: *Digital Creativity*; *Architecture_MPS*; *International Journal of Visual Design*; *Metalocus*; *Interfaces*; *Scroope Cambridge Journal of Architecture*; and *Architectural Issues*. Additionally, he has 35 international conference proceedings and exhibition catalogues (i.e. GSM II, eCAADe, ACADIA, ASCAAD, Hellenic Semiotics, Generative Art), and has presented in more than 29 international conferences and exhibitions (i.e. Art Expo, Art Tech Media, ARCO, GIROS, Image: Beyond Media).

Dr Ioannis Pissourios is a lecturer of Urban Planning and Design at the Department of Architecture, Neapolis University Paphos, and Visiting Lecturer at the Department of Civil Engineering and Geomatics, Cyprus University of Technology. He holds a Diploma of Architecture (Dipl. Eng.), and an MSc in Geography and Cartography. He also holds a PhD in Urban Theory, and pursued post-doctoral research in Urban Planning, both of which were funded: the first, by the State Scholarships Foundation of Greece; and the second, by the AUTh Research Committee. His research interests include the development of urban theory, as well as the analysis and planning of urban space with the use of indicators. Currently he is focused on the development of urbanology i.e. an analytical theory of urban uses. He has written 20 articles in peer-reviewed journals and collective volumes, published in *Land Use Policy*, *Ecological Indicators*, *European Spatial Research and Policy*, *Bulletin of Geography*, *Theoretical and Empirical Researches in Urban Management* and elsewhere. As an architect he has designed more than 30 residential buildings, while as an urban planner he contributed in 10 Greek and European Research Programs. He has also participated in the preparation of several urban plans, such as the planning of the EXPO 2008 World Fair in the Municipality of Thessaloniki, the relocation plan of the Aristotle University of Thessaloniki, and the planning of the Lachanokipi Business Center in Thessaloniki. Since 2003 he has lectured at various Greek and Cypriot universities on urban design and town and regional planning, at both the undergraduate and postgraduate level.

Dr Kathrin Golda-Pongratz is an architect, urban researcher and photographer. She holds a diploma from TU München and a PhD in architecture and urban planning from Universität Karlsruhe (KIT). She is a professor of international urbanism at the University of Applied Sciences in Frankfurt am Main (Germany) and visiting professor at the Universidad Nacional de Ingeniería in Lima/ Peru. She lectures at LaSalle-Universitat Ramón Llull and at the Master of International Cooperation Sustainable Emergency Architecture at the Escuela de Arquitectura EsArq in Barcelona (Spain). Her teaching and research focuses on urbanization processes and migration, Latin American urbanism, informal urbanism, housing policies, (post)colonial urbanism, public space, structural changes of urban societies, urban perception and urban memory. She has edited and published internationally, in *Architectural Design* (London), *werkundzeit* (Darmstadt), *ur[b]es* (Lima) and *MONU* (Rotterdam), among others. Her photographic work has been exhibited internationally, recently in a show at the Fundaciò Miró Museum in Barcelona.

www.ingramcontent.com/pod-product-compliance
Lightning Source LLC
Chambersburg PA
CBHW072130020426
42334CB00018B/1739